Saltwater Flies

of the Southeast
& Gulf Coast

text and photos by
Angelo Peluso

gyotaku artwork by
Charlie Brown

FAP

**Frank Amato
Publications**

Saltwater Flies

of the Southeast
& Gulf Coast

text and photos by
Angelo Peluso

gyotaku artwork by
Charlie Brown

FAP

**Frank Amato
Publications**

Dedication

Dedicated to all the pioneers of fly-fishing and fly tying who came before us and to all who will surely follow. To the memory and spirit of my cousin, friend and fly-fishing companion, Angelo Tirico. He was taken too soon from his beloved Florida waters. May he cast his flies upon eternal waters and to a never-ending procession of his favorite fish.

About the Author

ANGELO PELUSO has been a fisherman for more than 50 years—most as a fly-fisherman. He has balanced his love of this sport with a successful career in financial services, and is also an outdoor writer, lecturer, photographer and management consultant. Angelo is a frequent contributor to various local, regional and national magazines and newspapers. He is a member of the Outdoor Writers Association of America, the New York State Outdoor Writers Association, the Professional Outdoor Media Association, the Association of Great Lakes Outdoor Writers and the New England Outdoor writers. Angelo is also a founding member of the Long Island Outdoor Communicators Network.

In addition to *Saltwater Flies of the Southeast & Gulf Coast*, Angelo has also had other works published: *Saltwater Flies of the Northeast* and *Fly Fishing Long Island*. He is a published author of children's books and is currently working on his first novel and a memoir of his fly-fishing experiences in Alaska.

Over the years, Angelo has fished the entire East Coast from Maine to Florida, and many locations along the Gulf Coast. The Long Island Sound is now his family's home; Angelo spends much of his time on his boat, in his kayak and wandering the beaches fly-fishing for striped bass, bluefish, weakfish, false albacore and bonito. He also regularly fly-fishes for trout, salmon, large and smallmouth bass and travels frequently to fly-fish, Alaska being his favorite destination. Angelo has held several fly-rod tippet world records for Atlantic bonito, one of his favorite gamefish species.

All inquiries should be addressed to:
Frank Amato Publications, Inc.
P.O. Box 82112
Portland, Oregon 97282
www.amatobooks.com
(503) 653-8108

All photos by Angelo Peluso unless otherwise noted
Artwork by Charlie Brown
Cover and book design by Tony Amato

SB ISBN-13: 978-1-57188-478-7 SB UPC: 0-81127-00320-4

Printed in Singapore

1 3 5 7 9 10 8 6 4 2

Contents

Acknowledgements

An Extended Family

As I considered all the generous folks I need to thank to for their help and support in making this book a reality, a thought struck me squarely between the eyes. After all was said and done, my work on this book project put me in the enviable position of talking with and meeting not only some of the best fly-anglers and fly tiers in the world but some of the best human beings one could ever hope to meet. At first I was a bit skeptical that a guy from Long Island, New York could muster enough support and interest among top tier anglers and fly tiers throughout the entire Southeast and along the Gulf Coast to make a go of this book. I knew some great anglers and tiers from the region but not enough to fill the pages of this book. Human nature being what it is and unmatched southern hospitality rose to the occasion, and much to my delight and benefit I was welcomed with open arms and open fly boxes. I learned an important lesson: the bond between fly-anglers and fly tiers regardless of where they originate from is a very strong connection. Not one person I contacted denied my request for assistance; the response was greater than I had ever expected and for that I am forever grateful to all who contributed to this project.

The research phase of this book was a long one—almost two and a half years—but the process provided for unique opportunities to meet with and talk with literally hundreds of fly tiers, guides, captains, shop owners and various club members from Virginia and the Carolinas down through Florida and around the entire Gulf Coast to the grand state of Texas. Regardless of where this project took me, I was greeted warmly by both professionals and amateurs alike, all of whom graciously opened up to me their own personal fly-fishing worlds. This sharing is, in essence, very much an integral part of what we all pursue within our sport—the quest for continual learning. The clan of fly tiers and fly-anglers is not surprisingly a very close-knit network. Most of the folks I spoke with were well aware of one another's work and tying styles. What impressed me most was the sincere willingness of all to share their years of experience, skills and wisdom—and some even divulged their most closely guarded fly-tying secrets.

Over the decades, the sport of fly-fishing and the craft of fly tying have taken me on a remarkable journey of exploration and discovery. From the very moment that first fish ate a fly of my own creation, I was as hooked as the fish. It was amazing to me that a creation of feathers and fur I had clumsily tied upon a hook could actually stimulate a fish to strike at a fraudulent imitation of a life form. It was as close to a fishing miracle as I had experienced, and it was the beginning of a passionate and intimate obsession that has fortunately lasted more than four decades.

While I have been fishing somewhat longer than I have been fly-fishing, it has been the call of the fly that has given me my most memorable angling experiences. Whether pursuing striped bass, bluefish, bonito, and false albacore in Long Island Sound, salmon in Alaska, bonefish in the Yucatan, tailing redfish on Florida's west coast flats or snook in the mangroves, fly-fishing has been a guidepost, keeping life's obstacles and accomplishments in daily balance and perspective. For me, no finer fly-fishing can be had than that which is found in the medium of saltwater—and there is no more intensity to the sport than that which occurs in the waters of the Southeast and Gulf Coast.

As I traveled the path of this book project I encountered unmatched passion and dedication among all the fine craftsmen and craftswomen whose work is profiled on the pages that follow. From Virginia to Texas, their enthusiasm for fish and flies is a true hallmark of the Southeast and Gulf Coast fly-fishing communities. The greatest personal benefit from writing this book was the

opportunity to gather priceless insights from many of the most innovative fly-fishermen and fly tiers of our time. It was like being conferred a PhD in fly tying from an extraordinary faculty of professors. As I listened to fly tiers, guides and fly-anglers talk of their individual styles and approaches, I couldn't help but become totally engrossed in their philosophies. Each and every conversation broadened my own knowledge bank and profoundly affected the way I now view my personal involvement in the sport of fly-fishing. More important, what I learned from these tiers has in many ways enhanced my own style and approach to fly tying.

Now that this book is finally in print I would like to thank all of those wonderful *Masters of the Fly* that helped turn a vision for this book into a tangible product. With some folks I spent but an hour talking, others several days, and with some I shared time on the water. Regardless of the circumstance each one left an indelible mark. Their collective passion for the art of tying and their belief in the project was all the motivation I needed to get this book to press. Without their support and contributions this book would have remained but an outline on my computer.

My sincerest gratitude and appreciation are offered to the following members of my new and extended fly-fishing family, each of whom contributed in some way to the inspiration for this book: A.J. Forzano; Alan Caolo; Angelo Tirico; Anthony Hipps; Ben Furimsky; Bernard Lefty Kreh; Bill Murdich; Bob Clouser; Bob Lindquist; Bruce Marino; Buddy Rogers; Buzz Fender; Captain Adrian Mason; Captain Billy Trimble; Captain Chris Newsome; Captain Dino Torino; Captain Doug Sinclair; Captain Duber Winters; Captain Edward Wasicki; Captain Gary Dubiel; Captain George Beckwith Jr.; Captain Gordon Churchill; Captain Greg Arnold; Captain Greg Poole; Captain Gus Brugger; Captain Jim Blackburn; Captain Jim Hale; Captain Jimmy Albright; Captain Joe Blados; Captain John Hand; Captain John Turcot; Captain Lenny Moffo; Captain Marcia Foosaner; Captain Mike Starke; Captain Nick Angelo; Captain Pat Damico; Captain Paul Dixon; Captain Paul Strauss; Captain Randy Hamilton; Captain Rich Santos; Captain Rich Waldner; Captain Rick Grassett; Captain Roan zum Felde; Captain Ron Kowalyk; Captain Russ Shirley; Captain Scott Wagner; Captain Seth Vernon; Captain Steve Bailey; Captain Gus Brugger; Carlos Hidalgo; Catch Cormier; Charlie Brown; Charlie Chapman; Craig Riendeau; Craig Worthington; Dennis Ficco; Drew Chicone; Ed Story; Enrico Puglisi; Erwin Gaines; Feather-Craft; Gary Merriman; Glen Mikkleson; Gordy Hill; Harvey Cooper; Henry Cowen; Historic Ocean Springs Saltwater Fly Fishing Club; Joe Brooks; Homer Rhodes; Jack Gartside; Jack Samson; Janni Haney; Jeff DuBinok; Jim Hebert; Jim Seagraves; Joe McMahon; John Baker; Jon Adams; Jon Cave; Ken Bay; Kevin Arculeo; Kevin Cormier; Kyle Moppert; Lawrence Clemens; Leigh West; Lou Tabory; Matti Majorin; Mike Conner; Mike LaFleur; Mike Sfakianos; Murray Neames; New Orleans Fly Fishers; Oscar Feliu; Pat Dorsey; Paul Schwack Jr.; Paul Van Reenen; Peter Bongiovanni; Red Stick Fly Fishers; Reed Guice; Richard Schmidt; Richard Smith; Richard Steinberger; Rick Ruoff; Robert Ransom; Roger Del Rio; Ron Russell; Scott Hamilton; Scott Leon; Shell Creek Ink; Stu Apte; Tampa Bay Fly Fishing Club; Tim Borski; Tom Herrington; Tom Springer; Tom Tripi; Valerio A. Grendanin; and to all the great gamefish that keep us tying! To you all a most sincere and heartfelt, *Thank You!*

I am also grateful to Frank Amato, Tony Amato, Kim Callahan and the entire staff at Frank Amato Publications for their belief in this project and for their endless support in making this book a reality.

Foreword

by Henry Cowen

Angelo Peluso has once again unlocked many of the mysteries that continue to challenge fly-fishermen when trying to catch some of the most elusive gamefish our oceans have to offer. Only this time he set his sights far from his home waters of Long Island, NY. *Saltwater Flies of the Southeast & Gulf Coast* details the waters around the southern U.S. from Virginia and the Carolinas to the Texas Gulf Coast; this is where some of the greatest saltwater fly-fishing exists. It is fairly obvious that Angelo Peluso became enamored with this region's fly-fishing opportunities. The entire southeastern portion of the country, including Gulf Coast states are home to what must be considered some of the prettiest and best inshore flats, near shore and offshore fly-fishing available to saltwater anglers. Most anglers will at some point plan a trip to this region of the country to target such glamour species as bonefish, snook, permit, tarpon and redfish on a fly. *Saltwater Flies of the South East & Gulf Coast* will detail which fly patterns work best for this fishery. It will also give the reader a bit of an insider's look into this particular fishery. Some of the details you may have already known about, but much of what is in this book will enlighten you to many of the tips and tactics that its contributors have never discussed before. All species, regardless of stature are also given their due. This book goes far beyond that of your typical fly tying reference book. It helps answer the questions: Where do I begin? What do I do once I get there?

There is something in this book for all skill levels. It will become a reference for anglers who are in the novice stages of fly tying, as well as for the seasoned and accomplished fly tier. You may already be familiar with some of the patterns shown in the book. Those are classic saltwater patterns that have been around for many years, yet still continue to fool our finned friends. Others are subtle variations of classic flies that may get the fly angler an extra bite or two on those days when it appears the fish simply have lockjaw. Yet, it is these ever so slight variations of known patterns that make this book so unique and helpful even to the seasoned anglers among us.

There once was a bonefish fly designed by Keys guide Harry Spears called a Tasty Toad that had produced for him even when the most finicky of bonefish refused all other offerings. Many years later, angler, fly shop owner and one of the best tarpon fishermen on the planet, Gary Merriman designed a larger variation of this fly using rabbit to throw at Florida Keys tarpon. He named it the Tarpon Toad and the rest is history! It became THE "go-to" fly for Keys tarpon over the past eight years. This is how many of the new classics are uncovered.

Besides seeing the names of some of the most important fly-anglers/tiers in the world sharing their patterns, tips and general know-how in this book, we also see the names of many of the region's best guides participating with their own patterns and techniques that are specific to their local areas. It is this information that helps unlock many of the secrets that these pros have learned over the years all the while honing their angling skills. Many of these tips are brought forth in *Saltwater Flies of the Southeast & Gulf Coast* and will simply make you a better fly-angler no matter where you choose to toss feathers at spooky fish. There is even participation from members of some of the better-known saltwater fly-fishing clubs in the region. Anglers you may never have heard of are also in this book; they have turned over rocks and discovered things never previously discussed. It is this local knowledge that makes *Saltwater Flies of the South East & Gulf Coast* a must-have for any fly angler trying to unlock the secrets of the South's Atlantic and Gulf Coasts.

We have seen a renaissance of sorts in the area of fly tying during the past fifteen years. Previous to that almost all fly designs incorporated materials that were all natural. Buck tail, marabou, rabbit, chicken hackles and ostrich were the primary materials used to design the flies we whippy stickers fished. Flies by legendary anglers and tiers like Kreh, Clouser, Apte and Brooks are included in this book. More recently, synthetic materials have become extremely popular as the modern-day fly tier continues to find new materials and tying techniques previously overlooked by their predecessors to help catch more fish. Slinky Fibre, Puglisi Fiber, SF Flash Blend, Mega Mushy, Fluoro Fibre, Polar Fibre and Unique Hair are to name but a few of the synthetic tying materials that became popular from the mid 1990's to the mid 2000's. These materials had fly tiers creating some of the most realistic and productive patterns ever designed. Flies from tiers named Borski, Samson and Puglisi can be found within the pages of this book too. It is their flies that are now being labeled as the new classics. Over the past three to five years the new rage in fly tying has been to incorporate a mix of both natural materials along with synthetics into a fly pattern. This is how our sport continues to evolve and allows anglers to stay current with what seems to be the most important new discoveries in both the fly-fishing and fly tying worlds. Today's newest trends in fly design may one day give birth to the classics of tomorrow. *Saltwater flies of the Southeast & Gulf Coast* chronicles all of these trends giving you a history of sorts to this sports legacy. This should allow you to become a better fly tier as well as a more knowledgeable angler. A book of this caliber was long overdo and is simply one of the most useful fly pattern books ever published. My copy will sit next to my fly tying bench for years to come.

Prelude

Sea Level

Physically, I stand five feet and nine inches above sea level, yet my spirit dwells beneath the water's surface. I am drawn to water as naturally as magnetic poles exert influence, pulling in unison to move objects closer until they touch and join as one. At no time is that force more compelling than in the early morning hours of false dawn when the first streams of soft light filter through an eroding darkness. Like a Monet, it is an impressionistic depiction of reality. The experience is surreal, the absence of color exquisitely transforms into subtle and inspiring hues of yellow, red and orange. Fish and all nature come to life. I, too, come to life. Dawn is enchanting and enchanted, and I break its spell each time I step into the blurring of land and sea, where worlds sometimes collide and sometimes merge harmoniously in perfect transition. I need to be part of the dawn, to be in the scene rather an observer situated at its edge. Its magic knows no boundaries. Dawn, for me, is the same on a Long Island beach, the shores of an Alaskan river, the flats of the Yucatan Peninsula, the waters of Sanibel and Captiva Islands, or any tidal waters of the Gulf Coast. It has been this way always and I am blessed to share that small sliver of timelessness with those who came before me, and those who will follow a similar path long after I am gone.

I feel reborn around water—especially saltwater—and I can always find my spirit somewhere near it. I am summoned constantly to shorelines, numerous offshore haunts, quiet bays, flowing inlets and magical tidal flats, lured by the timeless, seductive sounds of water's graceful rhythms. I am never very far from water, particularly moving water. I am addicted to it. Whether the result of the north-south flows of a river, or the influences of eternal, perpetual tides, water in all its forms has proven to be a source of immense pleasure, an extraordinary elixir, medicinal. For as long as I can recall, fishable water has had that effect on me—even for a kid growing up in the big city. In "aqua veritae" I have always found truth, most often about myself. It has been a window on my soul, my sanctuary and my most intimate and dependable source of renewal. It revives my spirit like nothing else can. To cast a fly of my own making and have it graciously received by a magnificent gamefish is the pinnacle of sporting endeavors, the pure essence of the game we all so much enjoy.

I identify intimately with the gamefish I pursue. It is as if I have grown in harmony with their behaviors and seasonal migrations. From cold glacial waters of the far north to the warmth of the Southeast and Gulf Coast the fish and I travel parallel paths; we are on a similar journey. While instinct guides them in never-ending seasonal processions—to feed, to procreate or simply to find more fertile habitats—my instincts drive me with the same omnipresent urge to continually return to those same waters. I need to be physically part of the liquid medium and share with them their environment. I need to feel water, hear water—be on it, in it and have it surround me. Often, fish are secondary to my need, bit players in this liquid setting, players along with me in the watery ballet called fly-fishing.

—Angelo Peluso
At the water's edge…
January 2011

Introduction

The coastal waters of the Southeast United States and Gulf Coast represent some of the most fertile and prolific fisheries on our planet. From Virginia and the Carolinas all the way around to the Texas Gulf Coast multitudes of saltwater gamefish inhabit the encompassing waters, and challenge the fly angler at literally every turn. Always on the prowl, stalking vulnerable prey, these fish collectively represent some of the finest sport fisheries in the United States and in the world. When targeting flats, inshore or offshore species, this geographic region offers the avid fly angler some of the most diverse fishing opportunities available anywhere on planet earth. The year-round fisheries are truly world-class fly-fishing destinations.

Whether one pursues the addictive and magnificent Silver King, efforts to tempt nervous, tailing redfish, or chooses to cast flies deep among mangrove pockets in pursuit of aggressive snook, the Southeast United States and Gulf Coast offer an almost endless array of opportunities for the avid fly angler. Inshore and offshore waters, and expansive flats proffer some of the most magnificent gamefish to which one can cast a fly. Who among us has not marveled at the speed of a fly-hooked bonefish in shallow water? And what in the sport of fly-fishing compares with the spellbinding and often mesmerizing take of a permit as it inhales a fraudulent imitation of a crab? At moments like that one often needs be reminded of purpose, and remember to set the hook! And what in our angling world comes close to the tenuous connection we attempt to maintain while one hundred pounds of airborne tarpon or some rocket-launched "smoker"—the most regal mackerel of

them all—fights to regain its freedom? While there is majesty in the size and grandeur of species like sailfish, big dorado, bluefin tuna and sharks, anglers of the Southeast and Gulf Coast also enjoy a toy box just packed full with more diminutive species that are simply fun to play with; fish like speckled trout, ladyfish, bluefish, jacks, sheepshead, pompano, little tunny, Spanish mackerel and green Atlantic bonito. And lest we forget the middleweight division of brutes, the bull reds, big black drum and cobia, fish with substance that are all worthy adversaries on the fly. In the waters of the Southeast and Gulf Coast, the list of fly-friendly species is extensive and impressive.

The rich waters of the Southeast and Gulf Coasts are rife with enormous quantities of natural prey baitfish that attract and retain the equally varied and numerous game species. The bait are the catalyst—pilchards, pinfish, glass minnows, finger mullet, anchovies, sardines, threadfin shad, menhaden, crabs, shrimp, scads, silversides, ballyhoo and many other small baitfish and crustaceans. It is these baits and others upon which gamefish prey; and it is from these baits that fly-anglers receive inspiration to craft their fraudulent imitations of the real deal. Ours is a passion and a mission to create the illusion of a life form to motivate the targets of our angling efforts to eat and strike a fly.

Always attracted to these wonderful fish are those anglers who wield the long rod and toss about variations of hair and feather creations that often rival the abundance of bait they intend to imitate. These are flies crafted from natural or synthetic materials and combinations thereof, limited only by the creativity of the fly-

anglers who tie them. As fertile as the Southeast and Gulf Coast fisheries are, they are much more. The areas are blessed with a profusion of talented fly-anglers and are an absolute bastion of fly-tying creativity and innovation. The entire region has produced some of the most inventive and creative fly designs available to today's anglers, flies that are not only effective for local species of gamefish but as well for those that swim waters throughout the entire United States and beyond.

While the origins of fly tying in the United States are linked for the most part to freshwater trout fishing in the Catskill and Pocono Mountains of the Northeast, there is no doubt that much of the initial saltwater fly-tying inspirations have roots throughout the Southeast and Gulf Coast regions of the United States, where there is well-deserved recognition for their enormous contributions to the sport of saltwater fly-fishing. Flies for the ever-popular tarpon, bonefish, permit, snook, redfish and sea trout led the way as trailblazing anglers challenged creativity to craft effective patterns. Trial and error eventually let to success and resulted in a saltwater fly tying foundation that has had broad reaching effects all across the United States and wherever fish are pursued with the fly rod.

There is no question but that areas represented in this book formed and will continue to form the structural foundation for what will be built upon as the sport of saltwater fly-fishing matures even further. *Saltwater Flies of the Southeast & Gulf Coast* is first and foremost about productive saltwater patterns—flies that are designed to consistently catch fish. This volume was conceived

as a companion book to *Saltwater Flies of the Northeast*, and follows much of the same successful format and design. It profiles those patterns that professional and amateur anglers alike tie and reach for when there are fish to be caught.

The concept for the book was given life as I roamed an isolated beach on Sanibel Island—fly rod in hand—contemplating all the talented fly-anglers and fly tiers I met while writing and producing my *Northeast* volume of fly patterns. I wondered if a Southeast version of that book would be possible? As a northern angler whose thoughts turn south with the first chill of late fall I always look forward to my mangrove adventures. The exceptional fishing that I have experienced throughout the Southeast and Gulf Coast regions has opened up an expansive world of wonderfully talented anglers, all of whom share a common purpose: to dupe a fish into eating a fur and feathered fake as if it were real food! I have learned much from selfless and gracious tiers, guides, captains, fly shop owners, club members, all willing to share their time, experience, expertise—and most of all their wisdom and passion for the sport. I have been very fortunate through the sport of fly-fishing to have wet a line in many locations in this great country of ours and elsewhere, but I always return to the waters of the Southeast and Gulf Coast, lured by the hospitality of fish willing to eat a fly of my own making, and helpful anglers willing to show me the way. The reception and support I received for this book could not have been surpassed.

Intended to serve as a desk reference guide for both beginning and advanced fly-anglers and fly tiers, this book is also a window

on the world of some of the Southeast and Gulf Coast region's most successful fly-anglers. It presents a collection of flies that have been fished regionally from Virginia and the Carolinas down the entire southeast coast and around to the Texas Gulf Coast. The contributors to this book have graciously shared the remarkable products of their fly-fishing creativity and tying skills. Yet beyond just offering their most effective patterns, they have also shared their dedication to the sport and the art. Most of all, their fly patterns and tying techniques are a lens through which we can view literally hundreds of years of collective experience. Such fly tying and angling insight is priceless!

My objective in writing *Saltwater Flies of the Southeast & Gulf Coast* is a simple one: to present the reader with not only those fly designs that embody originality and creativity but also those that represent effective variations of existing patterns. Within the pages of this book are "go-to" designs that each contributing fly tier, professional guide and captain uses when the going gets tough and fish need to be caught. Those specific flies are quite revealing and enlightening patterns, both for their similarities and for their differences. At a minimum, the flies in this book will help the avid fly-fisher catch fish. It is my hope that *Saltwater Flies of the Southeast & Gulf Coast* will not only serve as a ready reference to those patterns, but that it will also inspire the readers to experiment with and explore new creations and variations in their own fly tying. In doing so they will help cultivate and perpetuate one of fishing's most creative and effective art forms.

The reader may notice that some patterns in this volume appear relatively close in design to others. Some patterns might even seem redundant. But for change to be effective it need not always be profound. Simple works too. At times it is but a minor tweak to materials or tying technique that allows a fly to look or behave differently, making it more appealing to fish under specific conditions. Fly tying is one of those endeavors where imitation is truly the finest form of flattery so some effective designs are built off the success of others. Very often simple and minor modifications to size or color can create a productive variation that may address unique fishing conditions or work to and attract a different species of gamefish. Small changes in design or material can often yield big results.

It becomes apparent to anyone researching the history of fly tying that there are but a few handfuls of what might be considered true originals, patterns so significant that they have directly influenced the sport and entire styles of fly tying. Lefty's Deceiver is one such design. This fly is more than just a pattern, it is a method of tying—it is the *Deceiver School* of fly tying, just like the school of impressionist art. One can tie this pattern true to the original recipe or modify it with creative license to meet one's own needs. The greatness of this art lies in our ability to build upon successful designs, and push a pattern to the next level of effectiveness. I often compare fly tying advances to the U.S. patent process, it acknowledges innovation that is truly new yet leaves the door open for someone else to come along with a meaningful improvement. So it is with fly tying—great original ideas followed by successful design modifications.

The only constraint on the modern saltwater fly tier is the limitation of one's imagination. Possibilities for modifications and variations can be quite boundless. New materials enter the marketplace at a steady pace and new techniques for crafting flies are constantly being devised. Industrious tiers can find inspiration in a variety of places: craft stores, hobby and gift shops, major retail outlets, yarn stores, and even super markets. The possibilities are endless. Creativity and a willingness to experiment are a hallmark of today's exceptional saltwater fly tiers. And nowhere is that more apparent than throughout the Southeast and Gulf Coast. The patterns presented in the pages that follow, continue to enhance a tradition of innovation that began many years ago by pioneers whose legacy we all work to honor.

The use of an artificial *fly* goes back a very long way and it is unlikely that we will ever know the identity of that first enterprising individual who experimented with fur, feathers and hooks as a means to catch fish. Fly-fishing's ancestry has been traced back to early Macedonia, but I suspect that the use of a fly-like lure extends back well before that. I am inclined to believe that an even earlier use of the fly extends back to at least the ancestors of those first ancients who crossed the great Bering Land Bridge from Asia to what is now Alaska. Armed with carved hooks made from bone, adorned with fur or feathers obtained from their hunting harvests, these early anglers would attempt to trick their next meal. I often wonder if they realized the remarkable, translucent and life-like qualities of polar bear hair or the buoyancy traits of caribou? I suspect their inquisitive minds pushed them to experiment, ever trying to improve those aboriginal patterns. Perhaps they were driven much like we are to find the perfect fly. I am sure that they were as elated as any of us when that first fish ate their handmade imitation. While survival instincts motivated those early fishermen, the contemporary angler is driven by sport and challenge. Yet, those primitive roots still connect us. Perhaps it is a throwback gene that influences us more today than we realize. As I wrote in *Saltwater Flies of the Northeast*, "It is an understatement to say that the art of tying has a long and distinguished tradition. Today's modern tiers owe much to those who came before them. We are simply adding yet another layer to that rich legacy for those who will follow us."

Saltwater Flies of the Southeast & Gulf Coast is a compilation of the best flies I have acquired during my travels and through my research. While it is a very comprehensive collection of exceptional regional patterns, there may be other flies worthy of inclusion that I unintentionally missed, or tiers who for some reason could not be contacted. The book pays tribute to all of the fabulous contributors whose work is herein profiled; it also is a tribute to those who may have been missed and whose contributions to the art and the sport are equally as significant. Above all, the book is homage to those pioneers of the sport who came before us, those of celebrity and those of anonymity.

The art of fly tying is a work in progress, and so too is this book. It is a snapshot of a point in time in our fabulous sport. I hope the flies profiled within the following pages help you catch more fish and spark your own imagination. May you enjoy perpetual tight lines.

—*Angelo Peluso*
Captiva, Florida
June, 2011

Saltwater Flies of the Southeast

Fly Patterns

Absolute Flea | Rick Ruoff

This shrimp pattern was tied to take large and difficult bonefish in the Keys. As is often the case with challenging fish the fly needs to be perfect in appearance and action. Keys bonefish can be most discerning, so the fly must be *absolutely* right, hence the name. It has proven so effective that Rick rarely fishes any other fly. Fly weight can vary to match conditions with the addition of lead or plastic eyes. The pattern can also be tied larger for permit.

Hook: Gamakatsu, SC15, size 2.
Thread: Tier preference.
Tail: Tie in a bump of white chenille at the hook bend. Tie in four strands of pearl Krystal Flash and then two bleached grizzly hackles on either side of the hook. The orientation of the hackles should be kicked up.
Hackle: Tie on one bleached grizzly hackle, trim the bottom flat and palmer forward.
Body: Tie in tan leech yarn, beach-chain eyes and the monofilament weed guard just ahead of the eyes. Wrap yarn forward, figure eight around the eyes and finish off the head.

AJ's Bendback | A.J. Forzano

This Bendback variation is tied on a wide-gap worm-style hook. It can be tied with natural or synthetic hair. The wide gap nicely accommodates a wide profile fly. All materials are tied on the hook platform immediately behind the hook eye. The fly is ideal for situations where a hook point riding up is advantageous.

Hook: Worm-style wide gap.
Thread: Clear, fine monofilament.
Throat: Tie in a small section of red natural or synthetic hair.
Wing/Body: In the natural hair version tie in a base of white bucktail over which is tied chartreuse or other color of choice.
Flanks: Tie in several strands of Krystal Flash on either side of the bucktail.
Topping: Tie in a bunch of peacock herl strands and add in a few additional strands of flash.
Head/Eyes: Build a head of epoxy. When dry, add stick-on eyes and apply an additional light coat of epoxy.

Arculeo's Action Baitfish | Kevin "Fluff" Arculeo

This pattern was created to reproduce the erratic movements of a wounded baitfish and the swimming action of a natural baitfish. This fly can be fished by using a one-handed strip or by tucking the rod under the arm for a two-handed, continuous retrieve. Using a one-handed strip creates an erratic, darting action similar to a wounded baitfish. Using the two-handed strip will cause the fly to wiggle like a swimming baitfish.

Hook: 3x to 4x long-shank hooks, size 6 through 3/0.
Thread: Monofilament, 6/0.
Body 1: Comb white Polar Fibre and cut a 3-inch width at base; comb out fluff from the bulky end. Tie in Polar Fibre Deceiver style. Tie one clump 2/3 down the hook shank towards the bend to create the tail, followed by another clump on the left side of hook just behind the eye. Tie in a clump on the right side just behind the hook eye, followed by another clump of white Polar Fibre on the top of the hook shank just behind the eye.
Back: Tie in a small clump of Polar Fibre, color of choice, on the top to create the colored back. Comb through all the clumps of Polar Fibre to form the body of the baitfish.
Lip 1: Crimp one end of 100-pound monofilament and tie in on the side of the hook shank with the mono pointing down towards the same side of the hook point. Measure the mono to the opposite side of the hook to form the lip and crimp the mono to tie in. Whip-finish to secure.
Body 2: Squeeze some silicone on a piece of paper and sprinkle in a generous amount fine glitter. Using a dubbing needle, mix the glitter and silicone to produce the hue of a baitfish. Using a dubbing needle apply the silicone to the fly body starting at the eye of the hook and spread it toward the back just past the bend in the hook. Lightly work the silicone into the Polar Fibre, spreading away from the eye and towards the tail.
Eyes: Place the 3D Molded Eyes on each side of the head, use some additional silicone to attach.
Body 3: Using the dubbing needle place a light coat of Photo Flo over the silicone. The Photo Flo will make the silicone dry clear.
Lip 2: Using the dubbing needle, spread a large amount of the Soft Body over the mono lip. Turn fly to keep the Soft Body glue from sagging. Continue to turn the fly until the Soft Body Glue dries enough not to sag.

Arculeo's Floating Crab | Kevin "Fluff" Arculeo

The Floating Crab was originally designed to imitate fiddler crabs for redfish in the waters of Charleston, South Carolina. These crabs can be found high in the water column climbing on spartina grass on the flats. The fly has evolved into a pattern to use for crabs that are swept out in strong current of bay and flats passes. This fly should be fished by using a one-handed, short, continuous strip in calm water and dead-drifted in a current with intermittent short strips.

Hook: Tiemco 811S, sizes 6 to 3/0.
Thread: Monofilament, 6/0.
Claws/Legs 1: Prepare claws by cutting two rubber tourniquet strips 3/16" wide and 3" long. Cut a slight taper in one end of strip for tying onto hook. Cut four double rubber leg strips 2" long. Tie an overhand knot in the middle of each tourniquet strip and rubber leg creating a 90-degree angle.
Body 1: Cut or stamp closed-cell foam and Furry Foam to the football shape of a crab matched to the hook size.
Claws/Legs 2: Tie in the tapered end of the first rubber tourniquet strip with the knot measuring about 1/2- from the hook and secure to the hook. Position claw angled out with the jointed knot section pointing inward and towards you. Tie in one rubber leg on back side of hook and angled toward the rear with right angle pointing towards back of hook. Leave a tag end on the rubber legs to use for positioning later in the process. Move forward and tie in the next leg pointing in same direction. Tie in the next leg pointing straight back with the jointed section pointing towards the eye of the hook. Move forward to just behind the eye and tie in the last leg pointing out away from you and towards the eye of the hook. Tie in the tapered end of the 2nd claw rubber tourniquet strip with the knot measuring about 1/2" from the hook; secure to the hook. Position claw angled out with the jointed knot section pointing inward and towards you. Cut a V shape on the end of the rubber tourniquet material to create the claw. Use a red permanent marker to color the inside of the V and the tips. Use the Prisma marker to add markings.
Body 2: Tie in the Furry Foam by using a dubbing needle to poke a hole through the end of the foam. Feed the hook point through the hole, pull the other end of the foam to the eye of the hook, and tie in the tip. This creates the underside of the crab.
Head: Tie in a tip of the closed-cell sheet foam just behind the eye. Tie in weed guard if needed, and whip finish. Add a drop of glue to finish head.
Eyes: Prepare the black plastic mono eyes by cutting off one of the eyeballs.
Finish: Spread 5-minute epoxy across the top of the Furry Foam and the underside of the closed-cell sheet foam. Saturate the hook area, including the rattle and the tie-in point for all legs and claws. Place the post of the eyes in the glue on the Furry Foam. As the epoxy starts to set, press the closed-cell foam to the Furry Foam, creating a sandwich. Continue to pinch foam cells together while positioning the claws, legs and eyes until the epoxy sets. Wipe off any excess epoxy before it sets.

Arculeo's Surface Action Baitfish

Kevin "Fluff" Arculeo

This fly was created to reproduce the erratic movements of a wounded baitfish being chased to the surface. It is similar to the Action Baitfish but with an upturned lip. This fly can be fished by using a one-handed strip or by tucking the rod under your arm for a two-handed continuous retrieve. Using a one-handed strip creates an erratic, darting action in an upward motion similar to a wounded baitfish swimming towards the surface. Using the two-handed strip will cause the fly to swim to the surface breaking the surface film and will erratically dart, jump, and splash water like a fleeing baitfish.

Hook: 3x to 4x long-shank hooks, size 6 through 3/0.
Thread: Monofilament, 6/0.
Body 1: Comb white Polar Fibre and cut a 3" width at base; comb out fluff from the bulky end. Shorten the Polar Fibre by pulling on the fibers at the pointed ends of the material, while also maintaining its pointed 3-D shape. Tie in Polar Fibre Deceiver style. Tie one clump 2/3 down the hook shank towards the bend to create the tail, followed by another clump on the left side of hook just behind the eye. Tie in a clump on the right side just behind the hook eye, followed by another clump of white Polar Fibre on the top of the hook shank just behind the eye.
Back: Tie in a small clump of Polar Fibre on the top to create the colored back. Comb through all the clumps of Polar Fibre to form the body of the baitfish.
Lip 1: Crimp one end of 100-pound mono and tie in on the side of the hook shank with the mono pointing up towards the opposite side of the hook point. Measure the mono to the opposite side of the hook to form the lip and crimp the mono to tie in. Whip-finish to secure.
Body 2: Squeeze some silicone on a piece of paper and sprinkle in a generous amount of fine glitter. Use a dubbing needle to mix the glitter and silicone to produce the hue of a baitfish. Use a dubbing needle to apply the silicone to the fly body starting at the eye of the hook and spreading it toward the back just past the bend in the hook. Lightly work the silicone into the Polar Fibre, spreading away from the eye and towards the tail.
Eyes: Place the 3D Molded Eyes on each side of the head, use some additional silicone to attach.
Body 3: Using the dubbing needle place a light coat of Photo Flo over the silicone. The Photo Flo will make the silicone dry clear.
Lip 2: Using the dubbing needle, spread a large amount of the Soft Body over the mono lip. Start turning the fly to keep the Soft Body glue from sagging. Continue to turn the fly until the Soft Body Glue dries.

Baby Tarpon Fly | Angelo Tirico

This fly was designed to mimic a fleeing baitfish or crab. It is especially productive in stained water when fishing for baby tarpon, snook and redfish.

Hook: Eagle Claw LO67S, Size 1 or 1/0.
Thread: Danville Flat Waxed Nylon.
Eyes: Secure bead chain eyes approximately 1/4 inch from the hook eye and on top of the hook, using figure-eight wraps.
Tail: Tie in a pencil-diameter bunch of Extra Select Craft Fur, it's full length extending past the hook bend, and forming a tapered tail.
Body: Secure gold Diamond Braid under the hook point just behind the eyes. Wrap Diamond Braid toward the hook eye taking several figure-eight wraps around the eyes to form the belly. Tie off Diamond Braid in front of the eyes, whip finish thread and cut. Use five-minute epoxy to form the body around the eyes, covering all exposed Diamond Braid, rotating in vise until dry. The body should lay flat on the side of the hook shank.
Wing/Head: Use a 3/8-inch strip of rabbit fur and secure hide with thread to form the head and wing.

Baby-T | Alan Caolo

Flies crafted with rabbit fur usually do well with tarpon. This fly reflects four key ingredients that create a reliable pattern for Florida's baby tarpon that can often be frustrating. This fly is the result of experimenting with different pattern ideas—a small black fly with lots of inherent movement tied on a hook perfectly suited for penetrating a tarpon's mouth emerged. This fly has been a reliable and consistent pattern for small tarpon.

Hook: 1/0 Gamakatsu SC-15.
Thread: Black Danville's Flat Waxed Nylon.
Tail: Wrap thread to cover the shank to a position over the barb and attach a 1 1/2-inch-long loop of stiff 30-pound mono that has been pinched to form a pointy loop to the back of the hook. Attach the Zonker strip over the mono loop with the rabbit fibers facing upward. The entire length of the strip should be about three inches from the attachment point to the tip of the tail.
Body: Secure a wide, webby black schlappen feather over the Zonker strip and palmer it in six or eight tight wraps to form a full, fluffy body, secure with thread and trim.
Head/Finish: Wind thread forward to the eye of the hook, forming a smooth, tapered head, secure, cut and coat the thread-covered portion of the hook with head cement.

Backcountry Brown Baitfish | Enrico Puglisi

This generic brown baitfish is representative of small, wide-profile dark baits that inhabit the backcountry. It is tied completely with EP Fibers. The pattern is an effective fly for all saltwater species that forage in backwater areas. It is popular for most southeast and Gulf Coast species. The overall length of this fly is either three inches or five inches, depending on the hook size.

Hook: Gamakatsu CS 15, size 3/0 or 2/0.
Thread: Mono, .004.
Body/Wing: Using white and brown EP fibers build a body and wing by tying in small batches of the fibers on the shank in layers. Begin at the bend and tie in the fibers on the top and bottom of the shank. Layer and taper fibers as you tie.
Flash: Tie in a few short strands of blue Magic Flash along both flanks.
Plastic Eyes: Black on yellow, 6mm.
Weed Guard: Tie in a two-pronged length of stiff monofilament.
Glue: Zap-CA, Hard as Nails, Goop.

Baker Bunker | John Baker

This menhaden fly is part of the Baker Baitfish Series. It is tied in a variety of sizes from three to six inches to replicate different sizes of bunker. It offers a realistic body width and profile. The pattern has proven effective from Delaware to Georgia as an excellent striped bass fly and from South Carolina to Florida as a productive tarpon fly.

Hook: Short shank big-game hook, size 1/0 to 4/0.
Thread: Color to match body.
Belly: Tie in a length of white Polybear by Larva Lace.
Body/Wing: Tie in combinations of white, pink, olive and dark gray Craft Fur, Polar Flash and Polybear to form the body and wing. Blend in strands of Polar Flash. Add the prominent black spot near the shoulder with a permanent marker pen.
Head/Eyes: Build a small head with a coating of Softex and affix plastic molded eyes.

Baker Mangrove Minnow | John Baker

This fly is a generic minnow imitation that is part of the Baker Baitfish series which can be used to replicate a variety of small to moderate size baitfish. It can be tied in a number of color combinations and sizes. This specific fly is tied to replicate small to midsize baitfish that inhabit the mangroves. The pattern design has proven effective from Delaware to Florida for a wide variety of gamefish.

Hook: Short-shank big-game hook, size 1/0 or larger.
Thread: Color to match body.
Body/Wing: Tie in combinations of tan and olive Craft Fur, Polar Flash and Polybear to form the body and wing. Blend in strands of Polar Flash. Add the prominent brown bars along the body with a permanent marker pen.
Head/Eyes: Build a small head with a coating of Softex and affix plastic molded eyes.

Baker's Mullet | John Baker

This is a great neutrally buoyant fly with a good overall mullet profile. The fly has enticing side-to-side actions and should be fished just under the surface. This pattern has taken fish from the mid-Atlantic to the Yucatan. It can be tied weighted or fished with a sinking line. The fly can be tied in several color combinations.

Hook: Standard saltwater hook, 1/0; big-game Hook, 3/0 to 7/0.
Thread: Matched to body colors.
Tail: Tie in Doug's Bugs Craft Fur, color of choice. Add in Flashabou.
Belly: Tie in a sparse amount of Craft Fur or Polar Fibre.
Wing: Tie in wing and topping of Craft Fur or Polar Fibre. Top wing can be barred with the use of a permanent marker.
Weed Guard: Tie in a length of 50-pound monofilament and form a weed guard.
Head/Eyes: Form a head using Softex. Affix doll eyes into the head.

Baker Minnow | John Baker

This fly is a generic minnow imitation that can be used to replicate a variety of small to moderate size baitfish. It can be tied in a number of color combinations but some of more effective presentations are: redfish orange, golden tan, purple, hot chicken and chartreuse over white. It is an excellent backcountry fly and has more than twenty-five species to its credit.

Hook: Standard saltwater, size 4 to 1 or big-game hook, size 1 to 4/0.
Thread: Color to complement materials.
Eyes: Tie in either dumbbell or bead chain on the underside of the hook shank.
Tail: Tie in four neck hackles at the bend of the hook and add a few strands of Flashabou on either side of the hackles.
Body/Wing: Tie in orange Doug's Bugs Craft Fur Plus, Polar Fibre or Craft Fur to form the body and upper wing.
Head: Tie in Doug's Bugs Crystal Chenille, Estaz or Estaz Grande and wind to form a head. Wind over the stem of the eyes.

Baker Pogy | John Baker

This fly is part of the Baker Baitfish Series and is tied as a variation of the bunker pattern. It is tied in a variety of sizes from three to six inches to replicate different bait species, and with a realistic body width. The pattern has proven effective from Delaware to Georgia as an excellent striped bass fly and from South Carolina to Florida as a productive tarpon fly.

Hook: Short-shank big-game hook, size 1/0 to 4/0.
Thread: Color to match body.
Anti-Fouling: Tie in pieces of heavy monofilament or fluorocarbon to form two anti-fouling loops at the bend of the hook. This will prevent wing material from fouling.
Belly: Tie in a length of white Polybear by Larva Lace.
Body/Wing: Tie in combinations of white, olive and black Craft Fur, Polar Flash and Polybear to form the body and wing. Blend in strands of Polar Flash. Add the prominent black spot near the shoulder with a permanent marker pen.
Head/Eyes: Build a small head with a coating of Softex and affix plastic molded eyes.

Baker Shad | John Baker

This fly is a generic minnow imitation that can be used to replicate a variety of small to moderate size baitfish. It can be tied in a number of color combinations and sizes. This specific fly is tied to replicate generic shad. The pattern design has proven effective from Delaware to Florida for a wide variety of gamefish.

Hook: Short-shank big-game hook, size 1/0 or larger.
Thread: Color to match body.
Body/Wing: Tie in combinations of gray and black Craft Fur, Polar Flash and Polybear to form the body and wing. Blend in strands of silver Polar Flash. Add the prominent black bars at the tips of the tail with a permanent marker pen.
Belly: Tie in a length of red Polybear by Larva Lace.
Head/Eyes: Build a small head with a coating of Softex and affix plastic molded eyes.

Baker Shrimp | John Baker

This pattern is a very productive and realistic imitation of a large-profiled shrimp. To enhance its effectiveness, it can be tied in a variety of strike-inducing color combinations.

Hook: Standard saltwater, size 6 to 1.
Thread: Color to match fly coloration.
Eyes: Tie in Spirit River I'balz eyes or bead chain.
Body and Extension: Tie in section of 80-pound monofilament on the underside of the hook shank. This will function as the foundation for wrapping the body and tail of Doug's Bugs Crystal Chenille.
Tail: Tie in Doug's Craft Fur Plus and cinch so that it forms a fanned tail.
Legs: Tie in Spirit River Krystal Wraps for the legs.
Wing: Tie in Larva Lace Polybear as wing material.
Weedguard: Tie in 50-pound fluorocarbon and form a weed guard.

Barracuda Needlefish | Glen Mikkleson

This seven-inch pattern has all the right stuff to attract toothy 'cuda. Its long, flowing hackles and bright chartreuse tones give it a most appealing needlefish look. The fly is also effective for any gamefish that forage large slender baits.

Hook: Long-shank SS, wide gap.
Thread: A Thread.
Tail: Tie in a platform of yellow bucktail with pearl Krystal Flash mixed in. Tie in several pairs of slender chartreuse/lime hackles and additional flash material. Tie in yellow hackles. Tie on long barred grizzly hackles high on the fly as shoulders. Add in additional flash.
Topping: Tie in a small bunch of lime bucktail.
Body: The body is tied on the hook shank from a point opposite the hook barb forward to the eye. Tie in pearl body material and wind toward the hook eye. Shape a small head at the rear of the shank. Tie off thread. Apply green and black markings to the topside of the hook shank with a permanent marker. Add a splash of red for gills.
Eyes: Affix small stick-on eyes, black on yellow.
Finish: Apply a coating of epoxy to the entire body and to the hair and hackles in the area of the eye. This will also serve to minimize fouling.

Bayou Diablo | Alan Caolo

Louisiana redfish feed heavily on shrimp and crabs in the fall. The Diablo Crab pattern was adapted for bayou waters based on Gulf habitat and for redfish food preferences. The pattern utilizes rust-colored feathers, bright orange and white legs, and added a little gold flash to give the pattern a lot of visibility in waters known for being off color (sometimes murky), and for fish not known for keen vision. The Bayou Diablo has been effective for redfish, black drum and sheepshead.

Hook: Mustad 3407, size 1, flattened barb.
Thread: Danville's flat-waxed nylon, red.
Eyes: Secure large dumbbell (1/16 oz) to the back of the hook shank, close to the eye of the hook. Wrap thread to cover the shank to a position over the barb.
Legs: Secure four Sili-Legs (two white and two orange/black) and four strands of Krystal Flash to the back of the hook, across from the barb (about a hook's length long—1/2 the length of the finished fly).
Tail: Attach a schlappen feather just ahead of the tail legs attachment and palmer it with four or five tight turns, secure and cut. Carefully back-wrap this hackle with a few thread turns so it lays back, flaring evenly over the leg's rust schlappen; gold Krystal Flash, two white and two orange/black Sili-Legs.
Body: Attach a second wide schlappen feather just ahead of the flared tail, and secure the chenille to the hook over that feather attachment. Wrap the chenille to a point about 1/4-inch back of the eyes. Attach the second set of Sili-Legs (one white and one orange/black) to the hook shank by carefully winding the chenille over and beyond. Continue winding the chenille and over-wrap the eyes, secure ahead of the eyes, and trim. Ensure the two legs protruding off each side of the fly angle back slightly toward the tail. Palmer forward the second schlappen feather over the chenille and around the legs with five or six wraps to just behind the eyes, secure with thread, and cut. Secure the thread ahead of the eyes, trim and cement. The body schlappen fibers should now be trimmed off the top of the fly to give it a flat, crab-like profile, leaving the long side and bottom fibers as is. The legs are trimmed to extend about 1/4" outside the body side fibers.

Beach Dweller Blue Darter | Oscar Feliu

This fly was designed to replicate the small blue darters that inhabit the edges of beaches. It can also imitate other translucent baitfish or those having mirror-like body surfaces. The pattern has been effective for snook, pompano and redfish. Many other predatory fish target this species of bait.

Hook: Mustad C70S D or C74S D, sizes 6 and 4.
Thread: Monocord 3/0, white.
Tail: Tie in four white feathers flanked by pearl flash material.
Skirt: Tie in sparse clumps of white calf tail hairs.
Top Wing: Tie in strands of white and colored Sea Fibers with mixed pearl flash. Use blue with barred markings for the top.
Bottom Wing: Tie in strands of white Sea Fibers mixed with pearl flash.
Eyes: 7mm molded eyes affixed to plastic tags.
Head/Finish: Build a head of thread. Cover head and eyes with a coating of epoxy.

Bead Butt Baitfish | Captain Pat Damico

This general baitfish pattern incorporates a unique method for utilizing a bead weight. The bead provides for well-balanced weight but also for additional flash attraction—a red bead could be used to represent a wounded baitfish. This fly has worked well for redfish and snook. In stained water, try a brass or copper bead.

Hook: Any large-gap, short-shank hook such as the Mustad 9174, 9175D, Eagle Claw 254 SS, size 2 or 4.
Thread: UNI-mono, size 4m clear.
Bead: Cyclops Eyes, size 5/32, nickel. Crimp the hook barb and insert the bead. Once the bead is positioned, wrap thread behind the bead forming a small ball of thread. Whip finish and slide the bead over the thread "bump". Place a drop of Flexament in the large bead hole.
Wing: White, yellow, green and brown Enrico's Sea Fibers, Mirror Image or Hi-Viz. Start thread in front of bead. Select a small clump of white Sea Fibers twice the length of the finished fly, and secure to the top of the hook at a position in front of the bead. Add a second clump of white fibers in the same manner in front of and close to the first bunch.
Flash: Tie in some Flashabou or silver Lite Brite fibers in front of the white Sea Fibers. Stroke back fibers and comb out.
Over-Wing: Place a small clump of yellow or chartreuse Sea Fibers in front of the Flashabou and secure in place.
Topping: Tie in a small clump of brown Sea Fibers in front of the Flashabou.
Head: Shape a head with thread and whip finish.
Eyes: Miracle Eyes, size 7/32. Affix eyes to the head and coat with thinned Flexament.

Bendback-Style Clouser

Roger Del Rio | Red Stick Fly Fishers

This Clouser variation was developed to fish deep in the Gulf of Mexico with sinking lines. The fly has been used in Louisiana to catch yellowfin and blackfin tuna, greater amberjack, pompano, little tunny, sheepshead, bluefish, Spanish mackerel and red drum. The fly should be tied sparse and stripped fast on the retrieve.

Hook: Mustad 3407/34007, sizes 1 through 4/0 or Signature C71S SS.
Thread: Danville's flat, waxed nylon, yellow.
Eyes: Tie in medium to extra large dumbbell eyes.
Body: Tie in red chenille or red yarn and wind toward the eyes.
Wing: Tie in successive bunches of white, chartreuse and yellow bucktail. Intersperse silver Flashabou between hair bunches.
Head: Build a head with thread. Tie off and apply head cement.

Bent Shank Baitfish | Captain Edward Wasicki

One of two bent fly patterns developed by Captain Wasicki, this version sports a rabbit fur wing. The pattern has been generally effective for many gamefish in the Mosquito Lagoon, North Indian River and Banana River areas. This style of fly is also very effective for bonito and false albacore.

Hook: Mustad 3407, Size 1 bent to form a belly approximately one-third from the hook eye.
Thread: White Monocord or fine monofilament.
Tail: Tie in a small bunch of fine synthetic hair with flash overtones.
Wing/Body: Tie in a small section of white rabbit strip at a point on top of the hook shank near the hook bend followed by a length of white Krystal Flash. Palmer the Krystal Flash forward and tie off immediately behind the hook eye. Trim the Krystal Flash flat on the tip of the hook shank and bring the rabbit strip forward. Tie off the strip immediately behind the hook eye.
Head/Eyes: Build a small head with thread and tie off. Affix stick-on eyes toward the back of the head area. Use either a super glue to affix the eyes or apply a coating of an adhesive like Softex.

Bent Shank Epoxy Baitfish

Captain Edward Wasicki

One of two bent fly patterns by Captain Wasicki, this is the epoxy version of the bent baitfish. The pattern has been generally effective for many gamefish in the Mosquito Lagoon, North Indian River and Banana River areas. This style of fly is also very effective for bonito and false albacore.

Hook: Mustad 34011, Size 1 or similar long-shank hook. Bend to form a belly approximately one-third from the hook eye.
Thread: White Monocord or fine monofilament.
Tail: Tie in a small bunch of fine synthetic hair with flash overtones.
Body: The entire body is formed with epoxy and shaped using a bodkin. Glitter can be added to the epoxy mix as it is being cured.
Eyes: Affix stick-on eyes toward the back of the head area and apply a light coat of epoxy or a coating of Hard as Nails.

Big Badger | Bill Murdich

This pattern began as a bonefish fly but has evolved into a very productive fly for sea trout, snook and redfish. It is especially effective when fished off a light, sandy bottom.

Hook: Mustad 3407, size 1.
Thread: White 3/0 Danville Mono cord or UNI-Thread for the body, tan to tie in the wings.
Weight/Eyes: Attach small lead eyes, white with black pupils, as you would for a Clouser Minnow. Leave a little extra room between the eyes and hook eye.
Tail: Tie in pearl Krystal Flash with white thread with an even thread base between the eyes and the bend of the hook.
Body: Tie in clear V-Rib and then pearl Flashabou. Tie in V-Rib with flat side facing out. Wrap Flashabou forward to the lead eyes. Wrap the V-Rib forward, curved side on the outside.
Upper/Lower Wings: Tie in a fairly large clump of badger fur behind the hook eye, using the tan thread. Tie off thread and cut. Transfer the thread behind the lead eyes and secure fur at that position. Tie off thread and cut. Turn hook over in vise and tie in another fairly large clump of fur behind the hook eye.
Head: Wrap head with thread and coat all wraps with head cement.

Silver is Better than Gold

You never quite forget your first dog, your first car, your first love or your first tarpon on a fly...and not necessarily in that order. My epiphany with *Megalops atlanticus* on a fly occurred many years ago in the backwaters of the Florida Everglades, somewhere in the neighborhood of Florida Bay. I say somewhere because after my skilled captain and guide made three or four instinctive turns in the maze of those back-bay creeks, I was totally lost. While I will admit, that is not a new feeling for me since I am a bit short when it comes to an inventory of directional genes, those mangroves were as close to wilderness as anywhere I've ever fished—including the remote Alaskan bush. Even a GPS would not

have helped me. I turned to my cousin and fishing partner for the day and yelled above the scream of the engine and the wind in my face, "Do you know where we are?" He shook his head, indicating a definitive no. He smiled as he said, "But he does," pointing toward the helm. So I sat back and enjoyed the ride, getting more lost with each passing minute. After a very long and scenic ride we arrived at a beautiful dark-water pond. The scenery alone was worth the trip but when my host said, *They are here,* my pulse quickened. I had to wait as a large black snake fly was tied to my reinforced leader. "Get up on the casting platform," was a simple enough instruction, "And strip out enough line... Now let me see you cast, out there in the middle." Having been through this drill before I knew my cast was about to be evaluated for distance and accuracy so that boat positioning could be determined. The 12-weight felt good and the cast was decent. I passed the first test.

The backwater area was shallow and the boat poled within range of a mesmerizing pod of tarpon rolling gently and then submerging into a tangle of root structure. "Get ready to cast," was my host's next instruction. The spirits of fly-fishers past must have been standing beside me guiding my fly line because buck fever had taken hold. Luckily, it was as perfect a toss as I had ever made. The black fly landed in amongst the trees and three strips later it was eaten. I really don't remember all the advice I was given from that point on but I strip struck as vigorously as I had ever done and kept doing so until my mind told me the fish was hooked. What happened next is a vision that I will take to my grave, and hopefully beyond, since the image of that tarpon leaping from the water and literally catapulting through the trees is permanently etched in my mind. All I could remember thinking is, *There's no way I am landing this thing.* When I say it was in the trees that is not hyperbole; I am almost certain that fish knocked a few dead branches into the water. For a moment the tarpon was suspended in time, gills flaring, water flying and the fish's muscular body contorting in gyrating movements in an attempt to free itself from the hook that I now prayed was securely embedded in its jaw. My concentration was so intently focused I vaguely remember hearing guidance coming from the aft of the skiff: *Stay tight; Bow to the king; More pressure; Reverse the rod angle; He's jumping, bow down; Now gain line... REEL!...*and so on. Amazingly, after all that the tarpon was still hooked. Runs, leaps, hard pulls, and the fish was still there. Now I was convinced my Guardian Angel had made the trip with me. And miracle of all miracles, I could feel the fish coming closer with each pull of the rod. I began to gather back line onto the reel. The monster herring was getting tired. Could it be that I would actually land the first tarpon I ever hooked on a fly? I had more pressure on that fish than I ever thought the fly rod could handle yet the fly line and leader still connected me to this fish with prehistoric lineage. It made one last valiant leap and slowly came boat side. I was in somewhat of a trance but I do recall seeing a gloved hand reach down and grab the leader and then grab the fish by the jaw. And then I heard my cousin hooting and hollering and say, "Can you believe he landed his first tarpon on a fly?" I was grinning, ear-to ear, and pretty darn proud of myself. Hey, I thought, *this is pretty easy.*

Fast forward to a relatively recent trip chasing tarpon on Florida's West Coast...

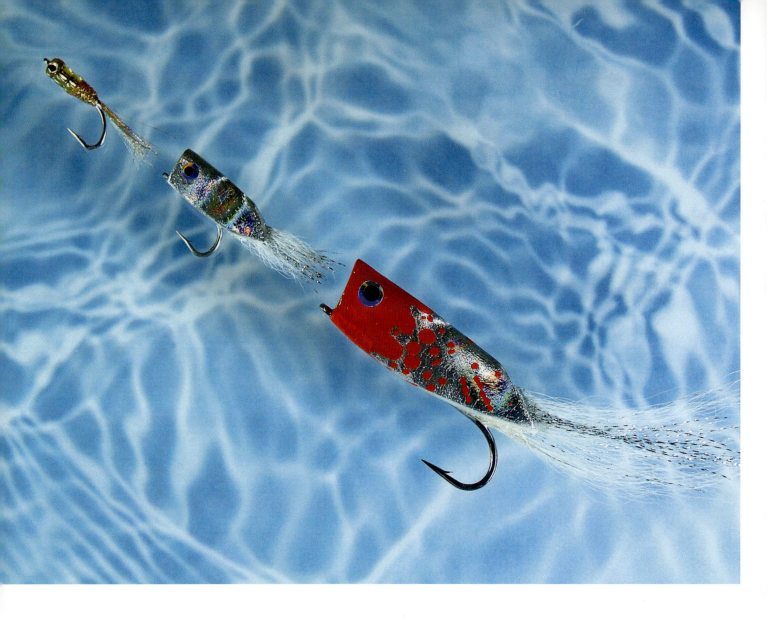

At one point during the day my captain and I were literally surrounded by little tunny. Captain Nick Angelo called them bonito—as do most anglers in the Southeast—but to a Long Islander they were false albacore, and there were acres of them. Yet, I didn't make a single cast! I was too preoccupied eying a pod of 100-pound tarpon to be side-tracked by masses of crashing albies. I must admit, the hardtails tempted me but the call of the tarpon was too great. They were what I was here for and I would not be denied. Such was an angling dilemma I would relish on any other fishing outing. Rather than play with little tunny we quickly chose to set up and wait for the tarpon to reach us. And come they did; I was ready. I did manage a few casts but had my ego trimmed down to size in short order. My fly was rejected. I was rejected. The harsh reality is that in the tarpon game you simply don't get many chances to make the perfect cast.

After a few straight out refusals of my fly I began to think about the hardtails that were still tormenting a raft of small rain bait. With the tarpon now a lost cause we slowly we worked out back to the albies. Just as I was readying myself for a cast, Captain Nick said, "Hold off. Don't cast!" Looking back I saw what he had seen— several permit cruising the edge of a rip. They appeared to be in feeding mood as evidenced by their energetic swimming behavior, and were most likely on the prowl for tasty crab morsels. While the permit may have been hungry they chose to totally ignore the crab pattern I offered them which, at times, had drifted seductively right in front of the pod of the cruising fish. We followed them down the edge of the rip line and halted as the water before us erupted in a football field of foam. It was the largest blitz of jack crevale I had ever witnessed. But tarpon were the only thing on my mind.

In the end and truth be told, the tarpon totally harassed me on that trip. I was humbled. Captain Nick successfully guided me to more than my fair share of shots at these magnificent fish. We saw plenty of big fish in areas known for numbers of big tarpon, but getting them to eat for me was an altogether different challenge. It mattered not that I had had other successes in getting tarpon to the boat using fly-fishing gear. That objective was not achieved. The closest I came to success was to stick flies into the bony maws of three 'poons, and I did jump a 100-plus-pound fish.

Both success and failure at the tarpon game teach valuable lessons. Those anglers who enjoy consistent success demonstrate a resolute will, patience and an unyielding determination; and achievement is

often measured in small victories. I've learned the hard way that the first challenge is to place the fly in the path of oncoming fish often moving at high rates of speed across open sand and grass flats. The fly must be presented at a correct angle so that it crosses the path of the tarpon in a natural way. This involves leading fish with the cast, much as a quarterback leads a receiver. Easier said than done. Despite their size, tarpon are surprisingly wary of anything—including flies—that comes at them from an unnatural direction, a residual imprint from their days as fry. Once the fly is cast and allowed to sink to the level of the fish, long, steady retrieves should get it to intersect the fish's route and capture its attention. Should the fish react to the fly in a positive way, chalk that up as a minor victory. But this is where the real fun begins.

When a big tarpon tracks a fly in thin water it is tough to maintain one's composure while watching the drama unfold. I can vouch for that from personal experience. Buck fever pales in comparison to this deal. But the fly must continue moving along steadily and in a way so as to maintain the *beast's* interest. Sometimes, tarpon will nose the fly or bump it. This is when one's self control needs to be at its peak. Often, a break in the retrieve with either a slight pause or some form of subtle seduction—like jiggling the fly with the rod tip—can excite and stimulate the fish. The goal at this stage of the presentation is to make the fly look alive, to get the tarpon to want to eat it. If the fish actually does inhale the fly, consider that another minor victory, or perhaps even a small miracle. When it does eat, one of two things will happen. The strike will either be an unmistakable, bone-jarring smash or a take so subtle you will think a small sea trout may have mouthed the fly. This latter strike is where it gets tricky. The natural inclination is to lift the rod. That is a big mistake. I've been there too. At this point in the game one needs to keep the fly in motion, even if you see the take and the accompanying flash of a turning fish. The key is letting the line go completely tight, as if you were hung up on a log. Once that happens, a few strip strikes just might seal the deal. If the fly angler makes it this far, congratulations on a job well done. But the mission is far from accomplished for this is when the difficult work begins. Tarpon can pull as hard as a Mack truck, and they will go missile ballistic as airborne acrobats. Should the fish choose to stay low and deep, just settle in for a long, hard fight. If you hook a flyer, all sorts of nasty things can happen. But that is a story for another time and perhaps another book. I remember thinking, *hey, this isn't so easy after all!*

Big Clydester | Buddy Rogers

This fly is a variation of the Clouser and a Big Eye Minnow. It is tied on an altered kahle hook. The higher profile of the hook allows for a taller fly without interfering with the hook gap. The fly is fished in the North Carolina surf for red drum, flounder and speckled trout. The most productive colors are brown over yellow.

Hook: Kahle, sizes 6 to 3/0. Modified by turning 1/4-inch of the eye up on the point side of hook.
Thread: Thread of choice.
Eyes: Tie in dumbbell eyes to the outside of the bend close to the hook eye.
Wing: Tie the bucktail on the point side of the hook just behind the eyes. About midway through the bottom color tie in four strands of gold Krystal Flash or Gliss and Glow. Bucktail is added until desired height of profile is achieved. Several strands of darker Krystal Flash can be added on the final hair layer.
Eyes: Affix stick-on eyes to the hair just behind eyes.
Head: Use five-minute epoxy to coat the entire head to a point slightly behind the stick-on eyes. When fly is about cured flatten the epoxy on the bottom of the head to provide a base for the fly to sit upright.

Big Poppa | Ben Furimsky

This soft-foam popper is ideal for large, surface-feeding gamefish that want a substantial offering.

Hook: TMC 600 SP.
Thread: White, 3/0.
Head: Soft foam popper head drilled and glued on a tube. Cover popper head with Mylar tubing and shape size. Color Mylar with a permanent marker and seal with Softex.
Eyes: Affix doll eyes and apply a light coating of Softex.
Tail: Tie in white strung saddle hackles and ten to twelve strands of Flashabou. Leader is threaded through the head and then tied on to tail hook.

Bikini Popper | Murray Neames | Red Stick Fly Fishers

This unique pattern is designed so that the body is threaded on and then the tail is tied on. The hook eye nestles into a hole in the body of the fly. The fly is fished in the Louisiana surf and marshes for speckled trout redfish.

Hook: Mustad 34007, size 2.
Thread: Flymaster Plus, color of choice.
Body: Cut 2-inch by 5/8-inch bobber to 3/4 inch. Use chamfer bit to make large end of bobber convex. Cut black peg to 1/8-inch and glue inside hole on convex end of bobber. Enlarge hole in peg to 3/32 of an inch. Paint bobber and clear coat if desired.
Tail: Tie in a clump of white Fish Fur two-inches long and then tie in five strands of doubled over Krystal Flash. Tie in a small clump of chartreuse Fish Fur. Top off with a few strands of black bucktail. Tie off, whip finish and cement.

Bizurk Baitfish | Captain Chris Newsome

This fly was designed to imitate a fleeing minnow as it splashes and darts on the water's surface. Most conventional surface flies use bulky foam to keep the fly on top of the water, however this pattern uses no floatation but instead incorporates a Fly Lipp. The lip causes the fly to rise and splash during the strip. Unique among top-water flies is how this pattern falls below the surface on the pause between strips. Fish this fly with fast, aggressive strips and it will gurgle and pop. Slow the strip and the fly will produce a V-wake. Go even slower and the fly will remain several inches underwater.

Hook: Mustad S71SSS or equivalent standard shank-hook, Size 1.
Thread: Danville Flat Wax—210 denier.
Lip: Tie in Fly Lipp in the up position, a direction opposite the hook bend. This will cause the fly to rise when stripped.
Tail: Tie in Polar Flash and rabbit strip at the hook bend.
Body/Wing: Wrap Polar Flash around hook bend toward the hook eye to give a flashy gill plate on the minnow. Coat Polar Flash on hook shank with Hard as Nails for durability. Tie in two clumps of calf tail—one on the top and one on the bottom.
Head: Wrap the head of the fly with Badger Creek Body Fur and trim as needed to give proper proportions.
Eyes: Attach 6mm Doll Eyes with Fletch-Tite Platinum.

Black and Purple Minnow | Captain Doug Sinclair

This synthetic-hair fly is a solid performer for many Southeast and Gulf Coast gamefish. Its effectiveness is in part attributed to the synthetic hair blend of black and purple, popular tarpon colors.

Hook: Gamakatsu or Tiemco, size 1.
Thread: Black.
Throat: Tie in a small tuft of orange synthetic hair material.
Lower Wing: Tie in a length of purple synthetic hair.
Flash: Tie in strands of silver flash material.
Upper Wing: Tie a wing of black synthetic hair material.
Eyes: Affix black eyes.
Head: Using dabs of epoxy build a small triangular head and allow to dry.

Blind Chicken | Captain Billy Trimble

This small crab and crustacean fly can be tied in a limitless array of colors. The original design was tied in pink over chartreuse. It has been fished successfully throughout the entire Texas Gulf Coast and has proven effective on a wide variety of gamefish. Redfish are especially partial to the pattern.

Hook: Tiemco 811 S, size 4. It can also be tied on sizes 2 and 6.
Thread: UTC 210, color to match cone head.
Head: Weighted cone head, color of choice. Insert cone head onto hook. Process is easier if hook is crimped barbless.
Body: Tie on short length of Crystal Chenille, color of choice, and wrap to form a body.
Under Wing: Tie in a small tuft of bucktail or material of choice on the underside of the hook. Materials should be tied to allow hook point to ride up.
Flash: Tie in several strands of flash material.
Over Wing: Tie in a long clump of bucktail approximately three times the length of the hook shank.

BMAR Almost Calamari | Bruce Marino

Originally designed for large Northeast striped bass, this fly has proven effective throughout the Southeast wherever gamefish forage squid. The fly is best fished on a sinking line using two techniques. The first is to allow the fly to sink deeply and simply let it flutter and drift in the current. The second also involves allowing the fly to sink deeply but requires a slow and long strip retrieve. Fish will often hit a squid fly with hard strikes.

Hook: Tiemco # 911S, size 4/0, 4X Long.
Thread: White flat waxed nylon.
Tentacles: Place a ball of Estaz or Cactus Chenille at the bend of the hook, and then tie in five or six pairs of hackles around the ball for tentacles.
Body: Wrap Estaz or Cactus Chenille over the hackles, pressing against the ball. Continue wrapping to a position about 1/2 to 1 inch from the eye of the hook.
Head: To create the fin, attach alternating colors of white, brown and pink Enrico's Sea Fibers using a figure-eight method. Fill the entire area to the eye of the hook. Trim fibers to a fin shape. Place a bunch of white Sea Fibers on top of the hook and an equal amount on the bottom.
Eyes: Trim out eye sockets in Cactus Chenille and affix glass stick-on eyes with epoxy.
Rattle: A rattle beneath the body material is optional.

BMAR Crab | Bruce Marino

This imitation is designed to mimic the fast descent of a fleeing crab. It is a durable pattern that has caught numerous species of fish including bonefish and permit. The use of modeling clay for a body, along with the addition of weight behind the eyes, has resulted in a fly that behaves quite naturally in water.

Hook: Tiemco thin-wire stainless, size 2.
Thread: White flat waxed nylon.
Eyes: Cut two pieces of 60-pound mono. Burn one end of each piece to form a bulb-shaped eye. Tie in both pieces on top of the hook shank. Paint the bulbs black.
Weight: Add in three wraps of lead behind the eye of the hook.
Claws: Strip the bottom from the stems of four brown grizzly hackles to the desired length for claws. Place them on top of the hook shank on the outside of the eyes. Whip finish and cut thread.
Upper Shell Body: Using Marblex self-hardening clay, shape a top shell. Place one form over the mono that forms the eyes and over the claws. Mix some 5-minute epoxy and fill the shell cavity.
Legs/Feelers: Place three sets of Sili-Legs or colored rubber bands and gold Polar Flash "feelers" in the wet epoxy, positioning between the eyes.
Bottom Shell: Shape a second shell for the bottom shell and place it over the top shell. Add clay to reshape as necessary.
Finish: Color the top of the crab with a Magic Marker. Tan, brown and a mottled coloration work well. Cover the entire crab with epoxy and let dry.

BMAR Floating Calamari | Bruce Marino

This pattern can be used to entice fish feeding on squid in the top layer of water. It is designed to cast easily and float high on the surface. It is especially effective when squid jump and skip along the surface. Fish this fly in fast-moving rips or current. Cast, let out additional line and retrieve with long, slow strips.

Hook: Gamakatsu, size 5/0 spinner bait hook.
Thread: White flat waxed nylon.
Rattle: Secure a glass rattle to the hook approximately half way down the length of the shank.
Tentacles: Tie in a large ball of pearl Estaz at the hook bend. This will allow the tentacles to splay outward. Tie in six pairs of matched saddle hackles (color of choice) evenly around the ball to form the tentacles.
Body: 3/4-inch open-cell packing foam, cut to size. Heat a dubbing needle and insert through the center core of the foam cell to form a hollowed-out area. Coat the hook shank with epoxy and push the foam body over the hook eye. Press the rear end of the foam against the ball and tentacles. Color the body with pink and brown permanent-ink markers.
Fins: Cut two matching triangles from 2mm white foam. Coat each piece with CA cement and place one fin on top of the fly at the eye and the other fin under the shank. Press together firmly to form the fin. Let dry and trim to shape.
Eyes: Affix large 3D eyes with epoxy to the rear of the body.

BMAR Shark Fly | Bruce Marino

This is a generic and easy-to-tie shark fly in the ever popular and effective white-and-red coloration. It is most often fished in a chum slick once there is a visual presence of sharks.

Hook: Gamakatsu 5/0.
Tail: Tie in two long white hackles Deceiver-style on the top and back of the hook shank. Place two shorter red grizzly hackles on either side of the white hackles.
Body: Place three white hackles over the hackles already on the shank, one on top and two parallel to the hook shank. Place two additional shorter red grizzly hackles down either side of the hook shank. Repeat this process until the hook shank is filled with hackles about 3/4 of the way toward the eye.
Head: Tie in a large white hackle and palmer it to the hook eye. Repeat this using red hackle or marabou. Tie off. An optional large dumbbell eye can be added for weight.

BMAR Shrimp | Bruce Marino

This generic shrimp pattern is effective when fish are feeding on small to medium sized crustaceans. Excellent pattern for redfish, sea trout and large bonefish. The fly can be fished by allowing it to drift in the current or with the use of a slow, intermittent retrieve.

Hook: Sizes 2 through 6, saltwater.
Thread: Flat waxed white nylon.
Extended Body: White and pink Ultra Hair with gold Sparkle Flash. Hair should be stacked and coated with Flexament.
Eyes: Burnt mono.
Body: Pearl Estaz.
Over Body: Mottled turkey.
Rib: Heavy pink thread.

BMAR Wounded Baitfish | Bruce Marino

This fly is a generic baitfish pattern, and is part of the Wounded Baitfish series. Its overall length is approximately 3 inches, with a wider body profile than the anchovy design. As with other flies in this series, this design uses packing foam, E-Z Body and lead to create the effect of a wounded baitfish that wobbles on the retrieve. It is a very productive pattern for most Southeast and Gulf Coast gamefish feeding on or near the surface. Cast the fly in the area of feeding fish. Allow it to lie on its side and strip slowly when fish return.

Hook: Any suitable hook, size 2.
Thread: White flat waxed nylon.
Tail: Cut a 1 1/2-inch section of pearl E-Z Body. Take a small bunch of gray Ultra Hair and slide it into the E-Z Body. This will form the tail. Make several wraps of thread around the E-Z Body to secure the Ultra Hair in place. Apply Super Glue to the wraps.
Underbody: Cut an anchovy-shaped body from 1/8-inch packing foam. Place silver tape along the bottom of the body on each side. This mimics the silver belly of the anchovy.
Color: With a Magic Marker, color the sides and top of the E-Z body to the colors of the baitfish being imitated. Apply gill marking with a red marker.
Weight: Place the hook in the vise and tie in two strands of lead wire, one on each side of the shank. Use smaller-gauge wire for the smaller baits.
Assembly: Take the prepared hook and thread it through the E-Z Body. Trim the tail to the desired length. Next, insert the colored foam body into E-Z Body, push to form a fatter body profile and tie off.
Head: Whip finish and tie off.
Eyes: Affix prismatic doll eyes with epoxy.

Body Fly Mini Anchovy | Oscar Feliu

This fly is a variation of the generic Body Fly series designed to imitate a number of small baitfish. This specific fly is designed to replicate a small anchovy and demonstrates the versatility of a pattern by simply changing color, size or materials.

Hook: Mustad circle hook, size to match fly.
Thread: Danville A plus or Monocord.
Body: This entire fly is tied as a body. It is tied totally with synthetic fibers and different color flash fibers, producing a translucent effect with subtle flash. Tie in white synthetic material and flash material on the bottom, sides and top of the fly forming the shape of the baitfish. Use darker tones for the top.
Markings: Using a permanent marker color the fibers to achieve the desired effect necessary to replicate the specific baitfish. For this fly use tones of dark and light blue, and barred markings.
Eyes: Add molded eyes affixed to small plastic plates attached to the fly in the region of the head.
Finish: Tie off and add head cement.

Body Fly White Bait | Oscar Feliu

This style of fly is designed to imitate any number of small baitfish. Two of the most popular are the generic White Bait fly and the Mini-Anchovy.

Hook: Mustad circle hook, size to match fly.
Thread: Danville A plus or Monocord.
Body: This entire fly is tied as a body. It is tied totally with synthetic fibers and different color flash fibers, producing a translucent effect with subtle flash. Tie in white synthetic material and flash material on the bottom, sides and top of the fly forming the shape of the baitfish.
Markings: Using a permanent marker color the fibers to achieve the desired effect necessary to replicate the specific baitfish. For this fly subtle tones of blue, purple and yellow markings are added. Red is added for gills.
Eyes: Add molded eyes affixed to small plastic plates attached to the fly in the region of the head.
Finish: Tie off and add head cement.

Bone Bug | Captain Lenny Moffo

This fly was designed for bonefish and permit in the Keys. Its success has made it a go-to fly when both species occupy the same flats.

Hook: Gamakatsu SC 15, size 2.
Thread: Color to match body chenille.
Body/Legs: Tie in holographic flash and tan Ultra Chenille. Double wrap so the butt is fat. Move back on top of the chenille with thread and tie in the rubber legs, trimming to desired length.
Wing: Tie in deer hair as you would for a caddis fly. Tie off and whip finish.

Bonefish Slider | Captain Greg Poole

This fly is a variation of Tim Borski's Bonefish Slider. It is tied heavier, with less hair and a weed guard. This fly has become a favorite pattern for redfish in the shallow water of the Banana and Indian River lagoons.

Hook: Tiemco 811S, size 4.
Thread: Flat waxed nylon.
Eyes: Tie in small or medium lead barbells.
Tail: Cut a bunch of EP fibers about the size of a matchstick and manipulate to form a tapered tail. Tie in on top of the shank about a third of the shank length back from the hook eye. Tie in several strands of Flashabou on either side of the tail. Add stripes with a permanent marker.
Body: Tie in one medium neck hackle and wind forward, tying off behind the eyes.
Collar: Cut, stack and tie in brown deer or elk hair.
Head: Tie in chenille in front of the eyes and wrap to form head.
Weed Guard: Tie in an inch-long length of stiff 15-pound monofilament and form a looped guard.

Bonnet Head Popper | Valerio A. Grendanin

This large popper works well for big bluewater and inshore species such as sailfish, jacks and cobia. This design causes a significant amount of surface commotion when stripped in combination with rod movement. A minimum 10-weight rod and floating line is recommended for best casting results. Marabou placed on the bottom of the popper provides added action when the popper is at rest.

Hook: Owner #5192-171, extra long shank, 7/0.
Thread: White or clear monofilament.
Body/Bonnet: Body is built from 25mm x 30mm marshmallow foam and the bonnet from 1/8-inch foam sheet. Add a line of Super Glue along the length of marshmallow foam, aligning with the end of the sheet. Apply glue to the gap between the marshmallow and the sheet and slowly roll until each side is fully wrapped. Make a 1/8- to 1/4-inch slit along the length of the marshmallow, in the gap between the ends of the foam sheet. Wrap entire hook shank with several layers of thread, crisscrossing back and forth. Coat threads with Super Glue and insert hook shank into slit. Squeeze bottom of marshmallow together closing slit.
Eyes: Create a small hole on each side of the head to accommodate the 12mm Animal Eyes (with stem). Apply a drop of glue on shank of eye and press into hole, firmly against body.
Tail: Tie in 1/8- to 1/4-inch thick bunch of 3-inch-long white Duster Fibers. Place around the hook shank and behind the popper. Add about 20 strands of 4-inch DNA Flash over the Duster Fibers. Follow with about 30 strands of 2-inch-long white Crimped Nylon, added to the bottom of the hook to prevent fouling.
Collar: Tie in and wrap large, red Ice Chenille.
Beard: Red marabou added to the bottom of the hook shank so it sticks downward.

Booby Fly | Ron Russell | Tied by Larry Clemens

This fly was designed to push water when fishing for puppy drum under muddy or murky water conditions. The two bulbous protrusions tied at the forward portion of the fly achieve that effect. The fly has also proved effective on black drum and striped bass.

Hook: Any suitable SS hook, sizes 1 through 2/0.
Thread: Flat-waxed nylon, red.
Tail: Tie in gold, copper or color of choice flash material on the underside of the hook shank followed by chartreuse bucktail.
Eyes: Plastic 9mm beads affixed to a stem of monofilament with super glue; use bead-chain eyes for a heavier fly.
Collar: Tie in cross-cut red rabbit strip—approximately three inches in length—and palmer forward toward the hook eye.
Head: Form a small head with red thread, whip finish and apply a coat of head cement.

Borski Backcountry Skunk | Tim Borski

This fly was originally designed for snook and baby tarpon but has also proven effective for redfish, pike, brown trout and smallmouth bass. The pattern can be tied in a number of different sizes and color combinations.

Hook: Tiemco 811S, size 1/0.
Thread: White flat waxed nylon.
Anti Fouling Loop: Tie in looped section of stiff monofilament at the bend of the hook and on top of the hook shank.
Tail: Tie in a moderate to long strip of white rabbit fur. You can vary color to preference.
Body: Tie in white tufts of marabou on top of the hook shank and along the flanks of the hook.
Head: Tie in and spin deer hair tightly forming the head. Leaving hair fibers flowing toward the rear of the fly. Trim head hair fibers to shape.
Weed Guard: Tie in stiff monofilament forming a two-pronged weed guard.

Borski Body Fur Bone Food | Tim Borski

This fly design is a recent adaptation as an alternative to bodies that require tying polypropylene yarn bodies in figure-eight style. The fly has been fished successfully in south Florida, the Bahamas and Mexico and has taken bonefish, redfish, smallmouth bass and carp as well as other gamefish species.

Hook: Tiemco 811S, size 1.
Thread: White flat waxed nylon.
Eyes: Tie in small dumbbell eyes, yellow with black.
Tail: Tie in a short length of synthetic fur with Krystal Flash intermixed. Tie on the underside of the hook shank.
Body: Tie in synthetic body fur material with blended flash, forming into a small crustacean body shape.

Borski Body Fur Seaducer | Tim Borski

This fly was inspired by the legendary Seaducer pattern. It is a variation that incorporates a bunny tail and body fur as a collar. This is a very effective snook pattern but works well for most any gamefish that range throughout the Southeast and Gulf Coast regions. It is also effective in the Northeast.

Hook: Tiemco 811S, size 1.
Thread: White flat waxed nylon.
Tail: Tie in a strip of white rabbit fur. You can vary color to preference.
Body: Tie in white Body Fur blended with flash material and wrap to form body.
Collar: Tie in hot pink Body Fur and wrap as collar.
Weed Guard: Tie in stiff monofilament for a two-pronged guard. Tie off thread, whip finish and apply head cement.

Borski Body Fur Slider | Tim Borski

This impressionistic pattern is effective for most fish that frequent shallow water to feed. While originally designed for redfish and snook, the fly has also taken brown trout and smallmouth bass. It is part of a series of patterns that incorporate body fur into the design.

Hook: Tiemco 811S, size 1.
Thread: White flat waxed nylon.
Eyes: Lead barbells tied in, yellow with black.
Tail: Tie in a strip of olive rabbit fur along with a few strands of gold flash.
Body: Rear portion of body is tied and palmered rabbit fur; forward portion is body fur with sparse flash intermixed.
Weed Guard: Tie in stiff monofilament for a two-pronged guard. Tie off thread, whip finish and apply head cement.

Borski Bunny Sliders | Tim Borski

This fly represents a variation of a Bonefish Slider from the early 1990's. The fly has taken redfish, snook, steelhead and carp.

Hook: Tiemco 811S, size 1.
Thread: White flat waxed nylon.
Eyes: Tie in medium barbell eyes, yellow and black.
Tail: Tie in a short to moderate length strip of barred tan rabbit fur. Hook rides point up so tie in rabbit strip with leather side facing downward.
Body: Tie in clumps of olive marabou or synthetic hair, encircling the hook shank.
Collar: Tie in and wind a short section of Crystal Chenille or similar material. Bring thread forward of the eyes, tie off, whip finish and add a dab of head cement.

Borski Chernobyl Crab | Tim Borski

This is literally one very hot crustacean pattern that is very effective for redfish. It has also been productive for flats-roaming striped bass and other gamefish that feed on crabs in shallow water. This impressionistic crab fly has developed into an all-around favorite skinny-water pattern. Vary weight, hook size and color scheme to suit fishing conditions.

Hook: Tiemco 811S, size 1.
Thread: White flat waxed nylon.
Eyes: Tie in bead-chain eyes.
Tail: Tie in a tuft of tan or very pale orange marabou followed by two furnace saddle hackles on either side of the marabou, concave hackle surface facing outward.
Body: Tie in and spin antelope or deer hair. Rib the body with two neck hackles, and palmer forward toward the eyes.
Weed Guard: Can be tied with or without a weed guard of stiff monofilament.
Finish: Apply a number of wraps forward of the eyes, whip finish and apply head cement.

Borski Dubbed Head Fur Shrimp | Tim Borski

This impressionistic shrimp pattern has been effective in saltwater and freshwater for all species that eat crustaceans. It is a pattern that has been part of the originator's process of tweaking Craft Fur shrimp patterns.

Hook: Tiemco 811S, size 1.
Thread: White flat waxed nylon.
Eyes: Tie in bead-chain eyes.
Tail: Tie in tufts of olive over tan Craft Fur on the underside of the hook shank
Body: Tie in a neck hackle and palmer forward toward the eyes.
Collar: Tie in Craft Fur and subtle flash around the hook shank.
Weed Guard: Can be tied with or without a weed guard of stiff monofilament.
Finish: Apply a number of wraps forward of the eyes, whip finish and apply head cement.

Borski Florida Bay Slider | Tim Borski

This slider design has been a work in progress from the 1990s. It has been fished successfully in freshwater and saltwater.

Hook: Tiemco 811S, size 1.
Thread: White flat waxed nylon.
Eyes: Tie in bead-chain eyes.
Tail: Tie in a moderate length of tan rabbit strip on the top of the hook shank. Hook rides point up so tie in strip with leather side facing down.
Body: Tie in and spin olive deer hair leaving tip extensions to form the body. Trim hair fibers, leaving bottom of rabbit strip exposed.
Head: Tie in and tightly spin chartreuse deer hair. Trim hair fibers to form the head.
Weed Guard: Tie in stiff monofilament forming a two-pronged weed guard. Tie off thread. Whip finish and apply head cement.

Bottom Shrimp | Bob Lindquist

A variation of the Woolly Bugger, this fly was originally designed for northern weakfish. It has become a very productive fly for large bonefish in the Florida Keys.

Hook: Gamakatsu bucktail or jig hook or Gamakatsu SP11 3L-3H, size 2.
Thread: 3/0 Monocord or Gudebrod.
Eyes: Lead eyes tied at the bend of bucktail hook or Clouser-like on SP11-3L3H. Mono eyes will be placed on either side of the tail.
Tail: EP Fibers or Llama. Mix with a bit of Angel Hair. Use a moderate length of material, but keep it a bit shorter than the body length.
Body: EP Fibers or Llama. Again mix with Angel Hair. This is best done on a dubbing machine with stainless-steel wire. Twist a dubbing brush of colors and materials to suit your needs. Llama and sparse pearl flash seem to be the most productive.

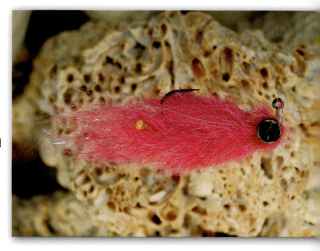

Briny Mullet | Bob Lindquist

This pattern was designed as a small mullet imitation for tarpon. It is tied with a dense deer-hair head that will push water and create low-frequency sound.

Hook: Gamakatsu SC15, size 1/0.
Thread: White Monocord or Gudebrod GX.
Flash: Tie in a couple strands of flash material.
Bottom Wing: Fold two shorter lengths of white EP fibers in a two-thirds/one third proportion and tie in on each side of the shank to form a body shape. Tie so that the longer length is up along the shank and the shorter is beneath it forming a belly.
Top Wing: Tie on a length of blue EP fibers on top of the white.
Head/Body: Stack and build olive deer hair as a head. Use white deer hair for the underside of head.
   To achieve a solid stack apply force with the thread in down, in, out and up motions only. Do not spin the hair. Figure-eight the thread to lock in the hair.
Eyes: Stick-on eyes affixed with glue.
Finish: Trim head to shape.

Brooks Blonde

Originated by Joe Brooks | Tied by A.J. Forzano

This is one of the true hair-wing classics. The Blonde made a first appearance on the fly-fishing scene in the 1950's and has been one of the most effective freshwater and saltwater files of all time. The fly can be modified to any size and color combination and is effective for gamefish from Maine to the Texas Gulf Coast, and beyond.

Hook: Mustad 34007 size 1 or sized to fly.
Thread: Black.
Tail: Tie in a clump of bucktail of desired color.
Body: Silver body flash or tinsel tied in at the hook bend and wound forward toward the hook eye.
Wing: Tie in a clump of bucktail at a point behind the eye, leaving enough room for the head.
   Variations of the original include multiple wings and/or a belly.
Head: Build a head of thread, tie off, whip finish and apply a dab of head cement.

Brush with the Devil | Captain Paul Dixon

This simple-to-tie shrimp pattern is a very effective fly for any number of flats species that feed on crustaceans.

Hook: Mustad 34002, sizes 4, 2 and 1.
Thread: Tan or fine monofilament.
Weight: Slide gold or brass bead or cone head. Tie in thread behind head and wind to the hook bend.
Nose: Tie in a small clump chartreuse marabou at the hook bend.
Feelers: Tie in a few strands of gold or chartreuse Krystal Flash.
Legs: Tie in two small, tan grizzly hackles.
Eyes: Tie in red or black monofilament eyes.
Body: Tie on tan EP Shrimp Brush fibers and wind thread to the bead. Wrap Shrimp Brush forward and tie off behind bead and whip finish.

Buckshot Bonefish | Captain Lenny Moffo

This fly was designed to take advantage of the uniformity benefits of epoxy. It has proved to be a very effective bonefish fly.

Hook: Gamakatsu SC 15, size 2.
Thread: Clear fine monofilament.
Tail: Tie in a small section of marabou followed by a small amount of Krystal Flash. Tie in two small barred hackles, splayed.
Body/Head/Eyes: Cut a section of clear plastic from a bubble pack into the shape of a kit and hot glue it on the back of the hook shank. Hot glue size 4 or 5 lead buckshot as eyes. Wrap a section of Krystal Flash forward in a figure-eight fashion.
Finish: Apply 5-minute epoxy to the body and head and place on a rotation dryer.

Bug-A-Bou | Captain Paul Dixon

This multi-purpose, generic crustacean pattern is easy to tie and presents a very buggy and effective look.

Hook: Mustad 34007, size 2, 4 and 1.
Thread: Fine monofilament.
Weight: Tie in a pair of black lead barbells at the eye of the hook and wind thread to the bend.
Eyes: Tie in red monofilament eyes.
Claws: Tie in a pair of chartreuse Hareline Dubbin marabou claws.
Feelers: Tie in a small clump of chartreuse marabou and a small clump of light tan yak hair.
Antennae: Tie in two strands of Krystal Flash.
Body: Tie in a length of Krystal Chenille and a tan hackle. Bring thread back to eye of hook. Wind the chenille forward and tie off. Palmer hackle forward and tie off. Whip finish.

Bunny Strip Cuda Fly | Kevin "Fluff" Arculeo

This fly was created to reproduce the action of the long, rubber tube lure. Barracuda respond to fast, fleeing prey. This fly can be fished by using long, fast, continuous one-handed strips, or by tucking the rod under your arm for a fast-as-you-can two-handed continuous retrieve.

Hook: Gamakatsu SP11-3L3H (front hook), size 3/0; Owner Aki Twist Hook (rear hook), size 2/0 or 3/0.
Thread: Monofilament, 6/0.
Wire Preparation: Tie in a piece of wire roughly 10 inches long by feeding the wire through the eye of the hook. The wire should run from the hook bend on the bottom of the hook shank through the eye across the top of the hook shank with the remaining wire hanging off the back of hook. Tie the wire in by wrapping thread from the hook eye to the hook bend and then back to eye.
Body: Tie in the Magnum Rabbit Strip in chartreuse, pink or orange. Wrap the thread to the hook bend and then back to eye. Using a dubbing needle, poke a hole in the rabbit strip about 1 inch behind the head and thread the wire through the hole on the leather side. Poke another hole through the rabbit strip about 1/2 inch behind the first hole and thread the wire back through the rabbit strip. Repeat again, threading the wire through the rabbit strip. The third threading of the wire should be back through the furry side of the rabbit strip coming out of the leather side. Attach the tandem back hook using a Haywire Twist. Poke a hole in the rabbit and stick the hook through the hole. Using 5-minute epoxy, glue the back hook to the leather of the rabbit strip.
Head/Collar: Holding the Polar Fibre comb out fluff from the bulky end. Measure the Polar Fibre so the pointed ends are 2 inches past the bend in the hook. Tie in Polar Fibre Deceiver style. Tie in a clump on the left side of hook just behind the eye. Tie in another clump on the right side just behind the hook eye. Tie in another clump of Polar Fibre on the top of the hook shank just behind the eye. Tie in a small clump of Polar Fibre on the top. Comb through all the clumps of Polar Fibre to form the 3-D body and head. The ends of the Polar Fibre will create a collar from the flexi-Cord head cover to the Rabbit. Attach the Flexi-Cord head cover. On one end of the flexi-Cord cut a 1/2-inch slit in the crease of the cord. Slide the flexi-Cord over the Polar Fibre head and tie in about 1/16 inch behind the hook eye. Cut the tag end off just behind the hook eye. Whip-finish the head.
Coating: Apply the silicone to the fly body starting at the eye of the hook and spread it toward the back just past the bend in the hook to the end of the flexi-Cord. Work the silicone into the flexi-Cord covering the entire head of the fly.
Eyes/Finish: Use 5-minute epoxy to attach the 3D Molded Eyes on each side of the head. Apply epoxy to thread on front of the fly. Place a light coat of Photo Flo over the silicone.

Buzz's Shrimp

Tied by Oscar Feliu | Originated by Buzz Fender

This shrimp pattern is very effective for tailing redfish and bonefish.

Hook: Mustad S74s SS, size 1 to 6.
Thread: Monocord, 3/0, burned orange.
Tail: Tie in shrimp-colored or beige Craft Fur.
Eyes: Tie in small barbell eyes on the top of the shank so the hook point rides point up.
Body: Peach Estaz tied in and wrapped to form body.
Legs: Tie in Sili-Legs, clear with copper specks.
Carapace: Tie in twelve strands of root beer Krystal Flash.
Weed Guard: Tie in 30-pound hard monofilament.

Cactus Pete | Captain Marcia Foosaner

This versatile fly was designed for small gear and smaller-sized Southeast species of gamefish.

Hook: Mustad 34007, size 1.
Thread: Any suitable thread.
Eyes: Make a few wraps of thread behind the eye of the hook and apply a dab of super glue. Tie in small dumbbell eyes on top of hook shank. Hook rides point up.
Body: Tie in Estaz or Cactus Chenille along the hook shank back to the bend. Wrap chenille forward to a point behind the eyes and secure thread in front of dumbbell.
Wing: Rotate fly and attach a section of streamer hair immediately behind the eye of the hook. Whip finish.
Eyes: Attach stick-on eyes and apply a dab of five-minute epoxy around the eyes.

Cajun Rattle Shrimp

Peter Bongiovanni | New Orleans Fly Fishers

This design incorporates a rattle to enhance the fish-attracting qualities of the fly. This pattern has been fished effectively for redfish and speckled trout in the Grand Isle, Delacroix Isle and Venice areas of Louisiana.

Hook: Mustad 34011, size 1.
Thread: Thread of choice.
Eyes: Wrap hook with a base of thread and tie in 7/32 lead or large bead-chain eyes.
Rattle: Tie in worm rattle behind eyes and on top of hook.
Legs: Tie in green Sili-Legs under the rattle.
Body: Tie in chartreuse Estaz over rattle and eyes and wrap entire hook.
Tail: Apply Super Glue to tail and insert a plastic shrimp tail onto the hook. Allow glue to set.

Cave's Li'l Wobbler | Jon Cave

The original Wobbler was designed as a fly-fishing counterpart to spoon-type lures. This is a smaller version of that fly. A unique trait is the fly's side-to-side oscillating motion that will not twist the line. The pattern can be tied to imitate shrimp, crabs, baitfish, worms, leeches, frogs, and a variety of other prey upon which fish feed. Although Wobblers were originally designed to catch redfish, the various styles have also been used as a favorite pattern for many other gamefish.

Hook: TMC 811S, size 2-8.
Thread: Flat waxed nylon (color to match prismatic tape portion of the body)
Tail: Tie in four strands of Krystal Flash or Accent Flash that are 1 1/2 times the length of the hook. Follow with a sparse clump of bucktail as long as the shank of the hook. Trim the excess bucktail, but do not trim the excess flash as it will be used later as ribbing to segment the body. Attach a sparse amount of bucktail at the same tie-in point as the flash. The bucktail should be roughly equal in length to the shank of the hook. Once the bucktail is secured, continue wrapping over it with thread, stopping just behind the eye. Trim any excess material.
Body: Twist the extra strands of flash into one long piece and spiral that single strand down the shank of the hook to form a segmented body. Tie off the twisted strand just behind the hook eye and then fold it back so that the leftover pieces form a wing that flows back toward the hook point. Whip finish the thread just behind the eye and trim the excess thread. Fold a small piece of prismatic or glitter tape so that the adhesive sides are stuck together back to back with the shiny sides exposed. Cut a small egg-shaped disk from the folded tape and attach to the hook shank with super glue. To be properly positioned, the rear edge of the disk should be even with the initial tie-in point at the rear of the hook. The front of the disk should stop at halfway down the shank of the hook.
Eyes: Fasten a pair of medium bead-chain eyes immediately behind the disk so the eyes are actually touching the rear of the disk. The weight and proper placement of the eyes help create the fly's wobbling action and prevent spin when stripped through the water.
Finish: Apply a thin coat of epoxy to the top and bottom of the disk.

Cave's Wobbler | Jon Cave

The weight distribution and placement of the eyes on this spoon fly helps create a unique wobbling action, and prevent a spin or rotation that causes detrimental line twist. The fly can also be tied bend-back style.

Hook: TMC 811S, size 2 through 2/0.
Thread: Flat-waxed nylon, color to match body.
Tail: Tie in four pieces of Krystal Flash or Accent Flash, one and a half times the length of the hook. Follow with a sparse clump of bucktail as long as the shank of the hook.
Body: Lightly coat the inside of the Mylar tubing with 5-minute epoxy, and then flatten and shape until glue is set with no air pockets in tubing. Recoat outside of tubing with epoxy. Fasten a two-inch-long piece of braided Mylar tubing at the tie-in point 1/3 of the way down the bend. Let 1/4-inch-long strands of Mylar extend past the tie-in point so they blend with the bucktail and flash. Tie-off the Mylar tubing directly behind the hook eye; make a jam knot and a whip finish. The epoxy will hold the fly together. Use fingers to flatten and shape the tubing so that it is wider at the end of the hook than it is next to the eye. Continue shaping the Mylar until the epoxy has cured and the inside walls of tubing are completely stuck together to form a wafer-thin body. Trim the excess tubing and finish the head with thread.
Eyes: Large bead-chain or smallish dumbbell eyes. Attach the bead-chain eyes at the tie-in point at the bend of the hook.
Weedguard: An optional weed guard of either .014 wire or a single strand of 20# mono can be added.
Finish: Use a coffee stirrer to apply a second light coat of epoxy over the Mylar tubing.

Chandeleur Special

Tied by Tom Herrington | Historic Ocean Springs Saltwater Fly Fishing Club
Style origins unknown

While the use of this versatile, easy-to-tie deep minnow pattern can be traced back to the 1960s in coastal Gulf States, and in freshwater for bass and bluegill, more modern versions of the fly are attributed to the Clouser Deep Minnow. Many variations of the Deep Minnow are a staple in the fly boxes of Gulf Coast fly-anglers as they are productive for a wide range of gamefish. This variation is an especially effective Chandeleur Islands pattern. It is tied to replicate the popular motor oil grub.

Hook: Mustad 34007 or similar. Small jig hooks can also be used. Size according to the species and bait.
Thread: Danville flat waxed nylon, olive.
Eyes: Tie on gold barbell eyes on top of the hook shank about 1/4 of an inch from the hook eye. Any form of weighted, dual-eye will work.
Bottom Wing: With hook point facing upward, tie in a bunch of olive bucktail at the eye and on the underside of the hook shank. Place the wing over and between the barbell eyes and secure with thread wraps behind the barbell. Snug hair firmly enough to hold hair in place, while not allowing it to flare.
Flash: Invert the hook and tie in pearl Krystal Flash.
Over Wing: Tie in another bunch of olive bucktail.
Head: Build a head with thread, whip finish and apply head cement.

Chaz The Yellow Weenie | Captain Russ Shirley

This fly was originally designed for the Bayport and Chassahowitzka tarpon flats in the Homosassa area. It is effective on bright days when the most popular colors aren't producing, especially if tarpon are hanging near or swimming around lime outcroppings surrounded by sand or light-colored bottom.

Hook: Mustad 3407 SS, size 3/0 or Owner 4/0.

Thread: Yellow flat-waxed nylon.

Tail: Tie in a 20-pound hard-nylon loop on top of the hook, near the rear. Divide six equally sized yellow or grizzly cock saddle hackles. Face each bunch outwards and high-tie on top of hook above the hook's barb. Coat feathers from tie-in spot back for approximately one inch with Flexament or Softex. This keeps feather wrapping to a minimum.

Collar: Once coated feathers are dry, add a sparse yellow squirrel tail collar.

Head/Eyes: Build-up a head with thread, affix Mylar stick-on eyes and coat with epoxy; turn until dry.

Cheryl's Brackish Water Shrimp | Tom Tripi

This highly effective shrimp pattern was designed for speckled trout. If it has one shortfall it is that trout attack it, and after several fish the trout's teeth begin to tear it up. While many tiers craft a sparse version of this pattern—using fewer materials and no silicone glue—the full version takes only about five minutes to tie, aside from the drying time. However you choose to tie the fly, the black eyes are considered a must.

Hook: Mustad 34007, size 1/0 or similar.

Thread: Fine, clear monofilament and 3/0 white.

Body: Cover hook with monofilament. This serves as an anchor for the body materials. Apply the materials as follows, progressively from the bend of the hood to the eye. First tie in mixed color Flashabou/Krystal Flash, followed by four to five fibers of ostrich plume. Tie in a bunch of pink marabou.

Pincers: Tie in quality dry-fly hackle tips, stripped and cut in center to shape a pincer, then edge with sparkle nail polish.

Eyes: Silk flower stamens painted black and varnished.

Antennae: Tie in black horsetail or moose mane.

Legs: Tied and palmered "webby" emu feather.

Carapace/Abdomen/Shellback: Use a thin, fine line of G. E. silicone glue. For the rostrum point, carapace and abdomen shell back use clear Swiss Straw. Start wraps at tail end above hook barb and make segmented turns, ending behind the eye of the hook. Extend Swiss Straw over eye of hook and form tail as shown. Coat Swiss Straw with a thin lacquer or sparkle nail polish.

Clearwater Fly | Leigh West

This Clouser-style pattern is based on a color combination of a productive rattling jig that was fished in the tannin-stained waters of the Everglades for snook and redfish. The fly was also used for summer beach snook fishing in the clear waters around Clearwater, Florida. This dark pattern works well over white sand bottom and has caught many large snook and trout. It also works well as a bendback pattern. Either pattern can be tied with a glass or plastic rattle in the body that helps when fishing dirty or tannin-stained waters.

Hook: Tiemco 811S or 800S, size 2-4.

Thread: Brown and fluorescent orange flat waxed nylon.

Eyes: Starting with the brown thread, tie in the extra small dumbbell (brass or lead) about 1/3 of the distance back from the hook eye.

Body: Tie in the gold, medium Mylar tubing near the curve of the hook, leaving a short tail, if desired. Wrap the tubing forward over the hook and secure in front of eyes. Apply head cement to the body for durability.

Wing: Tie in a small clump of root beer Fish Hair, then overlay with a generous amount of peacock herl.

Lateral Line: Tie in four to six strands of pearl Flashabou on each side of fly.

Head: Build up the head with thread and whip finish. Apply the fluorescent orange thread as an accent stripe in front of the wing, over the brown thread. Cover with head cement.

Clouser Deep Minnow | Bob Clouser

This pattern was first developed to fish smallmouth bass and stripers in the tier's native Pennsylvania rivers. It was quickly embraced by Southeast saltwater anglers as a very effective fly for a wide range of gamefish, such as redfish, bonefish, permit and sea trout. Since its introduction, this highly productive pattern has gained a distinguished reputation among saltwater fly-fishermen worldwide. The Clouser Minnow has spawned a myriad of modifications and variations of the original pattern design. It is a very adaptable fly and can be tied in numerous color combinations and sizes to suit the prevalent bait and fishing situations.

Hook: Mustad 34007 or equivalent, sizes 4 to 2/0.
Thread: White 3/0.
Body: None in the standard tie.
Eyes: Barbell lead eyes, sizes 5/32 or 3/16, tied in on the top of the hook shank, positioned approximately 1/4 to 1/3 of the way back from the eye of the hook. This fly is tied to ride hook point up.
Underwing: Tie in white bucktail or Ultra Hair in front of the eyes. Flash material such as Krystal Flash or Flashabou may be added on the sides of the underwing or between the upper and lower wings. The bucktail or Ultra Hair should also be tied down behind the barbell eyes, covering the center portion of the barbell.
Overwing: Chartreuse bucktail or Ultra Hair tied in at a point in front of the eyes.
Head: White thread.

Cobia Killer

Captain Paul Dixon | Inspired by Gordy Hill's Cobia Fly

This pattern was first used in the Florida Keys to cast to cobia following rays on the flats. The fly was brought north, modified and used for stripers on the flats of Gardiner's Bay. It is especially effective on the high tide, since it sinks very quickly and its descent gets it into the strike zone rapidly. Fish the fly by allowing it to bump the bottom during the retrieve.

Hook: SS of choice, sized to match bait.
Thread: Orange/brown.
Tail: Tie in Craft Fur and strands of gold Flashabou at the bend. Add Sili-Legs in on top of the tail.
Eyes: Wrap thread forward and tie in lead eyes.
Wing: Tie in splayed brown barred hackles (tarpon-fly style) and orange /black squirrel tail directly behind the lead eyes.

Coma Cockaho | Catch Cormier

The plastic H&H Cockaho Minnow is a favorite lure among speckled-trout anglers for fall fishing in Louisiana. The Coma Cockaho is a full-body fly designed to match the lure. Best colors for the Silli-Legs are chartreuse (green water) or black (dark or clear water). The fly has been fished effectively throughout Alabama and Texas.

Hook: Mustad 34011 stainless hook, size 1.
Thread: Thread of choice.
Eyes: Tie in 1/50-ounce lead hourglass eyes, painted.
Tail/Body: Cut a 1/4-inch section of pearl Mylar tubing and tie in at the bend of the hook. Tie in medium Ice Chenille and wrap forward to the eyes.
Legs: Trim off one end of the solid portion of the Silli-Legs so the "legs" move freely. Tie in just behind the eyes. Wrap the tag end of the chenille in front of the eyes and tie off. Next, tie in thread at the bend, just where the chenille begins, and pull half the clump of Silli-Legs back over the top and secure, and the other half over the bottom and secure. Trim the legs to same length as the Mylar tail. For added life, take a fine brush and apply a light coat of 2-ton transparent epoxy to the Silli-Legs on top and below the body.
Finish: Whip finish thread at the head.

Coma Spoon | Catch Cormier

Jon Cave's Wobbler inspired this pattern that is very simliar to the classic Colonel Spinner lure. The Coma Spoon has a longer, narrower body than the typical spoon fly allowing it to sink faster. With its twisted shape, on a strip, the fly rotates in one direction. During the pause between strips, the fly rotates back the other direction. The fly has been fished effectively for redfish from South Carolina to south Florida.

Hook: Mustad 34011 SS, size 1 or 1/0. Using pliers, make a series of slight bends in the hook until it assumes somewhat of a caddis shape.
Thread: Fluorescent red.
Body: Wrap thread back to halfway down bend of hook. Cut section of large Wapsi Mylar tubing and slide down shank from front until unraveled endings are past thread. Secure Mylar at bend with thread and knot off with a whip finish. Place thread around Mylar just behind hook eye and secure with several wraps. Trim excess Mylar on back and front, and then make a clean thread head on front. Using fingers, flatten out the Mylar.
Coating: Mix together a tiny amount of five-minute epoxy and, using a toothpick, spread it on both top and bottom. Cut a square of clear zip-loc bag material, enough to cover both sides of the fly, and use this to squeeze the epoxy into the Mylar being careful not to get the epoxy on your fingers. As the epoxy begins to set, press the Mylar flat. Allow to set. Later, using a brush, coat with thirty-minute epoxy to make it waterproof, durable and shiny.

Cooper's Offshore Squid | Harvey Cooper

This durable pattern is effective for all offshore gamefish that feed on squid.

Hook: 5/0 Gamakatsu Spinnerbait hook.
Thread: Danville flat waxed nylon.
Eyes: Black/silver 3D eyes.
Head: Cut a 1 1/2-inch length of 1/8" Flexi-Cord light pearl braid. Select two long white saddle feathers and align the tips. Place two pink marabou feathers on either side of the saddle feathers. Place two white marabou feathers on top of the pink feathers. Place white ostrich feathers around the white marabou feathers. Insert all the feather stems into the length of braid. Wrap all the materials together. Whip finish and cut the thread.
Body: Wrap a layer of thread over the hook shank. Cut a 2 1/2" length of 3/8" Flexi-Cord light pearl braid. Invert one end. Insert the feathers into the inverted braid. Position all the materials on top of the shank and tie down. Begin tying 1/2 inch from the feathers. Do not cut the thread. Mix a small batch of five-minute epoxy and glue the eyes to the head. Cut a 4 1/2-inch length of 3/8" Flexi-Cord light pearl braid and slide it over the hook shank. Overlap 1/4 inch of the head and the new length of braid material. Tie the braid down over the head. Whip finish and cut the thread. Invert the remainder of the braid creating the body.
Finish: Place color dots over the head, body, and feathers with the pink and purple markers. Mix a batch of two-ton epoxy. Add the color sparkles to the mix. Apply the first coat of epoxy over the head and body. Be careful not to cover the feathers. Place in drying wheel and rotate for one hour. Mix another batch of two-ton epoxy. Add the color sparkles to the mix. Apply the final coat of epoxy over the head and body. Place in drying wheel and rotate for one hour.

Cooper's Mantis Shrimp | Harvey Cooper

This mantis shrimp pattern was originally designed as a teaser for use in the Northeast, but it is also effective as a fly for various gamefish throughout the Southeast and Gulf Coast. This pattern requires two templates, one each for a carapace and a telson.

Hook: Tiemco 911S hook, 2/0 or larger.
Thread: Danville flat-waxed nylon, white.
Weight: X-Large dumbbells.
Eyes: Foam cylinders, 1/16 inch, black, glued in place.
Antennae: Two Sili-Legs, amber/gold flake glued on top of the foam and slightly under the eyes.
Carapace: Outer shell comprised of pearl Sili-Skin, 1/8" white foam and brown hackle. Cut out the carapace template approximately 1 3/4". The top half of the carapace should be 1/4" wide. The bottom half should start at 1/4" and end at 1/2" wide.
Claws: Create top claw by cutting 1" off a rubber band. Measure 1/4" from each end, fold the rubber band, and whip finish each end. Apply a drop of glue to the wraps. Create the bottom claw by cutting 1 1/2-inches off a rubber band. Glue the bottom claw slightly under the top claw. Spread the claws apart and glue the top half of the carapace down.
Body: The outer shell 1/2-inch natural pearl Sili-Skin. Cut a length of E-Z Body Braid. It should be long enough to overlap where the head is tied in and end just before the hook eye. Mix a small batch of epoxy and coat the inside of the E-Z body. Attach the Body Braid directly over the bottom of the head. Before the epoxy sets press the body flat. Continue applying pressure to the full length of the body until the epoxy sets. Palmer the brown hackle around the head assembly. Whip finish and cut thread.
Swimmerets: 1/8" tan rabbit Zonker strips.
Telson: Outer shell made from pearl Sili-Skin.

Cowen's Coyote | Henry Cowen

This fly was inspired by the Blakemore Roadrunner lure. Initially designed for striped bass it has since proven very effective for numerous species of gamefish, including redfish, sea trout, snook, cobia and small tarpon. A short and steady retrieve works best, as will allowing the fly to freefall. The movement of the rabbit tail and the vibrations caused by the spinner make this an ideal searching pattern.

Hook: Tiemco 811S, size 1/0.
Thread: Danville monofilament, fine.
Barrel Swivel: Slide the barrel swivel onto the hook, leaving it free swinging at the eye of the hook.
Eyes/Spike: Tie down the Real Eyes (with prismatic stick-on eyes) and the monofilament spike (40-pound test, clear) behind the eyes. Upon completion of fly burn a ball into the back of the spike to prevent the rabbit strip from coming undone.
Tail: Lay in the rabbit strip on top of the hook, hide-side up. Measure 1/4 inch past the bend in the hook and make a hole into the strip. Lash down the rabbit both in front of and behind the Real Eyes.
Body: Wrap gold Bill's Bodi-Braid or similar material around the rabbit strip from the hook bend to the eyes. Add in pearl Krystal Flash behind the eyes.
Wing: Tie in bucktail at a point near the hook eye and tie off. Apply head cement to all wraps.
Spinner Blade: Add split ring and spinner blade to swivel.

Cowen's Jigs Up | Henry Cowen

This pattern was inspired by the Popovics Surf Candy, Dan Blanton's use of jig-style hooks and Dave Sellars unique rear weighting system. The fly allows shallow-water anglers to fish an epoxy style without fear of snagging the bottom- the hook rides point up. It has taken redfish, speckled trout, snook, juvenile tarpon, striped bass, false albacore and even bonefish.

Hook: Mustad Ultra Point 32786BLN, size 1/0.
Thread: Danville monofilament, fine.
Underbelly: Tie in white bucktail on side opposite of hook point.
Wing: Tie in olive bucktail on top of underbelly tie-in point.
Flanks: Tie in pearl Krystal Flash along both sides of the fly.
Head/Body: Prepare the E-Z Body by pulling out one of the two white strings that hold the braid together. Trim the E-Z Body so that cut is slanted at a 45-degree angle, with the underside being a little longer. Apply E-Z Body over the fly with the remaining white string going on the underside of the hook. Lash down at the hook eye.
Eyes: Affix size 3 prismatic eyes, silver with black pupil and then apply a light coat of epoxy over the entire E-Z Body.

Cowen's Magnum Baitfish | Henry Cowen

This fly was inspired by Enrico Puglisi's peanut bunker. It was designed to target gamefish that eat large baits like pilchards and menhaden. While the fly was originally crafted for big striped bass, it has been used to catch tarpon, barracuda, bull redfish, large sea trout, sharks and offshore species.

Hook: Tiemco 600 SP, size 4/0.
Thread: Danville monofilament, fine.
Body: Wrap .030 lead wire around the hook shank and cover the wire with Bill's Bodi Braid or similar material.
Underbody: Starting at the rear of the hook and working forward, use a Hi-tie technique to lash white Flash-N-Slinky onto the top of the hook to form the underbelly.
Wing: Tie in lavender Flash-N-Slinky onto the top of the hook. All additional wraps after the lavender will be camouflage Flash-N-Slinky. As you work forward, measure each successive wrap a little shorter than the previous one.
Throat: Add some hot pink Fluoro Fibre at the hook eye and then cover with one last wrap of white Flash-Slinky. Tie off.
Eyes: Silver/black epoxy eyes, size 6, affixed with epoxy or Goop.
Finish: Trim fly to desired shape.

Cowen's Mullet | Henry Cowen

This pattern was inspired by Bob Popovics Surf Candy. It was originally designed to imitate juvenile finger mullet. Mullet is a favorite of striped bass, bluefish, weakfish, redfish and false albacore. This fly has also caught small tarpon, snook and freshwater bass.

Hook: Tiemco 811S, Size 1.
Thread: Danville monofilament, fine.
Eyes: Prismatic stick-on, size 2, silver with black pupil.
Underbody: Tie in natural Polar Fibre at the hook eye, leaving about an 1/8 inch between the tie-in point and the hook eye.
Wing: Tie in white Polar Fire on top of the hook shank and directly over the natural Polar Fibre. Tie in Grey Polar Fibre over the white fibers. Tie in peacock herl on top.
Flash Flanks: Blend both pearl and smolt blue Krystal Flash and tie in on both sides of the fly, running along the entire side of the fly.
Gills: Tie in a small, short amount of red Krystal Flash along both sides of the fly as a gill plate.
Body/Head: Prepare E-Z Body by pulling out one of the two white strings from within the body material. Trim the E-Z Body and apply over the fly with the remaining string on the underside. Lash down at the hook eye.
Eyes: Add silver/black prismatic stick-on eyes and cover some of the gill area. Lightly epoxy the entire E-Z Body Braid.

Cowen's Redfish Scampi | Henry Cowen

This pattern was originally designed for bonefish. This variation has been productive for redfish from North Carolina to Texas. It is very effective when used in semi-stained to stained waters. The fly can be fished to take any species that feeds on shrimp.

Hook: Tiemco 811S, size 1.
Thread: Danville monofilament, fine.
Eyes: Tie in large bead-chain eyes on top of the hook shank.
Tail: Tie in small gold Mylar tubing at the rear of hook, leaving the small extending tail.
Body: Palmer excess Mylar around the hook shank and up to the eye of the hook. Measure and cut a rust-colored Zonker strip. Pierce a hole in the strip and thread through the point of the hook, with point facing up. Lash Zonker strip down at the eye of the hook. The strip should lay along the hook shank with a small tail extending off the rear of the hook and opposite the side of the bead-chain eyes.
Wing: Add root beer colored Craft Fur at the hook eye as wing. Add two pieces of root beer colored Krystal Flash on top of the Craft Fur. Using a bodkin, fray the Mylar tail off the rear of the hook.

Cowen's Albie Anchovy | Henry Cowen

This fly was inspired by Bob Popovics surf candy and is used to match small bay anchovies found from Florida to Massachusetts. This pattern is especially effective for false albacore. The use of E-Z Body Braid allows for an easy and quick tie of an epoxy-style fly.

Hook: Tiemco 811S, size 2 through 6.
Thread: Danville Monofilament, fine.
Underbelly: Tie in shrimp Polar Fibre at the hook eye, leaving approximately 1/8 inch between tie-in point and the hook eye.
Wing: Tie in shrimp Polar Fibre on top of the underbelly at the same tie-in point.
Belly Sac: Tie in silver Gliss-N-Glow over the underbelly of shrimp Polar Fibre. Make certain the material extends only to the hook point.
Body/Head: Prepare the E-Z Body by pulling out one of the two inner strings. Trim the E-Z Body and thread over the fly with the sting-side on the bottom. Secure at the hook eye.
Eyes: Affix size 2 prismatic stick-on eyes, silver w/black pupil.
Finish: Apply a coating of 5-minute epoxy to the body.

Cowen's Crabbit | Henry Cowen

This pattern was inspired by the Cowen's Bonefish Scampi and the Merkin. The resulting fly incorporates Sili-Legs to give the hybrid design a more crab-like look. The fly has been proven productive for redfish, bonefish, permit, tarpon and striped bass.

Hook: Tiemco 811S, size 2.
Thread: Chartreuse, 140 denier or similar.
Eyes: Tie in small dumbbell eyes at the eye of the hook.
Rear Flash: Tie in a small tail of pearl Mylar at the hook bend.
Shell: Starting at the hook and working forward, tie in Aunt Lydia's rug yarn using figure-eight wraps. Use two pieces of cream, then two pieces of tan. Continue alternating colors until reaching the dumbbell eyes. Comb out rug yarn and trim to desired shape.
Legs: Using two half hitch knots to secure three sets of rubber Sili-Legs throughout the shell. Coat all wraps and knots with head cement.
Body/Tail: Using a bodkin, push a hole in the hide of a tan Zonker strip. Leave enough strip behind the hole for a short tail. Affix the Zonker through the hook point and lash down onto the hook at the eye and on top of the dumbbell eyes. Coat thread wraps with head cement.

Crab-a-licious | Captain Chris Newsome

This fly is a very effective crab-fly imitation that performs well from the mid-Atlantic region down throughout the entire Southeast.

Hook: Gamakatsu SC15, size 2-1/0.
Thread: UTC monofilament, .006.
Feelers: Tie in several strands of midge flash for feelers.
Mouth: Tie in a clump of orange Craft Fur as a mouth and trim close to the hook bend.
Eyes: Tie in monofilament eyes extending to the rear of the hook.
Body: Tie in and stack clumps of wool, forming the body. Trim wool to the shape of a crab.
Claws: Create two claws from mallard shank feathers. Coat the feathers with thinned Goop for durability. Glue claws to the underside of the wool shell.
Legs: Pull tufts of webby barbs from the stem of saddle hackle for legs. Glue legs to the underside of the wool shell.
Underbody: Flatten and trim soft lead to create the underbody. Glue to the wool top shell with 5-minute epoxy. Apply acrylic paint and coat when dry with Hard as Wraps.
Weed Guard: Tie in a two-pronged weed guard of 20-pound monofilament at the hook eye.

Crabalops Atlanticus Pass Crab | Captain Russ Shirley

This fly was tied specifically for tarpon that feed on the small pass crabs of Tampa Bay and Charlotte Harbor, and fish that don't respond to traditional flies and colors. Try varying degrees of packing the deer hair for different depth requirements. It is easy to shape the fly so that when stripped slightly it will ride upward and stay on top like the real thing.

Hook: Owner Aki 4/0.
Thread: White flat waxed nylon.
Antenna: Tie in a short tuft of green marabou and orange and peacock Krystal Flash (orange is the predominant color).
Mouth: Add one or two wraps of small or medium orange chenille for the mouth color. The wraps will also help kick-out and splay the feathers and eyes.
Claws: Tie in four (matching sets of two) light brown feathers, divided and splayed outward, and oriented more on top.
Eyes: Tie in two burnt, painted and epoxied eyes of 60-80 pound, kicked upward and out over the feathers.
Body/Legs: To start the crab body tie in olive-green belly strip deer hair. Tie in four Sili-Legs on top of the hook, interspersed between clumps of deer hair. Continue body with lighter bleached deer hair and additional legs. Trim the deer hair to shape. A properly shaped body will allow for a creative and natural swimming motion.

Crabe Voyant | Richard Schmidt/Jim Hebert

Inspired by Del's Merkin Crab, this flashy crab fly was originally tied for large Biloxi Marsh redfish. It has since proven effective for a wide array of gamefish such as striped bass, snook, large sea trout, weakfish, flounder and pompano. It can be tied in a variety of sizes and colors.

Hook: Mustad 34007, size 2-2/0.
Thread: Danville flat waxed nylon.
Tail: Tie in tan or light brown marabou and pearl Krystal Flash.
Mid-Body 1: Cut 1/8" to 3/16" gold Mylar tubing twice the length of the hook and tie in tip of Mylar tubing on top of the hook at the bend. Allow to hang loosely.
Main Body: Tie in brown Sparkle Yarn employing the Merkin body method. Brush out fibers.
Eyes: Tie in barbell eyes 1/8" from the hook eye.
Mid-Body 2: Work the Mylar tubing over the end of the hook and hook eye and over the barbell eyes. Tie down and whip finish. Pick out the gold Mylar, allowing it to flare to the hook point and out to the body.
Finish: Whip finish at head and apply head cement.

Crafty Cobia Baitfish Fly

Tom Herrington | Historic Ocean Springs Saltwater Fly Fishing Club

This is a fly designed specifically for enticing cobia out from under weed lines. It highlights the color orange, known to attract cobia. The pattern is easily modified and works well for various other pelagic species of gamefish.

Hook: Mustad 34007, or equivalent, size 2 through 6/0.
Thread: Danville flat waxed nylon.
Belly: Wrap the hook shank from the eye to the bend with thread. Coat with head cement to keep fibers in place. Tie in a bunch of white calf tail (two times the length of the hook shank) approximately 1/2" behind the hook eye.
Wing: Tie in bright orange Craft Fur (three to four times the length of the hook shank). Tie in another equal clump of Craft Fur slightly to the rear of the first wing clump.
Flash: Tie in pearl Krystal Flash, extending slightly past the wing.
Topping: Tie in several strands of peacock herl.
Head: Build a head with thread and whip finish.
Eyes: Affix eye with glue, then epoxy eyes and head.

Crease Fly

Joe Blados | Tied by Glen Mikkleson

This is a very versatile pattern design that is effective for a wide variety of gamefish throughout the Southeast and Gulf Coast. It can be tied in any number of sizes, with coloration to match different baitfish. This fly is designed to be fished both on the surface and deeper in the water column.

Hook: Standard Crease Fly tied on 4/0 or larger hook. Wrap the entire shank with several layers of thread.
Tail: Tie in bucktail and some flash. The tail on the original fly is tied sparse.
Body: Cut a small rectangular piece of stick-back foam, just a little longer than the length of the hook. Peel the protective paper from the back of the foam. Next cut a strip of silver foil (or color of choice) and place dull side onto the adhesive side of the foam. Trim the foam to shape. Place a small amount of C/A glue on the hook shank and pinch the bottom edge of the body onto the shank. When shaping the foam, make certain to keep an adequate gap between the hook point and the body.
Finish: A light coat of epoxy can be added to the fly body for durability.

Croaker Choker | Lawrence Clemens

As the name implies this fly was designed for croaker and juvenile red puppy drum. This pattern is both easy to tie and effective.

Hook: Daiichi X-Point, size 2.
Thread: Red.
Tail: Tie in several strands of bronze Krystal Flash, over which is tied a moderate clump of olive kip tail.
Body: For the rear portion of the body tie in and wrap white chenille. For the forward portion tie in olive hackle and olive chenille. Wrap the chenille forward and palmer the hackle over the chenille.
Eyes: Heavy dumbbell eyes, Real Eyes Plus. Tied in on the underside of the hook shank.
Head: Build a small head using red thread; whip finish and apply a coat of head cement.

Crocker Minnow | Captain Doug Sinclair

This synthetic hair fly is a solid performer for many Southeast and Gulf Coast gamefish. Its effectiveness is in part attributed to the synthetic-hair blend and the popular chartreuse and yellow color combination.

Hook: Gamakatsu or Tiemco, size 1.
Thread: Chartreuse.
Throat: Tie in a small tuft of orange synthetic hair material.
Lower Wing: Tie in a length of yellow synthetic hair.
Flash: Tie in strands of silver flash material.
Upper Wing: Tie a wing of chartreuse synthetic hair material and apply black spots and bars with a permanent marker.
Topping: Color the top hairs black.
Eyes: Affix black eyes.
Head: Using dabs of epoxy build a small triangular head and allow to dry.

Crystal Bunny Crab | Captain Edward Wasicki

This buggy-looking pattern is a new variation on an older design. It incorporates Trilobal Chenille as a body material.

Hook: Mustad 3407, size 2.
Thread: Monocord or fine monofilament.
Eyes: Tie in a small set of barbell lead eyes
Tail: Tie in a small tuft of marabou or rabbit fur and a length of rabbit strip.
Legs: Tie in four sets (eight legs) rubber fly legs.
Body: Tie in Trilobal chenille and wind toward the hook eye. Figure-eight thread over the eyes.
Weed Guard: Tie in a short length of stiff monofilament.

Flies from a Different Point of View

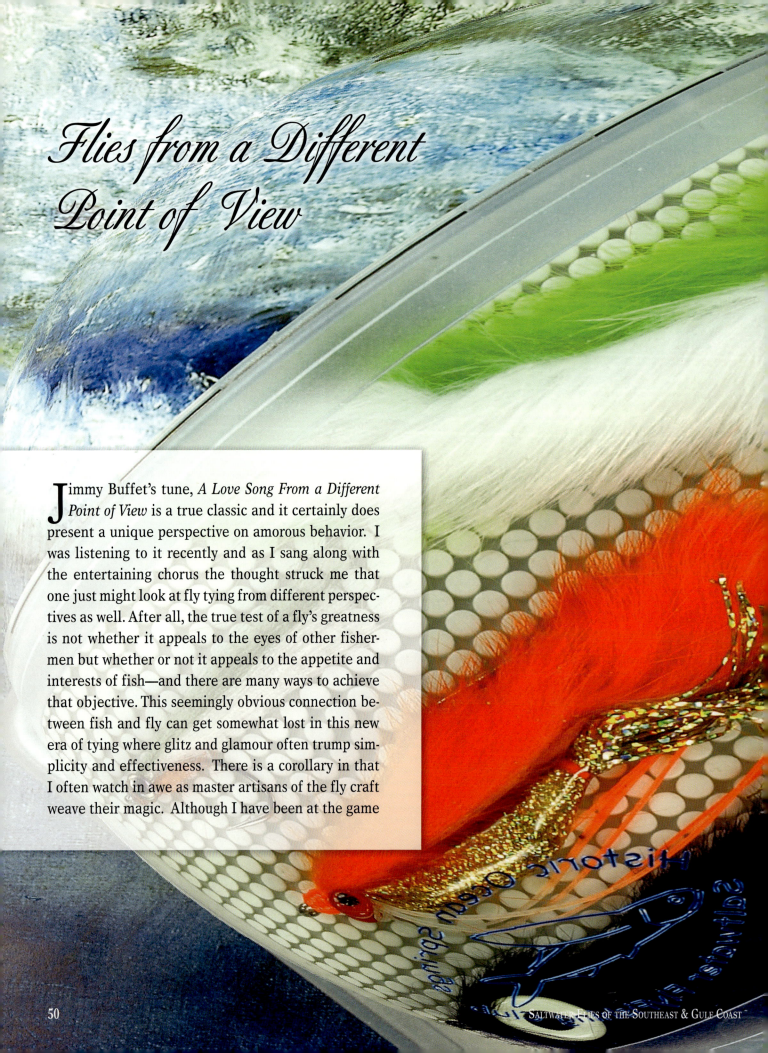

Jimmy Buffet's tune, *A Love Song From a Different Point of View* is a true classic and it certainly does present a unique perspective on amorous behavior. I was listening to it recently and as I sang along with the entertaining chorus the thought struck me that one just might look at fly tying from different perspectives as well. After all, the true test of a fly's greatness is not whether it appeals to the eyes of other fishermen but whether or not it appeals to the appetite and interests of fish—and there are many ways to achieve that objective. This seemingly obvious connection between fish and fly can get somewhat lost in this new era of tying where glitz and glamour often trump simplicity and effectiveness. There is a corollary in that I often watch in awe as master artisans of the fly craft weave their magic. Although I have been at the game

of fly-fishing for more than four decades I, nonetheless, still aspire to tie as well as some of these modern masters, for whom realism is a key component of their creations. Yet, with my own tying I cannot help but fall back on the uncomplicated functionality of a fly. I typically find myself following the lead of tiers that tie with the express purpose of tempting the senses of fish rather than creating anatomically correct replicas of various bait forms. I am firm in my belief that it is much better to get high marks for the compulsory requirements of structure, form and balance than a perfect score for artistic merit! Durability also speaks volumes about a fly's structure. As with many things in this world *pretty* fades over time, but substance endures. Some of today's flies actually look more realistic than the baitfish they are tied to replicate, and that is fine. But we have all learned from our own experiences that a fly need not be a precise imitation of bait to be effective. What a fly needs to achieve, in concert with angler intervention, is to motivate and stimulate a fish to strike. A fly that is durable, well tied, balanced and easy to tie is icing on the cake. I am a fan of the school of impressionistic flies as are many of the tiers profiled in this book, and when one considers the level of talent spread between these pages, it is undeniable that impressionism in fly tying works.

Ours is a sport and pastime that allows for and rewards creativity and freedom of expression. There is room for multiple approaches to fly tying. It fundamentally comes down to the schools of realism versus impressionism. In art circles there are proponents and patrons of both styles. And so it is in fly tying. Many newcomers to the art of fly tying can get somewhat mesmerized by the intricacy of some designs and patterns and perhaps get put off, believing that they cannot achieve that level of sophistication in their own tying. That is tantamount to the mystique that surrounded fly-casting when I first started in the sport. It all looked so complicated and so many of the writers of the day made it appear as though you had to be at least one part sorcerer and one part shaman to affect an adequate cast. Nothing could have been farther from the truth for when I finally had the technique demonstrated to me, all that remained was some consistent practice and the confidence that it would all eventually come together. It is well within the realm of possibility that an angler can be out there catching fish with a fly rod literally minutes after receiving the first casting lesson. Fly tying is no different. Those responding to the call of *tie a fly and catch a fish* need not wait years to perfect a set of skills to achieve the desired end result of fish on the end of the line that ate a personally tied fly. If given a choice of flies I will always select form and substance over artistically perfect renditions of baitfish. Pushing the edge of the envelope to produce the best possible fly is an admirable goal for that is how we advance the art but it need not become an all-consuming obsession, especially if you don't have endless hours to devote to crafting your flies. Some of today's fly tiers are inclined to forget the most basic fly-tying principle: a fly is an instrument of illusion. Simply put, it is a fraud, tied to accomplish trickery.

Two photographs hang on a wall above the desk where I am writing this piece. The images serve as reminders of great days spent fly-fishing. In each of the photos is a large striped bass, duped by flies that some might call appalling. The flies wouldn't turn a single head at a tying demonstration; nothing fancy, not much to look at but the big stripers obviously liked something about the design. It is that *something* which

should be the goal of every tier to include and emulate in his or her flies—the practical application of a natural design with one or more elements that stimulate a response. The flies used to take those bass were given to me by two exceptional captains, each often hesitant to open their boxes of "nothing special" flies. Most fly tiers I have talked with over the past ten years, while highly skilled and capable of producing works of art, told me hands-down they would take a representative fly that was simple and effective over one that was complex and anatomically true to form. Their go-to patterns are proof of that belief. Some may be more elaborate than others but all are tied to achieve the end result of being an impression of a bait form.

The most relevant personal example that I have of simplicity and effectiveness of a fly involves a pattern that was originally used for Pacific salmon in Alaska. It is a pattern that has since proven its effectiveness on a variety of fish species throughout the East Coast. I sat one winter's day at my tying bench crafting flies for a tidal-water coho salmon trip I would be taking later that year. The flies were rich in marabou and flash. My young daughter walked into my tying room and started playing with all the *pretty feathers*. She asked if we could make a fly together. She picked out colors and materials

that appealed to her and I tied them onto the hook. She was captivated by the allure of the feathers and even made a few wraps of the thread. The end result was a rather modestly tied creation—the *Jac Sprat*, a pink, purple, orange and white flash fly. We both liked it so I made a few more just in case it worked. As it happened, that fly salvaged the day with some reluctant silvers, and resulted in the best outing I had that trip. I have since modified that fly and have used it for applications on my home waters for school-sized stripers, simply changing colors until I hit upon the right combination.

While that salmon fly was quite simple in design, its effectiveness was inherent in its movement and colors. Though my daughter's initial response to the feathers was driven by serendipity and the eye candy effect, the attractor colors selected proved to be the ideal stimulator. Years of fishing for largemouth and smallmouth bass have taught me valuable lessons about the use and importance of lure coloration or, more importantly, the contrast effects of hues and tones in water. Those lessons were easily transferable to flies and fly-fishing in saltwater. There is no question but that some colors can and do motivate fish to strike when other colors come up woefully inadequate. As tiers we should focus on those proven combinations

that stimulate a strike response in fish. That trigger mechanism can be a reaction to a number of different stimuli: hunger, competition, aggressiveness territorialism or just simple opportunity. Colors and the perception of those hues and tones can act as a catalyst to gain the attention of fish. Multiple, contrasting and complementary colors often have an edge over lures, flies and baits of a single color. Just take a look at any common baitfish, whether in freshwater or saltwater. Within varying degrees there is typically a light underbelly, a darker top and sort of blended transition shading on the flanks of the body. In most cases the flanks of the bait appear almost translucent. So what does that mean to the fly tier? In essence, it means simplicity. Some of the best flies that I have used are tied with three colors: a light material for the underbelly, a darker material for the top and a transition material for the body of the fly. Just take a look at any of the classic saltwater flies—highly effective, brilliant in their simplicity and enduring over time. Colors and the perception of those hues and tones can act as a catalyst to gain the attention of fish. So too can a fly's design appeal to other senses. For example, specific materials can push water, creating vibrations that stimulate the lateral line and increase interest in the fly. So too

can techniques like adding rattles to a fly body or tying an articulated tail that sways seductively when retrieved.

To some extent, the art of fly tying is synonymous with duck decoy carving, an American folk art. Some decoys are carved as representative facsimiles while others are crafted with intricate detail. Both work, yet crudely carved and painted blocks of wood effectively rigged will often account for as many if not more ducks coming to the stool than decoys, which look like they too can fly. What is important are size, silhouette, coloration and the ability to present the decoys in a lifelike manner. The same is true of flies. A fly that meets the basic requirements of design and is fished effectively will perform as well as a more realistic counterpart. The key lies in our abilities as anglers to make that fly appear alive. Even the most realistic of patterns cannot do it all on its own. Angler intervention in the form of the retrieve is the essential ingredient. After all is said and done that is the essence of *fishing*.

I would encourage all tiers, novice and professional alike, to continue the quest for the perfect fly. Not only is that fun but it also keeps us sharp and on top of the game. And let's not forget that simplicity in fly tying, as it is in fishing, can be divine!

Crystal Bunny Shrimp | Captain Edward Wasicki

This shrimp pattern tied with Crystal Chenille and bunny has proved very effective on tailing redfish. Tan and olive are two favorite colors.

Hook: Mustad 34011, sizes 2, 1.
Thread: Match to body coloration.
Eyes: Tie in a pair of small bead-chain eyes on the underside of the hook shank at a point opposite the barb.
Body/Carapace: Tie in a section of Crystal Chenille and a length of rabbit strip, colors of choice. Wind the chenille forward and tie off behind the eye of the hook. Trim the chenille slightly on the top of the shank. Bring the rabbit strip forward and tie off behind the eye.
Weed Guard: Tie in a section of stiff monofilament extending to the barb.

Crystal Crustacean | Captain Greg Poole

This fly was designed for shallow, off-color waters of central Florida. The pattern was originally conceived for redfish but in various colors it is also effective for seatrout, ladyfish, black drum, juvenile tarpon, jacks and tripletail. Favorite colors are white and grizzly, tan, brown, and tarpon seem to be partial to orange.

Hook: Mustad, 34007, size 2.
Thread: Flat waxed nylon.
Eyes: Tie in large bead-chain eyes.
Tail: Tie in Mylar tubing and unravel strands for tail.
Wing: Tie in bucktail and a lower wing and then two medium neck hackles on either side and on top of the bucktail. Splay the hackles curved side out. Tie in flash material on either side of the wing.
Finish: Tie off thread at hook eye, whip finish and apply a dab of cement.

Crystal Shrimp | Tom Springer

What began as a specific pattern for seatrout under the lights on the Emerald Coast has become a very versatile pattern. The species list for this fly includes: panfish, bass, oscars, peacocks, coldwater trout, snook, baby tarpon, drum, and mullet. It's even credited with a 28-pound redfish that once topped the Louisiana state fly rod records! Although there are several flies that bear a similar name and look, this pattern was designed for ease of tying.

Hook: Size 2-6, Mustad 3406 or similar style.
Thread: Flat-waxed nylon in white or pearl.
Eyes: Tie in 1/4-inch sections of 50-pound monofilament, burnt at each end and crimped in the center.
Tail/Antennae: Tie in several strands of Krystal Flash, long enough for antennae and allow to protrude past the hook eye.
Body: Tie in small or medium Crystal Chenille and do one wrap in front of the eyes, then wrap back to hook eye. The first wrap helps to separate the eyes outward. Tie off the chenille at the hook eye and whip finish.
Finish: Tie off and whip finish.

Cuda-Needle | Alan Caolo

Barracuda are often difficult to fool in bright sun and shallow water. While they are readily taken with bright or flashy patterns over deep-water structure and during twilight hours near shore, fishing the mid-day flats is a different game. Their incredible eyesight and careful nature make them tough targets. This pattern has proven deadly on tropical flats wherever needlefish are present. A simple combination of bright green synthetic material and Holographic flash, with a *less is more* tying philosophy, led to the creation of this simple-to-tie yet effective fly.

Hook: 1/0 Gamakatsu SC-15.
Thread: Danville's flat-waxed nylon, lime.
Wing: Wrap thread to cover the shank to a position over the hook point and over-wrap forward 1/8 inch ahead of the point. Attach a layered 6 1/2″-long wing consisting of twenty strands of baitfish green Kinkyfibre followed by four strands of silver Holographic flash followed by another twenty strands of Kinkyfibre and topped with four strands of pearl Flashabou to the back of the hook. Secure thread and trim the fibers and flash evenly so the Holographic flash extends 1/8 inch beyond the other material.
Eyes: Yellow prismatic, size 2.
Throat: At the same attachment point, secure an eight-strand cluster of 3/4-inch-long silver Holographic flash to the underside of the hook, wind the thread forward to the eye, secure and cut. Trim the cluster at varying lengths to form a flared throat.
Eyes: Stick the yellow Prismatic eyes, size 2, to the sides of the hook at the wing attachment and coat the head and eyes with 5-minute epoxy.

Da Bayou Mega Crab | Jim Seegraves

This large Merkin-style crab pattern incorporates a tail and was designed for big Louisiana red and black drum. The fly's success has extended to two world records and approximately 250 large drum over twenty pounds.

Hook: Gamakatsu Jig 60 Flat Eye, size 2/0.
Thread: Monofilament or heavy duty, brown.
Eyes: Tie in a pair of dumbbell eyes.
Tail: The tail consists of a fly tail and shortened rubber legs blended with several strands of gold flash.
Body: The entire body of this fly is built from segments of carpet yarn, tied on with series of figure-eight wraps. Use enough batches of yarn to form a body. You can trim the yarn to shape. The entire body is coated with clear nail polish.
Weed Guard: Tie in 30- to 40-pound Mason monofilament and form a loop.

Dancin' Diver | Captain Chris Newsome

The fly was designed with a built-in action similar to that of diving plugs used by conventional fishermen. The lip causes the fly to dive and "dance" on the strip. A foam popper head forms an intricate part of the pattern. Foam on the topside of the hook shank is critical to ensure proper tracking and enhance wiggle when the fly is stripped. This is a good pattern to have in the box when fish refuse traditional flies. Fish with long, fast strips followed by a two-second pause.

Hook: Mustad S71SSS, size 1/0.
Thread: Fine monofilament.
Lip/Flash: Tie in a Fly Lipp in the down position. Tie in two clumps of Polar Flash on the topside of the hook just in front of the hook bend. Secure and cut thread. You can trim the Fly Lipp to adjust the dive and wiggle.
Head: Widen slit in the foam head with a file so that the head will slip over the hook shank. Place the foam head on the hook shank with the cupped portion facing the rear of the hook. Keep all but a small portion of the foam on the topside of the hook and leave a small gap between the head and hook eye. Adhere with 5-minute epoxy.
Body: Attach thread between the hook eye and the Wapsi Perfect Popper foam head. Cut a portion of Polar Flash then fold and cut in half. Work the hair back and forth in your fingers to give a tapered effect. Tie in the portion so that a slightly shorter length is facing forward of the fly. Continue applying portions of Polar Flash until you have worked your way around the head; use four portions. Secure and cut thread. Apply Hard as Wraps around the head portion of Polar Flash. Pull the forward half of Polar Flash back toward the rear of the fly. Wet the rear of the fly or use a twist-tie to keep the Polar Flash pulled back. Apply another layer of Hard as Wraps around the head of the fly.
Eyes/Gills: Affix 1/4-inch stick-on eyes and draw on gills with red permanent marker.
Finish: Coat with a final application of Hard as Wraps. Let dry. Trim hair to give a tapered profile from the side and top.

Deer-ceiver | Tom Tripi

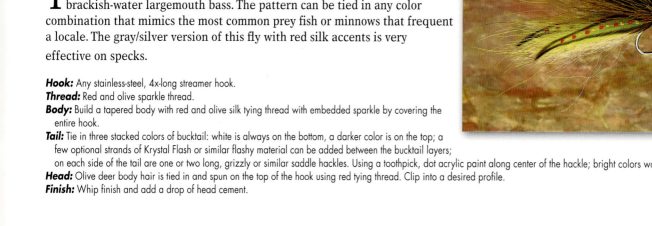

This fly was designed to target species such as redfish, speckled trout and brackish-water largemouth bass. The pattern can be tied in any color combination that mimics the most common prey fish or minnows that frequent a locale. The gray/silver version of this fly with red silk accents is very effective on specks.

Hook: Any stainless-steel, 4x-long streamer hook.
Thread: Red and olive sparkle thread.
Body: Build a tapered body with red and olive silk tying thread with embedded sparkle by covering the entire hook.
Tail: Tie in three stacked colors of bucktail: white is always on the bottom, a darker color is on the top; a few optional strands of Krystal Flash or similar flashy material can be added between the bucktail layers; on each side of the tail are one or two long, grizzly or similar saddle hackles. Using a toothpick, dot acrylic paint along center of the hackle; bright colors work best.
Head: Olive deer body hair is tied in and spun on the top of the hook using red tying thread. Clip into a desired profile.
Finish: Whip finish and add a drop of head cement.

Dino's Albie Fly | Captain Dino Torino

This fly is also known as the Albie Whore. It was designed especially for false albacore. It is an easy-to-tie and effective pattern.

Hook: Mustad 3407, Size 3 though 1/0.
Thread: White 3/0 monofilament.
Tail: Tie in two small white hackle feathers.
Body: Pearl Estaz tied in followed by a single white hackle feather. Wind Estaz forward. Tie in a few strands of pearl flash, then palmer the white hackle forward. Tie off and whip finish thread. Hot-glue body.

Dino's Marabou | Captain Dino Torino

This fly is tied Clouser-style. It can be tied in a number of sizes and colors and is effective on most gamefish in moderate depth ranges of the water column. Captain Torino has enjoyed success with this pattern along the east coast of Florida as well as in the Northeast.

Hook: Mustad, size 2 through 1/0.
Thread: White monofilament, size 3/0.
Tail: Tie in a moderate clump of white marabou.
Body: Tie in pearl Bill's Body Braid at the rear of the hook and wind forward toward the hook eye.
Wing: Tie in sparse bunch of Krystal Flash extending to the tips of the marabou, followed by a moderate clump of chartreuse bucktail slightly shorter than the white marabou.
Head: Build up a head from thread, tie off and apply head cement.

Dixon's Mini-Me | Captain Paul Dixon

This pattern was conceived from a desire to create a hybrid pattern between a lobster and a shrimp. The fly is best fished with a twitch-and-strip retrieve, to impart a fleeing-type action. It can also be fished with a strip and pause allowing the fly to sit on the bottom.

Hook: Long shank, stainless steel.
Thread: Pink or fine monofilament.
Tail: Tie in pink Craft Fur at the bend of the hook. Follow with pink Krystal Flash and then wrap in the lead eye.
Claws/Legs: Bring the thread back to the eye and tie in Puff Claws and red hackle. Wrap the hackle to the eye of the hook. Tie off and trim the top hackle.
Head: Bring the thread back to the lead eyes and tie in more pink Craft Fur. Wrap five wraps back to the hook eye and leave fur lying over the eye of the hook.

Dock Light Shrimp | Captain Dino Torino

This fly was designed for fishing under dock lights when small shrimp and baitfish swim about attracted by the illumination.

Hook: Size 2 though 1/0.
Thread: White 3/0 monofilament.
Tail: Tie in a small tuft of white marabou and several strands of pearl flash.
Body/Legs: Tie in a length of pearl Estaz at the tie-in point of the tail followed by one white hackle feather.
Eyes: Tie in small, black bead-chain eye-s on top of the hook shank at a point opposite the hook point.
Body Wrap: Wrap the Estaz over and around the eyes and forward toward the hook eye. Leave enough room for the wind and tie-off. Palmer the hackle feather forward and tie off on top of the Estaz.
Wing: Tie in a short wing of white Polar Fibre that extends almost to the tips of the tail.
Head: Build a small head with thread, tie off and coat with cement.

Doobee Minnow Glow | Captain Duber Winters

This fly is a variation of the Clouser Minnow. It is a very effective glass minnow pattern and was designed to fish dock lights at night for snook. It is also a great fly in the daytime since this material reflects light beautifully. The fly has caught snook, trout, baby tarpon, little tunny, mackerel, pompano, jacks and sea trout. Match the color and size of the fly to the bait in your area.

Hook: Mustad 34007 or Gamakatsu SL11-3H, size 2 - 2/0.
Thread: Clear monofilament, medium.
Eyes: Tie in silver lead barbell eyes on the underside of the hook shank so the hook rides point up.
Body Ribbing: Wrap a thread base back to the bend of the hook. At this point tie in a piece of white glow tinsel and then spiral wrap the thread back to the lead eyes. Wrap the tinsel over the thread base towards the lead eyes and tie off. Trim at that point.
Wing/Lateral Line: Wrap the mono thread to a point between the lead eyes and eye of the hook and tie in a 2-3" of Flash 'n Slinky. Wrap thread back under the eyes and tie down material right behind the lead eyes. Tie in several strands of Krystal Flash, the glow Flashabou and another 2-3"-long piece of Flash 'n Slinky. Finish and coat all exposed thread. Trim to shape.

Doobee Pilchard | Captain Duber Winters

This pattern was created to simulate a somewhat neutrally buoyant juvenile pilchard style fly. Initially it was created as a snook fly to fish the middle and upper water column but has since evolved. By varying the hook size, bulk and length of materials the fly has been effective for roosterfish, jacks, sea trout, bluefish, Spanish mackerel, king mackerel, little tunny, dolphin and tarpon.

Hook: Gamakatsu, SC15, Size 1. Vary according to fly size.
Thread: Medium, clear monofilament.
Belly: With hook point is facing up wrap a small bump of thread about 1/4 down the hook shank from the eye. Tie in a 2- to 3-inch clump of white flash blend and allow 1/2 to 1 inch of material to remain forward of the tie-in point. Pull that end of the material back towards the hook point and tie-in so all material is facing in the same direction but at different lengths.
Wing: Invert the fly and tie in Krystal Flash and Flashabou. Tie-in gray flash blend on top of the hook the same as you tied the white. The gray material should be at two different lengths as well. Wrap thread from the tie in point and create a head that tapers to the hook eye and whip finish. Apply Hard as Hull thread cement.
Lateral line: Pearl Krystal Flash and Flashabou in glow.
Eyes: Affix Prismatic holographic mirage eyes glued to a tapered thread-wrapped head. Apply epoxy, coating entire head of the fly.
Finish: Trim the material on both the top and bottom. Color the wing or back of the fly with an olive marker and color the thorax with an orange or red marker.

Drifting Crab | Tom Tripi

This simple yet effective fly was designed for small redfish, speckled trout and brackish-water largemouth bass. The pattern is typically fished on a 12-foot leader, in clear, skinny water, with a sandy bottom. The fly is allowed to drift with a slow current, and then settle on the sand. Very short twitches are used to entice redfish. Weed guards and lighter hooks are options depending on conditions.

Hook: Any 2x short saltwater hook.
Thread: Red tying silk.
Eyes: Silk flower stamens sealed with super glue.
Body/Eyes: Wrap bend of hook with red tying thread embedded with red and green glitter. Then tie in and wrap a small clump of fox hair on either side of the bend. Tie in eyes (either plastic or crafted from burnt monofilament), and then tie in and wrap soft brown hen hackle between the eyes. Tie off and dot knot with super glue.
Finish: Whip finish and apply a small amount of super glue to the knot.

Dubiel's Finesse Fly | Captain Gary Dubiel

This fly was originally designed for striped bass but has since evolved into an effective pattern for more than eighteen different species of gamefish. It is very productive for false albacore, Atlantic bonito and Spanish mackerel. The pattern is adaptable to a variety of sizes and colors.

Hook: Varivas 990S or equivalent, size 2.
Thread: UNI-Products fin monofilament.
Wing: Tie in white Craft Fur Select. Two wings are tied to the hook shank in even proportions with the Craft Fur secured to the rear portion of the shank.
Weight: Secure .025 lead wire and make ten wraps forward.
Body: Tie in silver Bill's Bodi-Braid and wrap forward. Tie in five strands each of silver and pearl Flashabou on top of the braid.
Over/Body: Slide a segment of medium, green E-Z Body tubing over the hook shank, covering the shank from the eye to a point in front of the hook bend.
Eyes: Affix #3 adhesive metallic eyes, silver.
Finish: Coat body with 30-minute epoxy. Rotate fly until dry.

Dubiel's Lil' Haden | Captain Gary Dubiel

This fly was originally designed for fishing the Pamlico Sound Estuary and to replicate the shape of juvenile menhaden. The pattern has had success with many species of gamefish from the Northeast through the Southeast including, red drum, spotted seatrout, flounder, weakfish, striped bass, false albacore, bluefish, Spanish mackerel, snook and tarpon.

Hook: Varivas or equivalent, size 1. For tarpon, size 3/0.
Thread: UNI-Products fine monofilament.
Weight: Tie in ten wraps of .025 lead wire.
Body: Tie in and wrap silver Bill's Bodi-Braid.
Underwing: Tie in a moderate amount of white Craft Fur Plus.
Flash: Tie in ten strands of Kreinik's silver flash material.
Overwing: Tie in green, olive, tan or chartreuse Craft Fur Plus.
Eyes/Head: Using Super Glue, affix 3-D, #3.5, molded eyes in pearl, silver or chartreuse. Fill in the areas around eyes and head with five-minute epoxy and rotate fly until dry.

Dubiel's Red-ducer | Captain Gary Dubiel

This is a shallow-water redfish fly that fishes well on the flats, using a floating line. It is an adaptation of the Seaducer. The addition of bead-chain eyes allows the fly to fall into the grass when the retrieve is halted. The pattern is also effective when tied in all white, red and white and chartreuse.

Hook: Mustad 34007 or Tiemco 811S, size 1.
Thread: UNI-thread 3/0, brown or tan.
Eyes: Tie in large, gold bead chain.
Tail: Tie in ten strands of gold or copper Flashabou. Tie in two Whiting rooster cape grizzly hackles, dyed tan.
Body: Tie in tan Estaz and a single hackle feather. Wrap the Estaz forward to the eye and tie off. Palmer the saddle hackle to the eye and secure.
Head: Build a small thread head in front of the eye; whip finish and coat with Hard as Hull.

Duct Tape Minnow | Kevin "Fluff" Arculeo

This fly was created to reproduce multiple types of small to medium size baitfish. Because of its design it flips on its side when stripped, mimicking an injured baitfish. Fish the fly by using a one-handed short strip, pausing briefly between strips.

Hook: 3x to 4x long shank, size 1 through 3/0.
Thread: Monofilament, 6/0.
Tail: Measure Farrar's Flash Blend so it hangs off the end of the hook about 1 to 2 inches. Tie in white Farrar's Flash Blend onto hook shank by securing with the mono thread from the hook eye to the hook bend and back to the hook eye. Tie in the colored Farrar's Flash Blend on top of the white Farrar's Flash Blend using same method.
Body: Cut a piece of clear, silver or white duct tape so it can be folded to create the body but short enough so it will not cover the hook point. Also cut the piece of duct tape so it will cover the hook shank from the hook eye to a 1/4 inch past the hook bend. Place the middle of the sticky side of the Duct Tape on top of the back of the fly and fold over sticking the Duct Tape together. Whip-finish the Duct Tape to the hook just behind the hook eye. Starting at the hook eye cut the Duct Tape to match the body of the baitfish of choice. Cut around the hook bend to end of the tape at back but leave enough tape so it continues to stick together at the tail. Apply Angler's Choice Soft Body glue to tail section of the fly where the Duct Tape meets the Slinky Fiber and at the hook eye. Also apply glue to the seam of the Duct Tape to keep it from separating in the water. While Duct Tape is very durable it can separate when kept in the water for long periods of time.
Eyes: To attach the 3D molded eyes poke a hole through the Duct Tape in the area where you want to place the eyes. Using a dubbing needle place 5-minute epoxy inside the hole and on the Duct Tape. Place the eyes on each side of the hole, gluing the eyes together through the hole in the Duct Tape.
Finish: Trim the tail to match the bait. You can cut it square or trim it with a "V" cut in the shape of an actual fish tail.

Duval Crawler | Drew Chicone

This fly was designed for Keys tarpon and was inspired by a green bead necklace.

Hook: Owner 5470-111, sizes 1/0, 3/0.
Thread: Flat-waxed nylon, chartreuse.
Eyes: Tie in green bead eyes with a series of figure-eight wraps.
Tail: Tie in chartreuse rabbit Zonker strip. Form anti-fouling loop from 20-pound hard Mason monofilament by placing loop under strip and tie tips on top of Zonker. Tie in three plumes of yellow marabou about an inch long, concealing the monofilament loop.
Body: Tie in chartreuse Estaz Grande and wrap forward, leaving room ahead of the eyes for the collar.
Collar: Tie in two yellow neck hackles and palmer them to the eyes. Advance thread in front of the eyes and whip finish.

Eat Me Fly

Captain Adrian Mason | Inspired by Scott Hamilton

This fly is a variation of Scott Hamilton's original Eat Me fly. It is tied on a short-shank hook with all materials tied on top. This generic baitfish imitation has accounted for many species of Southeastern and Gulf Coast gamefish as well as many species of Northeast gamefish. Fly size and coloration can be adapted to any number of baitfish situations.

Hook: Mustad C47S D, size 1/0.
Thread: Fine clear mono.
Belly: Wrap the fine mono from the hook eye to a point just ahead of the barb. Trim the ends of the Ultra Hair straight and tie in, positioning the cut ends just beyond the hook bend. Wrap back to the hook point and make two wraps behind the hair. Cut the butts at an angle and wrap forward to the eye and back to the tie-in point. Tie in two more layers of Ultra Hair—each layer tapered a bit longer than the previous. Tie in five pieces of Flashabou as long as the longest Super Hair.
Wing: Tie in two separate layers of olive Ultra Hair, with the second layer longer than the first.
Topping: Double over ten pieces of Sparkle Flash and trim as long as the previous layer of Ultra Hair. Tie off and trim to shape.
Head/Eyes: Affix 3D eyes with epoxy with half the eye above the hook shank. Build a head with epoxy, going around, not over the eyes. Hand rotate to achieve proper shape and place on a drying wheel.

Electric Kwan

Pat Dorsey | Tied by Rich Santos

This fly was originally designed as a crab pattern for the back waters and flats of south Florida but quickly proved itself in many other waters. The Kwan fly is a very effective redfish fly in various conditions. It makes a good shrimp imitation for tailing redfish or those cruising or crashing bait. This fly is also productive when stripped as a streamer pattern for blind casting around oyster bars, points, deeper holes and cuts for redfish, spotted sea trout and flounder. It is most successful in the dark muddy colored waters in northeast Florida's backcountry mud flats and creeks. Its profile and dark color show up well in the stained water.

Hook: Daiichi 2546, size 4. Bend the hook eye so the hook point rides up.
Thread: Black Danville's 210 Denier Flat Waxed Nylon.
Eyes: Wrap tying thread back to approx. 1/8"-3/16" from hook eye. Tie in black bead-chain or mini dumbbell eyes on opposite side of hook point with a series of figure-eight and random circular wraps to secure firmly. Add a couple drops of glue of your choice.
Tail/Body: Continue wrapping thread to the rear of hook shank where the bend of hook begins. Select two matching small 1 1/2 inches to 2 inches long narrow grizzly neck hackle feathers and lay flat together. Flatten the stem ends. Secure the butt end of the hackle stem on the very top of the hook bend. Then palmer the dual hackles tightly together for only 3/4 of the length of the hackle and tie off. Tie in a small amount of Craft Fur approximately 1/4-inch thick directly in front and over the top of the palmered hackle. Place short pieces of the two synthetic fibers no thicker than 1/16 inch wide across or perpendicular to the hook shank. This is tied with a series of figure-eight thread wraps around the fibers and hook shank. Alternate the colors for the barring effect. Continue wrapping thread to the rear of hook shank where the bend of hook begins. Wrap the thread forward in front of the eyes and tie on the weed guard. Trim the body to desired shape and mark three black bars on Craft Fur tail.

Emerita

Tom Herrington | Historic Ocean Springs Saltwater Fly Fishing Club

This pattern was developed to simulate the mole crab or sand flea, a favorite food source for pompano and large, beach-dwelling sea trout.

Hook: Mustad tarpon hook, size 2.
Thread: Danville flat waxed nylon, tan.
Eyes: Tie in barbell eyes about 1/4 inch from the hook eye. The eyes should be painted brown.
Butt: Tie in a 1/2-inch-long length of small orange chenille and wrap as a small ball. Tie in the tip of a small tan hackle that will later be palmered up the chenille body.
Body: Tie in a 1/2-inch-long length of small tan chenille and wrap to a point behind the barbell eyes. Palmer the saddle hackle up the body and secure in place.
Carapace: Tie-in two small hen saddle hackles with fluff on either side of the hook and tie in between the hook eye and the barbell eyes.
Head: Build a thread head, whip finish and apply head cement.

Enrico's Mantis Shrimp | Enrico Puglisi

This mantis shrimp pattern is representative of a crustacean that is neither shrimp nor mantid but one that fish love to eat. The fly can be tied in any number of colors from various shades of browns to neon hues. Any gamefish that feeds on this food source will find the pattern appealing.

Hook: Wide gap, size 1/0, 2.
Thread: Waxed chartreuse.
Weight: Tie-in a small set of barbell eyes on the bottom of the hook shank.
Tail: Tie-in three tufts of EP Fibers forming a tail with the middle section slightly longer than the two side sections.
Legs: Tie-in several strands of Sili-Legs.
Eyes: Tie-in a pair of EP Shrimp Eyes.
Body: Add a small tuft of orange EP Fibers on the underside of the hook shank below the barb. Tie in small bunches of EP Fibers across the underside of the hook shank with figure-eight thread wraps. Build a body progressively with additional bunches to a point behind the lead barbells. Tie in several pairs of Sili-Legs between bunches.
Weed Guard: Tie-in a section of stiff monofilament and form a two-pronged weed guard. Tie off, whip finish and add cement.

EP Crab | Enrico Puglisi

OLIVE/TAN

This generic EP fiber pattern is a natural for all gamefish that feed on crabs. It is effective throughout the entire range of the East Coast and Gulf Coast and is especially productive for redfish, bonefish, permit and striped bass. The crab can be tied in many sizes and colors.

Hook: Wide-gap saltwater hook matched to size of fly, size 1-8.
Thread: Waxed, chartreuse.
Eyes: Tie in lead barbell eyes on the top of the hook shank. Hook rides point up.
Tail: Tie in a tuft of marabou and several strands of pearl Krystal Flash.
Body/Legs: Beginning at the hook bend tie in small bunches of EP fibers across the underside of the hook shank with figure-eight thread wraps. Build a body progressively with additional bunches. Tie in several pair of Sili-Legs between the fiber bunches. You can also use two different colors of EP fibers to give a striped effect to the crab. Leave fibers untrimmed until fly is finished.
Weed Guard: Tie in a section of stiff monofilament and form a two-pronged weed guard. Tie off, whip finish and add cement.
Finish: Trim EP fibers to shape.

EP Everglades Fly | Enrico Puglisi

This fly is tied with a large conical head that creates fish-attracting turbulence. Since it is tied completely with EP fibers it has a subtle and soft presentation when entering the water but pushes water when retrieved.

Hook: Gamakatsu CS 15, size 3/0 or 2/0.
Thread: Mono, .004.
Body/Wing: Using white and brown and olive EP fibers build a body and wing by tying the fibers on the shank in layers. Begin at the bend and tie in the fibers on the top and bottom of the shank. Layer fibers as you tie.
Flash: Mix-in Pearl Magic flash, #23 and Holographic Silver Flash #14.
Head: Tie in stacked bunches brown EP building a conical head much like a spun deer-hair head on a bass bug.
Gills: Tie in EPSF fibers, #07 red.
Plastic Eyes: Black on white, 6mm.
Weed Guard: Tie in a two-pronged length of stiff monofilament.
Glue: Zap-CA, Hard as Nails, Goop.
Markings: Apply barred markings with a brown permanent marker.

EP Ghost Shrimp | Enrico Puglisi

This pattern is a generic design effectively used in situations where any form of small shrimp is the food source. It is effective throughout the entire range of the Southeast and Gulf Coast states. It can be tied in a variety of sizes and colors.

Hook: Saltwater, sizes 2 and 6.
Thread: Monofilament, fine.
Eyes: Tie in a pair of bead-chain eyes.
Body: Tie in a short section of small pearl body braid material at the hook bend. Tie in a moderate bunch of long EP Fibers. Wind the strands of fibers forward forming a densely packed body. The forward portion of the body should be formed with a slightly larger diameter. Wrap fibers around the eyes, cut and tie off. Wind the pearl braid forward to a point in front of eyes, cut and tie off.
Legs: Tie in several Sili-Legs at a point forward of the eyes.
Wing: Tie in a moderate tuft of EP Fibers. The base of the fibers should be longer than the top.
Eyes: Tie in a pair of EP Shrimp Eyes and finish off the head of the fly.

EP Mangrove Baitfish | Enrico Puglisi

This generic mangrove baitfish is tied completely with EP Fibers. The pattern is an effective fly for all saltwater species that forage in mangrove areas. It is popular for most Southeast and Gulf Coast species The overall length of this fly is either three inches or five inches, depending on the hook size.

Hook: Gamakatsu CS 15, size 3/0 or 2/0.
Thread: Mono, .004.
Body/Wing: Using white and brown/root beer EP fibers build a body and wing by tying the fibers on the shank in layers. Begin at the bend and tie in the fibers on the top and bottom of the shank. Layer fibers as you tie.
Flash: Mix in Pearl Magic flash, #23 and Holographic Silver flash #14.
Gills: Tie in EPSF fibers, #07 red.
Plastic Eyes: Black on white, 6mm.
Weed Guard: Tie in a two-pronged length of stiff monofilament.
Glue: Zap-CA, Hard as Nails, Goop.

EP Mullet | Enrico Puglisi

Tied with EP fibers this mullet imitation is both resilient and lifelike. The pattern is an effective fly for all saltwater species that forage mullet-like bait. It is especially popular for snook, tarpon and pelagic species such as Atlantic bonito and false albacore. The overall length of this fly is three inches for the 2/0 version and five inches for the 3/0 tie.

Hook: Gamakatsu CS 15, size 3/0 or 2/0.
Thread: Mono, .004.
Body/Wing: Using slate and white EP fibers build a body and wing by tying the fibers on the shank in layers. Begin at the bend and tie in the fibers on the top and bottom of the shank. Layer fibers as you tie.
Flash: Mix in Pearl Magic flash, #23 and Holographic Silver flash #14.
Gills: Tie in EPSF fibers, #07 red.
Plastic Eyes: Black on white, 6mm.
Weed Guard: Tie in a two-pronged length of stiff monofilament.
Glue: Zap-CA, Hard as Nails, Goop.

EP Pinfish | Enrico Puglisi

Tied with EP Fibers this pinfish imitation is durable and lifelike. The pattern is an effective fly for all saltwater species that forage ion pinfish. It is popular for most Southeast and Gulf Coast species. The overall length of this fly is either three inches or five inches, depending on the hook size.

Hook: Gamakatsu CS 15, size 3/0 or 2/0.
Thread: Mono, .004.
Body/Wing: Using light olive and and white EP fibers build a body and wing by tying the fibers on the shank in layers. Begin at the bend and tie in the fibers on the top and bottom of the shank. Layer fibers as you tie.
Flash: Mix in Pearl Magic flash, #23 and Holographic Silver flash #14.
Gills: Tie in EPSF fibers, #07 red.
Plastic Eyes: Black on white, 6mm.
Weed Guard: Tie in a two-pronged length of stiff monofilament.
Glue: Zap-CA, Hard as Nails, Goop.

EP Tarpon Streamer | Enrico Puglisi

This fly is a very popular and effective tarpon pattern, especially in black and purple. It has a track record of getting spooky tarpon to eat. It is tied either as a three-inch or four-inch fly. The pattern is also effective for many other gamefish. Combinations of black, purple and red fibers are often the most productive.

Hook: Gamakatsu CS 15, size 3/0 or 2/0.
Thread: Mono, .004.
Body/Wing: Using black EP fibers build a layered body and wing by tying the fibers on the shank in successive layers. Begin at a point approximately half way down the hook shank and tie in the fibers on the top and bottom of the shank. Layer fibers as you tie.
Flash: Mix in Pearl Magic flash, #23 and Holographic Silver flash #14.
Head: Tie in stacked bunches red EP fibers building a head that completely encircles the hook and the body and wing.
Gills: Tie in EPSF fibers, #07 red.
Plastic Eyes: Black on yellow, 6mm.

Epoxy Baitfish | Glen Mikkleson

A very versatile generic fly suggesting small to medium baitfish, this fly is a modern version of the vintage Joe Brooks fly, the Blonde. The tighter silhouette of this pattern also resembles Lou Tabory's simple sand eel fly. It can be tied in numerous color combinations and is very effective for most gamefish species. For a productive night fly, tie a version in red and black. To fish the flies deeper, slide a conehead weight onto the leader before tying on.

Hook: Gamakatsu SL11-3H or TMC 800S, size 4 to 1/0.
Thread: A thread.
Tail: Attach thread and wrap a tight base down the shank, ending directly above the barb. Tie in white bucktail, extending 2 1/2 to 3 times the shank length. Add a mixture of Krystal Flash on top of the tail. Tie in some strands of pearl Flashabou and silver Mylar braid.
Under-body: Wrap the braid to the eye followed by all but one of the Flashabou strands. The silver will now shine through the pearl.
Wing: Tie in a wing of bucktail extending to the end of the tail. Pull the wing down and bind it to the body with the remaining strand of Flashabou.
Head: Whip finish and color the head with nail polish.
Finish: Brush coat the body with three light coats of 30-minute epoxy.
Eyes/Gills: Affix the stick-on eyes and red Flashabou into the second coat after about twenty minutes.

Epoxy Keel Fiddler | Captain Edward Wasicki

This epoxy crab fly is another keel design that rides point up and does not spin when retrieved. While it has taken many species of fish in the Mosquito Lagoon, Indian and Banana River area it is especially effective for tailing redfish on the flats.

Hook: Mustad 3407, size 2.
Thread: Monocord, brown.
Tail: Tie in a pair of small tuft of brown marabou.
Keel: Cut a piece of lead wire a bit longer than the hook shank. Straighten and flatten one end and tie on top of the tail. Apply a small drop of glue to secure. Bring thread forward toward the hook eye and secure the wire with thread. Use a bodkin to form the curve of the keel.
Frame: Tie in a length of 20-pound coated wire and shape a uniform and symmetrical frame.
Eyes: Tie in a pair of burnt monofilament eyes, colored black, laterally on the hook shank.
Legs: Tie in four sets of rubber legs to the outer edge of the frame. Knot legs to form segmentation.
Weed Guard: Tie in a short length of stiff monofilament at the eye. Extend to the barb.
Body: Build a body using Devcon Clear 5-Minute Epoxy. Add a very small amount of craft paint, color of choice, to the mixed epoxy and sprinkle in ultra-fine craft glitter. Use a rotating drying wheel to set the epoxy. Shape the sides and curvature with a bodkin as the epoxy sets.

Epoxy Keel Fly | Captain Edward Wasicki

This fly is a smaller version of the Epoxy Keel Wobbler. It is useful for more subtle presentations to wary fish feeding on micro baits. It enjoys the same characteristics of the larger pattern. It has been an extremely productive fly on the flats for redfish.

The most effective colors are metallic gold, cooper and bronze. Tail material can vary and includes flash, bucktail, rabbit strip and marabou. Tie on with a loop knot so it will wobble freely.

Hook: Mustad 34011 smaller sizes 6 and 4.
Thread: Monocord, 3/0.
Tail: Tie in a substantial bunch of Flashabou strands or other suitable tail material on the top of the hook shank. The tail should be as long as the hook shank.
Keel: Tie in .032 lead wire and form a curved keel on the underside of the hook shank. The curve should be uniform with the highest part 1/3 of the hook shank length behind the eye.
Frame: Tie in a length of 20-pound coated wire and shape a uniform and symmetrical frame.
Body: Build a body using Devcon Clear 5-Minute Epoxy. Add a very small amount of craft paint, color of choice, to the mixed epoxy and sprinkle in ultra-fine craft glitter. Use a rotating drying wheel to set the epoxy. Shape the sides and curvature with a bodkin as the epoxy sets.

Epoxy Keel Shrimp | Captain Edward Wasicki

This fly was patterned off the Epoxy Keel Wobbler spoon and is effective in situations where fish feed on small shrimp. Like its predecessor the fly rides point up and does not spin when retrieved. While it has taken many species of fish, the fly is especially effective for redfish on the flats.

Hook: Mustad 3407, sizes 4, 2.
Thread: Fine monofilament.
Tail: Tie in a pair of small, splayed barred hackle feathers. Tie in another small hackle and palmer at the rear of the hook as you would a small collar. A tail variation can also be tied with synthetic hair and hackle.
Keel: Cut a piece of lead wire a bit longer than the hook shank. Straighten and flatten one end and tie on top of the tail. Apply a small drop of glue to secure. Bring thread forward toward the hook eye and secure the wire with thread. Use a bodkin to form the curve of the keel.
Weed Guard: Tie in a short length of stiff monofilament at the eye. Extend to the barb.
Body: Mix epoxy and add glitter. Apply epoxy to form body shape.

Epoxy Keel Wobbler | Captain Edward Wasicki

This fly design is an epoxy variation of a spoon fly. The fly rides with the hook point up, does not spin when retrieved, is easy to cast and its effective. The fly has taken twenty species of fish including bonefish, redfish and striped bass. The most effective colors are metallic gold, copper and bronze. Tail material can vary and includes flash, bucktail, rabbit strip and marabou. Tie on with a loop knot so it will wobble freely.

Hook: Mustad 34011, sizes 6 to 1/0.
Thread: Monocord, 3/0.
Tail: Tie in a substantial bunch of Flashabou strands or other suitable tail material on the top of the hook shank. The tail should be as long as the hook shank.
Keel: Tie in .032 lead wire and form a curved keel on the underside of the hook shank. The curve should be uniform with the highest part 1/3 of the hook shank length behind the eye.
Frame: Tie in a length of 20-pound coated wire and shape a uniform and symmetrical frame.
Body: Build a body using Devcon Clear 5-Minute Epoxy. Add a very small amount of craft paint, color of choice, to the mixed epoxy and sprinkle in ultra-fine craft glitter. Use a rotating drying wheel to set the epoxy. Shape the sides and curvature with a bodkin as the epoxy sets.

Estaz Collared Tarpon Fly | Oscar Feliu

This fly was designed to create fish-attracting vibrations. It is ideal for use in discolored or murky shallow waters. User a loop knot to secure fly to the leader.

Hook: Mustad C47S D or C70 D, size 3/0 to 7/0.
Thread: Danville A plus, white.
Tail Center: Tie in a blend of Krystal Flash of contrasting colors.
Wing: Tie in three or four matched diverging feathers per side.
Flank: Tie in six strands of pearl Krystal Flash under a clump of calf tail in a contrasting color.
Collar: Tie in pearlescent Estaz, or color of choice, and make seven winds forming a collar.
Head: Build a tapered head with thread.
Finish: Apply clear epoxy to cover all head threads and the first two wraps of Estaz. The epoxy will stiffen the Estaz and allow the head to push water.

Faux Toad | Captain Paul Dixon

This pattern is referred to as the two-minute toad. It is a simple and very effective fly for tarpon. The fly was inspired by the original Toad design and can be tied in a variety of productive color combinations.

Hook: Gamakatsu SL12S, 1/0 or 2/0.
Thread: Chartreuse, 2/0.
Eyes: Tie in black monofilament eyes.
Tail: Tie in a moderate clump of yellow marabou and several strands of pearl Krystal Flash.
Body: Tie in chartreuse Body Fur at the bend of the hook and wrap forward to the eyes. Whip finish and trim to desired size.

F-C Salt Shaker | Ed Story | Feather-Craft

This easy-to-tie streamer pattern was first developed for Spanish mackerel feeding on small rain bait. It performs well in freshwater, and is an excellent speckled trout fly. When fished, allow the fly to sink to the desired depth and then strip retrieve to impart swimming and darting motions. The flash creates enticing shimmer effects.

Hook: TMC 811 or Mustad 34007, Size 1, 2 or 4 or Dai-Riki 0707 bronze, sizes 6-8.
Thread: UNI-Thread, white 3/0 or flat waxed floss.
Body: Silver tinsel or pearl Flashabou tied in and wrapped along the hook shank.
Wings: Cut small clumps of four-inch "salt and pepper" Flashabou and tie in behind the hook eye with 1 1/4 inches of Flashabou wing extending beyond the hook bend, and the balance of the clump extending out forward of the hook eye. Fold this shorter clump over and tie in, forming the top wing.
Head: Form a head with the thread.
Gills: At the rear of the head, use red thread wraps to form the gills.
Eyes: Small Decal-Eyes are optional. Finish with a light coat of epoxy.

F-C Sand Shrimp | Ed Story | Feather-Craft

This pattern is very effective for redfish, sea trout and pompano. It is tied to represent a fleeing sand shrimp and is best fished sub-surface, on the bottom and stripped over weed beds.

Hook: TMC 811S, sizes 1, 2 or 4.
Thread: UNI-Thread, red, 3/0.
Eyes: Tie in small barbell eyes (red with black pupils) on top of the hook shank, just behind the hook eye.
Tail: Tie in eight to ten strands of pearl Krystal Flash, 1 1/2 to 2 inches in length. Tie in an equal length of tan or rust F-C Craft Fur on top of the Krystal Flash. Also tie in a four-inch length of root beer Estaz Crystal Chenille for use as the fly body.
Body: Wrap the Estaz chenille up the hook shank, forming the body. Tie in behind the barbell eyes and cut away any waste.
Top Wing: Tie in behind the eyes a clump of Orangutan Orange Rust F-C Craft Fur. The fur should extend over the top of the fly body and most of the tail. Cover butt ends with thread wraps and figure-eight the barbell eyes.
Finish: Cement thread wraps with penetrating head cement. Using a black Sharpie marking pen, place three black bars across the Craft Fur tail.

F-C Shiner | Ed Story | Feather-Craft

This white-bait streamer pattern is effective for a wide variety of gamefish including ladyfish, speckled trout, jacks, bluefish, bonito and false albacore.

The fly can be fished on floating or sinking lines. In moving water strip, skip and swim the fly, imparting additional action with the rod tip. In still water, allow the fly to sink to the desired depth.

Hook: TMC 9394, nickel finish, sizes 2, 4 and 6; TMC 911S, 3x long.
Thread: UNI-thread, red, 6/0 or 3/0 or flat waxed floss in red.
Weight: Wrap front half or full shank length with lead or non-toxic wire, .020 or .025.
Body: Pearl Crystal Chenille or pearl Estaz wrapped to form a shiner or small bait-shaped body.
Tail: Tie in eight to ten strands of white ostrich herl on top of an equal amount of pearl Krystal Flash. An alternative tail can be tied with a clump of #9 Flashabou.
Eyes: Affix small decal eyes.

Fender Fly

Tied by Richard "Doc" Steinberger | Originated by Robert Ransom

This fly is fundamentally a large white-bait imitation. It suggests and highlights the gill plates of the baitfish and presents a rather unique eye structure. Different templates allow the use of a wide variety of materials and styles. As examples, fenders can take the shape of hearts, leafs, diamonds, circles, oblong, etc. Fish the fly on a high-density, full-sinking line, using a short butt section and 20-pound tippet.

Hook: Mustad 34007, size 4/0 or 34011 or Eagle Claw 254.
Thread: Monocord A or Danville flat waxed nylon.
Support: Tie in a hard mono anti-fouling loop at the rear to support the wing.
Keel: Tie in two pieces of .035 lead wire under the shank from rear of headspace to bend.
Tail/Wing: Bucktail, Saddle Hackle, Fish Hair or similar synthetic, Flashabou or Krystal Flash, long dense fur strip such as fox. For this specific fly, EP Fibers were used in polar white, pink, lavender, yellow, gray, gold, olive and black. Hi-tie and Lo-tie all materials from the rear forward, folding material around hook before tying in.
Flash: Pearl, multi-light, multi-dark Glimmer.
Throat: Red flat metallic polyester braid.
Body: Diamond Braid.
Fender Face: Prismatic Mylar tape or equivalent, reinforced with fiberglass strapping tape. Prism tape is bonded to strapping tape, adhesive-to-adhesive. Pre-cut template for fender cutout. Pattern and size vary with hook size and style of dressing. Fender is installed by mounting with the fold under the shank, using Goop. If desired, coat outside of fender with Hard As Nails.
Eyes: Punch hole in fender for eye and insert Dritz sew-on snaps. Fill each eye well created by the snaps with epoxy, and use acrylic paint and glitter to color the eyes.
Adhesive: Thinned Goop or other multi-purpose cement.
Coating: 5-minute epoxy and glitter pigmented acrylic paint.

Feral Oyster Crab | Captain John Turcot

This is another of the Turcot series of small flies for Mosquito Lagoon redfish. It is tied in natural looking colors and presented to feeding reds.

Hook: Mustad 34007, size 4 and 6.
Thread: Waxed 6/0.
Eyes: Lead eyes are tied in behind the hook eye as weight. Burnt monofilament stubs for the actual eyes at the bend of the hook.
Tail: Four rooster neck tips splayed outward with arctic fox hair tied in forming the tail.
Body/Legs: Tie in four strands (clumps) of yarn "Merkin" style along the bottom of the hook shank. Soft grizzly saddle wound through the yarn forms the legs. The hackles are pulled outward and trimmed on top of the crab. Tying cement applied to the bottom of the crab helps secure the legs flat.

Feral Shrimp | Captain John Turcot

This simple-to-tie and effective shrimp pattern was designed for redfish, sea trout and baby tarpon.

Hook: 34007, size 4, 6.
Thread: Waxed, 6/0.
Eyes: Plastic dumbbell eyes tied in 1/3 up the hook shank.
Tail: Tie in four to six rooster neck tips splayed outward forming a 1-1/2-inch tail.
Body: Tie in fluorescent orange calf tail forward of the hook bend. Tie in natural grizzly saddle hackle and palmer around the hook shank.

Fire Tiger | John Baker

This fly is a generic minnow imitation that is part of the Baker Baitfish series. It can be used to replicate a variety of small to moderate size baitfish. It can be tied in a number of color combinations and sizes. The Fire Tiger is tied in the hot attractor colors of yellow, chartreuse and orange. The pattern design has proven effective from Delaware to Florida for a wide variety of gamefish.

Hook: Short-shank big-game hook, size 1/0 or larger.
Thread: Color to match body.
Body/Wing: Tie in combinations of yellow and chartreuse and dark gray Craft Fur, Polar Flash and Polybear to form the body and wing. Blend in strands of Polar Flash. Add the prominent black bars at the shoulder with a permanent marker pen.
Belly: Tie in a length of yellow Polybear by Larva Lace.
Head/Eyes: Build a small head with a coating of Softex and affix plastic molded eyes.

Flapper | Captain Edward Wasicki

This pattern is crafted similarly to a Crease Fly with a rattle sealed inside the body and a spoon blade affixed at the tail. The Crease Fly is a notoriously effective fly and this variation enhances that effectiveness. The Flapper can be tied in many sizes and numerous color combinations.

Hook: Mustad 3407, sized to pattern dimensions.
Tail: Tie in a loop of stiff monofilament that has been threaded through split ring and spoon blade configuration. The spoon will be positioned as the body is formed.
Weed Guard: Affix and tie in a pre-fabricated, spring-type weed guard.
Rattle: Affix a small rattle inside the body cavity before sealing it.
Body: Build the body Crease Fly-style using a foam underbody and a mylar outer shell. Apply epoxy to inside of the foam and seal the edges, making certain to position the spoon blade properly.
Finish: Apply desired paint, affix plastic eyes, apply a coating of epoxy and sprinkle on glitter.

Flashy Pin Fish | Captain Paul Dixon

This fly is a modification of Captain Dixon's Jumping Jack Flash. It is tied with barred marabou and is very effective for snook, tarpon and sea trout. This is a very versatile and easy-to-tie pattern.

Hook: Gamakatsu SL 12 S, 1/0.
Thread: Clear heavy monofilament.
Tail: Tie in barred marabou at the hook bend forming the tail.
Body: Tie in strands of pearl Krystal Flash at a point immediately behind the eye to form the body and whip finish. Trim flash to a triangular shape.
Eyes: Optional stick-on, prismatic eyes can be added.

Flashy Shrimp | Joe McMahon | New Orleans Fly Fishers

This fly was inspired by Tim Borski's Craft Fur Shrimp. It is a simple, flashy inshore pattern designed for the silt-laden waters of southeast Louisiana salt marshes. The fly rides hook point up and pushes water. It has proved very effective for redfish and speckled trout. Retrieve with short, erratic strips and moderate pauses.

Hook: Mustad 34007, size 2.
Thread: 280 Denier, red.
Eyes: Tie in gold Dazyl-Eyes, 5/32-inch.
Body: Tie in Orvis Holographic & Tri-Lobal Hackle, root beer. Palmer the material forward to the eyes. Tie-off and trim.
Wing: Tie in over the eyes a small piece of thinned Craft Fur. Whip finish and cut the thread.
Markings: Blot the Craft Fur with a waterproof marker. Let dry and then comb out the fibers.
Weed Guard: Place fly back in vise and install a weed guard of 15- to 20-pound Mason hard monofilament.
Finish: Build a small head with thread and whip finish. Apply head cement.

Flat Tail Cockroach | Captain Edward Wasicki

The cockroach fly was inspired by the flat-wing tying style of Ken Abrames. The pattern has proven to offer an effective profile in situations where the fly is moving away from the fish.

Hook: Mustad 3407, 1/0.
Thread: Brown Monocord.
Tail: Tie in flat-style two short grizzly or barred hackle feathers at top of the hook shank. Add a few sparse strands of sparkle flash.
Underwing: Tie in a short, sparse bunch of brown bucktail or calf tail on the underside of the hook shank.
Top Wing: Tie in a longer bunch of brown bucktail or calf tail on the top of the hook shank.
Head: Build a head with thread, whip finish and apply a coating of head cement.

Flat Tail Variant | Captain Edward Wasicki

This fly is a variation of the Flat Tail Cockroach. It is tied for a much more subtle presentation and softer delivery with a palmered hackle body. A small set of bead-chain eyes tied to the underside of the hook shank allows the hook to ride point up. This is a good fly for skittish thin-water fish.

Hook: Mustad 3407, sizes 4, 2.
Thread: Monocord, brown.
Eyes: Tie in a pair of very small bead-chain eyes on the top of the hook shank.
Tail: Tie in two barred grizzly hackles flat on the top of the hook shank. Tie in a few strands of Krystal Flash.
Body: Tie in one grizzly hackle and palmer toward the eye, forming the body. Tie off thread immediately behind the bead-chain eyes.
Finish: Figure-eight thread over the eyes and make a number of wraps ahead of the eyes. Tie off and apply head cement.

Flats Feast | John Baker

This pattern is tied as an all-purpose flats fly. It is effective for redfish, bonefish and permit. It is especially productive for large bonefish, and when a small-fly presentation is needed for redfish.

Hook: Standard saltwater hook, size 4 or 2.
Thread: Color to match body.
Tail: Tie in Sili-legs, colors to match fly.
Body/Legs: Tie in and wrap Krystal Wrapz.
Wing: Tie in Craft Fur or Polar Fibre.
Weed Guard: Tie in 50-pound fluorocarbon for a weedguard.
Head: Form a head with thread and apply Softex.

Flats Pirate | Drew Chicone

This fly is a modification of a Hiromi Kuboki crab pattern. It was designed for redfish, bonefish and permit in Florida and the Bahamas, and can be tied in tan, olive or brown.

Hook: Stainless steel, sizes 2,4, 6.
Thread: 3/0 to match body color.
Body: Start thread near the back of hook and spin deer hair (color of choice) on the entire shank. Whip finish at the hook eye. The fly will ride hook point up. Clip the underside of the fly flat and close to the hook. Trim to shape the top shell of crab.
Claws: Cut a 2-inch piece of scud back for each of the claws and swim fins. Fold over on top at a 90-degree angle and glue. Shape the claws and fins with scissors.
Underside: On the flat underside of the fly, glue on 50-pound-test monofilament eyes, legs, claws and antennae. Once dried, roll lead wire into a flat pad shape and glue on top of other body components. Cut to form and affix a felt pad to the underside of body. Color claws and legs with permanent marker.

Flats Rascal | Angelo Peluso

This fly is a hybrid crustacean pattern that was initially tied for both redfish and striped bass feeding on shallow sand flats. The fly is an impressionistic tie and works especially well when fish are keyed on crabs and small crustaceans.

Hook: Mustad 34007, size 1.
Thread: Clear, fine monofilament.
Eyes: tie in medium bead-chain eyes.
Tail: Tie in two splayed burnt furnace hackle feathers, over which are tied two wide brown hackle feathers on either side of the furnace hackle.
Flash: Tie in several strands of gold holographic flash.
Body: Tie in one brown hackle and a length of root beer Crystal Chenille. Wind the chenille forward to a point immediately behind the eyes, and then wind the hackle feather forward to the same location.
Head: Build a small head with thread, tie-off and whip finish.

Fleeing Crab | Captain Lenny Moffo

This fly was designed for bonefish and imitates a crab trying to escape. It has proven a very effective impressionistic pattern when attempting to match small crabs. In addition to Florida the fly has worked very well in the Bahamas, Belize and Mexico.

Hook: Gamakatsu SC 15, size 2.
Thread: Flat waxed 3/0, color of choice.
Legs: Tie in two or three pumpkin-colored Sili-Legs, combined with six or seven round, tan rubber legs. Tie all in one bunch and well into the bend of the hook.
Eyes: Tie on dumbbell eyes.
Body: Build up the thread so it is uniform and tie on small sections of craft yarn to build the body, progressing from the tail to the eyes.

Floating Finger Mullet | Captain Jim Blackburn

This mullet pattern has been effective catching a wide variety of gamefish, including snook, sea trout, ladyfish, tarpon and jacks.

Hook: Any short- or medium-shank saltwater hook, size 2/0 to 4.
Thread: Thread of choice.
Head: Wrap a thread base on hook shank and coat the front third of shank with Super Glue. Insert and thread-on a foam cone head of appropriate size and color.
Weed Guard: With a heated bodkin make two holes in the bottom of foam cone. Glue a short piece of stiff monofilament in the holes forming the weed guard.
Tail/Body: Tie in a blend of Kraft Fur and Krystal Flash, about 2 1/2 times the length of the hook shank. Tie in Zonker rabbit strip of desired color and wrap toward the head, leaving enough room to tie in an Estaz collar.
Topping: Krystal Flash of desired color.
Markings: Using permanent marker, make vertical bars on both sides of the tail.
Finish: Apply head cement.

Floating Micro Crab | Kevin "Fluff" Arculeo

This smaller Floating Rattle Crab was originally designed to imitate micro-crab hatches. It should be fished dead-drifted in a current with intermittent micro-short strips.

Hook: Tiemco 811S, size 8.
Thread: Monofilament, 6/0.
Claws/Legs 1: Cut two double rubber legs 2 inches long. Tie an overhand knot 2/3 down the rubber legs. Separate the legs on the short side of the knot. Cut the ends to form a point to make the claws. For the legs, cut four single rubber leg strips 2 inches long. To give the legs a realistic jointed look, tie an overhand knot in the middle of each rubber leg creating a 90-degree angle.
Body 1: Cut or stamp two pieces closed-cell foam to the football shape of a crab, matched to the size hook you are using. You can also use Rainy's pre-cut crab foam bodies.
Claws/Legs 2: Wrap mono thread back to bend in hook. Tie in the tapered end of the first rubber leg claw 1/4" from bend in hook. Position claw angled out with the jointed knot section pointing inward and towards you. Tie in one rubber leg on back side of hook and angled toward the rear with right angle pointing towards back of hook. Leave a tag end on the rubber legs to use for positioning later in the process. Then move a little forward and tie in the next leg pointing in same direction. Tie in the next leg pointing straight back with the jointed section pointing towards the eye of the hook. Move forward to just behind the eye and tie in the last leg pointing out away from you and towards the eye of the hook. Tie in the 2nd claw rubber leg with the knot measuring about 1/4 inch from the hook. Position claw angled out with the jointed knot section pointing inward and towards you.
Body 2: Tie in the 2nd piece of closed-cell foam by using a dubbing needle to poke a hole through the end of the foam. Feed the hook point through the hole, pull the other end of the foam to the eye of the hook, and tie in the tip. This creates the underside of the crab. Tie in a tip of the closed-cell sheet foam just behind the eye. Tie in weed guard if needed, and whip finish. Add a drop of glue to finish head.
Eyes: Prepare the black plastic mono eyes by cutting off one of the eyeballs.
Finish: Use a dubbing needle to spread 5-minute epoxy across the top of the bottom sheet foam and the underside of the top sheet foam. Saturate the hook area, including the tie-in point for all legs and claws. Place the post of the eyes in the glue in-between the top and bottom sheet foam. As the epoxy starts to set, press the closed-cell foam top and bottom together, creating a sandwich. Continue to pinch the sandwich together while positioning the claws, legs and eyes until the epoxy sets. Wipe off any excess epoxy before it sets.
Markings: Use the red permanent marker to color the inside of the V and the pointed tips. Use the Prisma marker to add dots and marks for realistic look.

Floating Rattle Crab | Kevin "Fluff" Arculeo

The Floating Rattle Crab was originally designed to imitate fiddler crabs in Charleston, South Carolina waters, and to target redfish. The fly has evolved into a pattern to use for crabs that are swept up in the strong current of bay and flats passes. This fly should be fished by using a one-handed short continuous strip in calm water and dead-drifted in current with intermittent short strips.

Hook: Tiemco 811S, sizes 6 to 3/0.
Thread: Monofilament, 6/0.
Claws/Legs 1: Prepare the claws by cutting two rubber tourniquet strips 3/16 inches wide and three inches long. Cut a taper in one end of strip for tying onto hook. Cut four double rubber leg strips two-inches long. Tie an overhand knot in the middle of each tourniquet strip and rubber leg creating a 90-degree angle.
Body 1: Cut or stamp closed-cell foam and Furry Foam to the football shape of a crab matched to the size hook you are using. You can also use Rainy's pre-cut crab foam bodies.
Claws/Legs 2: Tie in the tapered end of the first rubber tourniquet strip with the knot measuring about 1/2 inch from the hook. Position claw angled out with the jointed knot section pointing inward and towards you. Tie in one rubber leg on back side of hook and angled toward the rear with right angle pointing towards back of hook. Leave a tag end on the rubber legs to use for positioning later in the process. Then move a little forward and tie in the next leg pointing in same direction. Tie in rattle at the midpoint and backside of the hook shank. Tie in the next leg pointing straight back with the jointed section pointing towards the eye of the hook. Move forward to just behind the eye and tie in the last leg pointing out away from you and towards the eye of the hook. Tie in the tapered end of the second claw rubber tourniquet strip with the knot measuring about 1/2 inch from the hook. Position claw angled out with the jointed knot section pointing inward and towards you. Cut a V shape on the end of the rubber tourniquet material to create the claw. Use a red permanent marker to color the inside of the V and the tips. Use the prisma marker to add dots and markings.
Body 2: Tie in the Furry Foam by using a dubbing needle to poke a hole through the end of the foam. Feed the hook point through the hole, pull the other end of the foam to the eye of the hook, and tie in the tip. This creates the underside of the crab.
Head: Tie in a tip of the closed-cell sheet foam just behind the eye. Tie in weed guard if needed, and whip finish. Add a drop of glue to finish head.
Eyes: Prepare the black plastic mono eyes by cutting off one of the eyeballs.
Finish: Spread 5-minute epoxy across the top of the Furry Foam and the underside of the closed-cell sheet foam. Saturate the hook area, including the rattle and the tie-in point for all legs and claws. Placed the post of the eyes in the glue on the Furry Foam. As the epoxy starts to set, press the closed-cell foam to the Furry Foam, creating a sandwich. Continue to pinch the sandwich together while positioning the claws, legs and eyes until the epoxy sets. Wipe off any excess epoxy before it sets.

Fluorofibre Red Minnow

Tom Herrington | Historic Ocean Springs Saltwater Fly Fishing Club

This fly was designed to replicate the bay anchovy, a favorite forage fish of little tunny. The anchovies are often referred to as red minnows since their translucent bodies reveal the hues of the red and brown algae they eat.

Hook: Mustad C68SS, size 2 or similar hook.
Thread: Monofilament, clear.
Belly: Tie in a clump of red Fluorofibre on the underside of the hook shank and the length of the hook shank.
Wing: Tie in a length of white Fluorofibre on the top of the hook shank, three times the length of the shank.
Topping: Tie in green Fluorofibre on top of the white wing, a length equal to the wing.
Eyes: Affix small molded silver eyes with epoxy.

Flying Fish | Captain Doug Sinclair

This top-water popper was designed to appeal to gamefish that feed on small flying fish. The pattern is easy to construct, it's durable and easy to cast.

Hook: Long-shank stainless-steel popper hook, size 1/0 or 2/0.
Body: The entire body is constructed from a foam cylinder shaped to form a flying fish facsimile.
Tail: Glue in short strands of pearl Krystal Flash in a slit formed at the rear of the body.
Wings: Bore two sets of holes through the body, one about 1/3 the length down the body, the other about 2/3 down the length of the body. Pair off two sets of green hackles and insert through each of the openings.
Eyes: Affix black over yellow eyes with glue.

Foamback | Captain Edward Wasicki

This is a terrific little bonefish fly that can be tied in many sizes and colors with contrasting thread tones.

Hook: Mustad 3407, sizes 6, 4, 2.
Thread: Match or contrast to body coloration. When wrapping hook leave a small tag of thread immediately after the hook bend.
Eyes: Tie in small bead-chain eyes behind the eye and on the bottom of the hook shank. Leave enough room to build ahead.
Body: Tie in foam on the bottom of the hook shank and segment with thread. Typical segmentation is three.
Wing: Tie in a small section of wind material. Soft hair like fox works well.
Head: Build a small head with thread, tie off and apply head cement.

Foamback Shrimp | Glen Mikkleson

Quite similar in pattern to other shrimp flies, this design uses foam on the back to keep the flies riding upright. Elements of this fly were influenced by one of Bob Sater's patterns. This fly can also be tied weighted with the hook riding up and in a variety of colors. It is best fished in dead-drift fashion, and is especially productive for sea trout.

Hook: Mustad 34011, size 4 to 10.
Thread: A thread.
Antennae: Tie in antennae of Krystal Flash. Two will be as long as the shank and two will be half that length.
Mouth Parts: Tie in mouth parts of marabou half the length of the short antennae.
Eyes: Tie in burnt thirty-pound monofilament eyes on either side of the marabou, curve outward and extend half the length of the marabou.
Thorax/Rib/Abdomen: Dub a small amount of Pseudo Seal and Angora goat fur and tie in the saddle hackle. Dub along the shank to form a thick thorax. Tie in four-pound mono for the rib. Palmer hackle over thorax and dub the abdomen down the rest of the shank, tapering it thinner toward the eye.
Shellback: Crinkle clear pearl wrapping film by twisting it and sticking it to the foam. Cut to a shape about 1 1/4 times the length of the shank. Color the back, edges, under the tail and under the tip of the nose with a Sharpie marker. Place a drop of CA glue on the top front of the thorax. Tie in shellback at its tail joint at the end of the abdomen, hold down front end and let glue set. Bind the shellback down with four-pound mono. Rib from the back of the thorax to tail.
Finish: Whip finish at the eye and coat the entire back, under the tail and the whip finish with liquid acrylic. After the acrylic has dried, touch up color and add speckles to the shellback.

Foamy Slider | Captain Edward Wasicki

This pattern is a blend of two designs: the Slider and the Deceiver. It is an easy effective fly to tie and works well as a surface pattern for many species of gamefish.

Hook: Mustad 34011, size 1 or 1/0.
Tail: Tie in a white bucktail, short white saddle hackles Deceiver-style and add several strands of silver flash.
Head/Body: Form a white foam head and body into the shape of a "cardinal's hat". The foam should be sized equal in length to the hook. Slip the foam inside a small section of drinking straw to form the head. Apply epoxy to the inside of the head. After the epoxy dries remove section of straw and paint.
Eyes/Glitter: Affix stick-on eyes to head. Coat with a light coat of epoxy, Hard Head or Softex: Apply a light coat of adhesive material to the foam back and sprinkle on glitter.

Foxy Bone | Angelo Peluso

Developed specifically for Atlantic bonito, the fly design intended to elicit quick strikes from fish feeding on large silversides. The fly is a blend of flash, weight and supple natural fibers that allow it to pulsate on the descent. The fly is best fished on an intermediate or high-density sinking line by casting in the direction of feeding bonito. Allow the fly to descend as if it were a stunned baitfish, imparting a slight twitching motion. Often, a fast two-handed retrieve works well. This fly has produced numerous bonito, false albacore and Spanish mackerel.

Hook: Mustad 34001 long shank, sizes 1 and 1/0.
Thread: Monocord clear or chartreuse.
Tail: Tie in a small bunch of fine white bucktail as a foundation and overlay with a moderate-sized tuft of fox fur at the bend on top of the shank. The original pattern uses Blue Fox but other foxy furs or tails are also suitable.
Body 1: Tie in a length of gold Electra Braid and wrap forward several turns. This step will be repeated three times as the wing is layered along the shaft. The braid should be long enough to wrap three segments of six turns each.
Body 2: Tie in another moderate tuft of fox fur at the point of the last braid wrap and secure. Add several strands of gold tinsel, making certain the tinsel extends approximately 1/4 inch beyond the tips of the bucktail. This allows the tinsels to flutter as the fly descends. Repeat two additional times winding the braid, adding a tuft of fox fur and adding the tinsel, leaving enough room for the bead-chain eyes and a head. You can add one final tuft of fur over and between the bead-chain eyes. The fly will have three layered Hi-Tie wings and will ride hook point up.
Eyes: Tie in gold bead-chain eyes and invert the fly in the vise.
Wing: Tie in a base wing of chartreuse bucktail topped with an overwing of light olive bucktail.
Head: Whip finish and cement.

Frankee-Bell Bonefish Fly

Leigh West | Originated by Captain Jimmie Albright

The Frankee-Bell has been attributed to the late Florida Keys guide, Captain Jimmie Albright. It is considered to be one of the oldest and best bonefish patterns. This fly is tied as a color variant of the original and incorporates a subdued color combination of a tan wing and yellow body. This simple, easy-to-tie fly is effective for tailing redfish and tailing sheepshead, especially in the winter months and in clear water. The fly can be delivered almost on top of tailing fish, as it lands on the water surface with a slight, attractive splash. Changing the body and thread color to tan or brown, however, results in a very effective fly for Keys bonefish.

Hook: Tiemco 811S, Size 4.
Thread: Danville flat-waxed nylon, fluorescent nylon.
Body: Place hook in vise and lay down a base wrap of thread ending slightly behind the shank on the curve. Attach the medium, yellow chenille, and wrap the thread forward. Wrap the chenille forward until near the eye. Tie down chenille and cut off excess.
Wing: Tie a small bunch of tan calf tail (bend-back style, covering the hook point) extending just beyond the length of the hook.
Sides: Attach a small grizzly saddle hackle to either side of the wing, just a bit shorter than the wing length.
Weed Guard: Tie in 20-30-lb monofilament line (optional).
Head: Build up the head just slightly with thread and whip finish.

Furimsky's Floating Minnow | Ben Furimsky

This fly was designed for sea trout, bonito, false albacore and striped bass. It replicates any number of small species of baitfish.

Hook: Gamakatsu SC15.
Thread: White, 3/0.
Tail: Tie in six to eight strands of pearl Krystal Flash.
Body: Tie in successive layers of white, pink, and tan Craft Fur. Blend in Krystal Flash between layers.
Head: Build a head from foam packing wrap colored to match body. Cover with tan Midge Krystal Flash and pearl Angel Hair on belly.
Eyes: Affix stick-on eyes and seal with Softex.

Furimsky's Mangrove Minnow | Ben Furimsky

This fly has been especially productive for baby tarpon, snook, sea trout, redfish and snappers.

Hook: Eagle Claw LO54 bent to about 15 degrees to create a bendback style.
Thread: White, 3/0.
Tail: Tie in six to eight strands of pearl Krystal Flash.
Body/Wing: Tie in chartreuse over white Super Hair. Top with chartreuse over white bucktail.
Topping: Tie in eight strands of peacock herl.
Eyes: Affix 3D stick-on eyes.
Head: Build a small head with thread, tie off and apply head cement.
Gills: Color gills with a red permanent marker.

Fuzzy Flash Bunker | Captain Chris Newsome

This fly was designed to imitate Atlantic menhaden. A combination of tying technique and specific materials allow for a high-profile pattern without adding excessive bulk to the fly. It can be tied 3-12 inches long to match size of bait. The fly can also be used any time fish are keyed on high profile bait like shad or pinfish. The pattern has been productive for striped bass, speckled trout, flounder, bluefish, gray trout, red drum and cobia snook, tarpon, jacks, barracuda, kingfish and tuna.

Hook: Mustad C68SSS, TMC 600SP, size 2 to 6/0.
Thread: Monofilament.
Body/Wing: Blend of Fuzzy Fiber and Polar Flash. Begin "hi-tie" process by adding a small portion of blended material on the topside of the hook near the rear of shank. Continue tying in portions of materials on the top and bottom of the hook shank working down to the eye of the hook. Use small amounts of material because the goal of this fly is a high profile without a large amount of bulk. Majority of the materials should be added on to the top of the hook shank to provide proper tracking of the fly when fished with a fast strip, as well as preventing the material from fouling around the hook shank. Adjust the length of material added to give a tapered shape to the fly. Once the material has reached the eye of the hook, secure and cut the thread.
Eyes: Secure small plastic doll eyes with Fletch-Tite Platinum glue. If necessary, trim the material to achieve the fly's best profile. A fly that is properly tapered during the tying process should require very little trimming.

The Fuzzy Flash Bunker with Tail

Captain Chris Newsome

This fly was designed to imitate Atlantic menhaden. It can be tied 3-12 inches long to match size of bait. The fly can also be used anytime fish are keyed on high-profile bait like shad or pinfish. The pattern has been productive for striped bass, speckled trout, flounder, bluefish, gray trout, red drum and cobia snook, tarpon, jacks, barracuda, kingfish and tuna.

Hook: Mustad C68SSS, TMC 600SP, size 2 to 6/0.
Thread: Monofilament.
Body/Wing: Blend of Fuzzy Fiber and Polar Flash. Begin "hi-tie" process by adding a small portion of blended material on the topside of the hook near the rear of shank. Continue tying in portions of materials on the top and bottom of the hook shank, working down to the eye of the hook. Use small amounts of material because the goal of this fly is a high-profile without a large amount of bulk. Majority of the materials should be added on to the top of the hook shank to provide proper tracking of the fly when fished with a fast strip, as well as preventing the material from fouling around the hook shank. Adjust the length of material added to give a tapered shape to the fly. Once the material has reached the eye of the hook, secure and cut the thread.
Eyes: Secure small plastic doll eyes with Fletch-Tite Platinum glue. If necessary, trim the material to achieve the fly's best profile. A fly that is properly tapered during the tying process should require very little trimming.
Tail: Optional. Cut a shallow V-shape into the top portion of a turkey neck feather. Strip the bottom portion of webbings off the quill until the remaining webbing forms the fork-tail shape and size of the desired bunker tail of the fly. Insert the stripped quill into 20# braided mono until the newly created tail butts against the braid. Add a few drops Fletch-Tite Platinum to keep the tail from sliding out of the braid.

Ghostly Grass Shrimp | Captain Chris Newsome

This fly was designed to imitate the translucent traits of shrimp.

Hook: Mustad S71S SS, size 6.
Thread: UTC monofilament, .006 or equivalent.
Weed Guard: Tie in 20-pound monofilament and form a loop.
Legs: Create the walking legs by palmering a neck hackle at the bend in the hook shank.
Feelers: Create feelers by adding a small clump of bucktail on top of the palmered neck hackle.
Eyes: Add the mono eyes so that they extend off the rear of the hook.
Antennae: Add the antennae by tying in two strands of Krystal Flash.
Swimming Legs: For the swimming legs of the fly, tie in frosted yarn at the rear of the hook.
Body/Tail: Take a clump of Slinky Fiber/Angel Hair blend to be used as the body of the fly. Tie in the clump at the rear of the hook. The clump should extend off the rear of the hook and off the eye of the hook. Palmer the frosted yarn forward to the hook eye and secure. Tie off the blended material body at the hook eye, in a manner that pulls the material extending off the hook below the hook eye. Trim to create the tail.
Head: Trim the rear portion of blend to create the point head.
Carapace: Apply Tuff Fleye glue to the top of the fly to create a hard carapace shell.
Trim: Trim the palmered yarn to create the short swimming legs of the shrimp. At the hook eye, tie in the loose end of mono to complete the looped weed guard.

Glades Minnow | Mike Conner

This fly was developed for snook and tarpon feeding selectively on gambusia minnows, also known as mosquito fish and found in the waters of Florida's backcountry.

Hook: Tiemco 811S or Mustad 34007, size 4 or 6.
Thread: Tan or brown, 3/0 or 6/0.
Body: Wrap a thread base from mid-point of hook shank to top of bend and back. Tie in a 6-inch length of Mylar braid, wrap to bend and back and tie off.
Wing: Tie in a sparse 1 1/2-inch layer of cream Fly Fur topped by slightly longer, fuller layer of tan Fly Fur. Top off with sparse layer of olive Fly Fur. Tie in 20 strands of minnow-green Lazerlights to each side of wing. Top off with 20 to 30 strands peacock herl-colored Lazerlights. Fine peacock herl can be used.
Head: Build a head from tan Fly Fur or Craft Fur and trim into a bullet shape, allowing hair at rear to blend into the wing.
Eyes: Affix 1/8-inch Mylar decal eyes.
Gills: Add a gill slash with red permanent marker.
Finish: Shade top of head with olive marker and tie in two-pronged weed guard of 15-pound Mason hard monofilament.

Glimmer Ghost | Captain Chris Newsome

This fly was designed for clear water, bright sunlight and selective fish. It is an effective fly whenever fish are keyed on high-profile bait like shad or pinfish. The pattern has been productive for a wide variety of Southeast and Northeast gamefish species.

Hook: Mustad C68 SSS or Gamakatsu SC 15, size 4 to 1/0.
Thread: UTC Monofilament .006.
Preparation: Make a blend of Slinky Fiber and Angel Hair. Select a small portion of material, blending so that some tapered hairs are shorter or longer than others. This allows for a fly that has little bulk and enhanced action.
Body/Wing: Tie in the tapered portion near the hook bend. Taper and tie in small portions of material on the top and bottom of the hook shank, working toward the eye of the hook. The majority of materials should be added to the top of the shank to allow for proper tracking. Adjust length of material for desired baitfish profile. Cut the thread at the eye of hook.
Eyes: Secure dome eyes with Fletch-Tite Platinum Glue.
Finish: If necessary trim the fly to shape.

Golden Shad | John Baker

This fly is a generic minnow imitation that is part of the Baker Baitfish series that can be used to replicate a variety of small to moderate size baitfish. It can be tied in a number of color combinations and sizes. This specific fly is tied to replicate golden shad. The pattern design has proven effective from Delaware to Florida for a wide variety of gamefish.

Hook: Short-shank big-game hook, size 1/0 or larger.
Thread: Color to match body.
Body/Wing: Tie in combinations of tan and black Craft Fur, Polar Flash and Polybear to form the body and wing. Blend in strands of Polar Flash. Add the prominent black bars at the tips of the tail with a permanent marker pen.
Belly: Tie in a length of yellow Polybear by Larva Lace.
Head/Eyes: Build a small head with a coating of Softex and affix plastic molded eyes.

Goony | Captain John Turcot

This fly and its variations work well for Mosquito Lagoon redfish. It was designed to present a small fly in natural colors to feeding reds.

Hook: Mustad 34007, sizes 4 to 6.
Thread: Waxed, 6/0.
Eyes: Lead eyes are tied in behind the hook eye for weight. Burnt monofilament stubs form the actual eyes at the bend of the hook.
Tail: Tie in four rooster neck tips splayed outward to form a 1-inch-long tail.
Body: Tie in four strands (clumps) of yarn Merkin style on the bottom of the hook shank, with sparkle dubbing tied in on top. The clumps build the body as you tie. Use figure-eight wraps of the thread. Natural grizzly saddle hackle wound around the hook shank forms the back of the body.

Goon Muddler | Captain John Turcot

This fly is an effective Muddler variation used for Mosquito Lagoon redfish.

Hook: Mustad 34007, size 4, 6.
Thread: Waxed, 6/0.
Wing: Tie in brown Craft Fur, banded with brown Prisma-Color pen. Add a few strands of copper Angle Hair and form a tail.
Head: Tie in brown deer body hair and spin around hook shank Muddler Minnow-style to form the head. Whip finish and tie off.

Grass Crab | Captain Gordon Churchill

This fly was inspired by the design of the Borski Chernobyl Crab. It was crafted to suggest life rather than imitate it. The fly is fished with the point up in weedy areas that are extremely shallow. Dumbbell eyes can be added for weight in deeper areas. Redfish eat this fly as will bonefish and other fish that feed on crabs or shrimp.

Hook: Standard saltwater hook
Thread: Clear, fine monofilament.
Tail: Tie in flash (copper, gold, pearl or silver).
Claws: Tie in three stiff grizzly hackles.
Body/Legs: Tie in a small amount of deer hair on point side of hook. Spin the deer hair and tie in rubber legs so they hang off either side of hook shank. Tie on and spin an additional clump of deer hair and stack it snug against the first bunch. Clip deer hair flat on top and bottom and close to the hook shank.
Wing: Tie in a sparse clump of squirrel tail as a wing.
Overwing: Tie in hackle feather over the primary wing.
Weedguard: Tie in double post sections of 40-pound monofilament as a weed guard.

Grassett's Flats Minnow | Captain Rick Grassett

This fly was developed for fishing shallow grass flats for reds, snook and trout. It is a hybrid half-shrimp and half-minnow pattern with a wide profile. The fly has some weight so you get a jigging type action similar to a Clouser. The smaller version of this fly is light enough to be used for tailing reds on a thick grass bottom. It can be tied in a variety of colors; olive is the favored color, but success has come with white, tan, rootbeer and pink. The thread and wing match the body.

Hook: Mustad 34007 hook, sizes 2 or 4, bent slightly 1/4 way down from the hook eye.
Thread: Chartreuse.
Eyes: Tie in medium gold bead-chain eyes on the #2 hook and small gold bead-chain eyes on the #4 hook. Tie in eyes at bend of hook shank on top of the shank (fly rides hook up like a Clouser, so bead-chain eyes are on the side of hook opposite the point).
Body: Wrap thread back to bend of the hook and tie on olive Ice Chenille or Estaz. Wrap forward to just in back of bead-chain eyes and tie off.
Wing: Tie in wing of white bucktail, followed by six or eight strands of gold Flashabou (doubled over), then olive bucktail and top with three or four strands of peacock hearl. Wing should be about 2 1/2 inches on the #2 hook and 1 1/2 inches or 2-inches on the #4 hook.
Weed Guard: Add weed guard of 20-pound-test Mason Hard Mono. Flatten ends before tying to head of fly. The finished weed guard is 2 strands of 20-pound Mason Hard Mono that extend just beyond the point of the hook. Start by tying a loop on (twist a 1/2 turn to get it to stand up) and then cut to the appropriate length.
Head: Finish fly by making the head of the fly and coating with Flexament.

Grassett's Grass Minnow | Captain Rick Grassett

This fly was developed primarily for snook fishing around lighted docks and bridge fenders at night, but it has also been used successfully for false albacore, Spanish mackerel, bluefish, trout and ladyfish. It is a half shrimp and half-glass minnow pattern that has some weight to get it down in a fast current.

Hook: Mustad 34007 hook, sizes 2, 4 and 6.
Thread: Chartreuse.
Eyes: Tie in medium or small bead-chain eyes, depending on hook size, on top of hook just behind the eye of the hook. Lead eyes should be tied on the bottom and are used in very fast currents or following cold snaps when fish may be deeper. This fly rides hook down and lead eyes tied on top will turn it on its side.
Tail: Wrap thread back to bend of the hook and tie on a sparse clump of synthetic polar bear or white EP Fibers. Tail should be about 1" long (total length of fly will be 2 inches). Put six or eight strands of Flashabou, either pearl or night glow, in tail.
Body: Tie on white or pearl Estaz or Ice Chenille at base of tail and wrap forward to just behind eyes and tie off.
Weed Guard: Tie in weed guard of 20-pound Hard Mason monofilament. Cut about 2" long, flatten ends and twist 1/2 turn before tying each end on sides of head. Cut to the proper length so it extends just past the point of the hook.
Head/Finish: Finish fly by making the head of the fly and coat with Flexament.

Graveline Shrimp

Tom Herrington | Historic Ocean Springs Saltwater Fly Fishing Club

This shrimp pattern was designed as a weedless seatrout fly. It is tied bendback style with the hook point facing upward. Red fluorescent beads enhance the shrimp look of the fly—a tungsten cone allows for a quick descent and an increased noise factor as it comes into contact with bottom matter. The cone suggests the telson or middle lobe of the tail.

Hook: Mustad 34007, size 2. Bend back first 1/2 inch of the hook shank at the eye.
Thread: Monofilament, clear.
Tail: Tie in a clump of pearl Polar Flash at the end of the hook shank.
Telson: Slide a medium tungsten cone onto the hook, covering a portion of the tail tie. The barb may have to be flattened.
Body: Tie in long pearl flash chenille at the base of the cone and wrap to a point about 1/4 inch from the hook eye. Wrap to ensure leggy or buggy look. Tie off and secure with a whip.
Wing: Tie in a length of pearl Polar Flash—three times the length of the hook shank—at the hook eye.
Stalk/Eyes: Cut two sections of 30-pound monofilament to a length three times the hook shank. Insert a red fluorescent bead onto one end of each stalk of monofilament, gluing in place with epoxy. Flatten the non-bead end of each stalk and tie in at the hook eye and alongside the Polar Flash.
Head: Whip finish and apply head cement.

Green and Gold | Leigh West

This pattern was first fished on a flat in Tampa Bay in the early spring. It caught several snook that were holding in sand holes surrounded by grass. It has since become a go-to fly for snook, trout and redfish. As a bend back, it's virtually weedless. It is very effective when tied Clouser-style as it can be used more effectively in deeper water, and it has won several fly-fishing tournaments.

Hook: Mustad 34007, #4-2/0. Bend to form bend back shape.
Thread: Brown Kevlar or flat waxed nylon.
Body: Where the hook starts to bend around towards the point, secure five long strands of gold Flashabou, followed by a 3-4 inches piece of vinyl rib (can substitute clear or brown 30-40-pound monofilament). Wrap the thread to the bent area just behind the hook eye. Wrap the Flashabou forward, covering the thread base wrap completely. Secure at the bend. Do the same for the vinyl rib, with the flat side of the material towards the hook. Secure the front of the body, and coat the body with head cement for durability.
Wing: Tie in bucktail (the brown hair near end of tail) or brown-dyed bucktail, gold Flashabou, peacock herl. Wing the fly with alternating layers of Flashabou and brown bucktail, and top that with a generous amount of peacock herl. The wing should be about one and a half times the length of the hook. Finally, place a lateral line of a few strands of gold Flashabou on the sides, between the bucktail and herl. Build up the head and coat with head cement.

Hairy Fodder | Craig Riendeau

This fly was originally designed as a snag-resistant crawdad pattern. It has since evolved into a very effective baitfish pattern and has accounted for a wide array of gamefish including striped bass, redfish, seatrout and flounder. By varying colors and sizes this fly is adaptable to many fishing situations.

Hook: Eagle Claw 413-60-degree jig hook, sizes 4 to 3/0.
Thread: Monofilament, .006 diameter.
Weight: Tie in dumbbell or bead-chain eyes to backside of the hook shank. You can also tie in a Riendeau's Ringer for interchangeable weighting.
Rattle: Tie an appropriate-size glass rattle to the backside of the hook shank. Secure well with thread wraps.
Tail: Cut and tie in a length of Sili-Legs for the tail and add strands of either Krystal Flash or Holographic Flashabou on both sides of the hook shank.

Body: Tie in a piece of crosscut rabbit strip on the top, back edge of the rattle with the skin side facing down. Make one wrap of the rabbit at the back of the rattle and tie off. After wings and body flash are tied in, two more palmered wraps of the rabbit will be made around the hook.
Wings: Tie in two sets of wing Sili-Legs along the sides of the hook, starting directly behind the dumbbell eyes. Pull legs toward the rear of fly, make one wrap of rabbit strip over the legs and tie in place.
Body Flash: Tie in a piece of UV Polar Chenille directly in front of the rabbit strip and make a wrap. Make wraps depending on the size of the fly.

Hamilton China Back Spoon Fly

Captain Randy Hamilton

Spoon flies are very effective throughout the Southeast and Gulf Coast region. Redfish and trout are especially partial to this small spoon-pattern design.

Hook: Any small stainless-steel hook, in sizes 6 and smaller.
Eyes: Very small bead-chains-eyes, tied in at the rear of the hook on the bend.
Tail: Tie in a small tuft of hair like squirrel or some other similar material.
Body: The entire body of the pattern is crafted from Mylar and epoxy. Tie on a shaped body foundation of Mylar, paint black and apply light coatings of epoxy. Rotate spoon until dry.
Weedguard: Tie in stiff monofilament at the hook eye.

Hamilton Copperhead | Captain Randy Hamilton

This all-flash fly is effective for a number of southwest Florida gamefish, especially redfish. The pattern can be tied in all-copper or in root beer.

Hook: Mustad 34007, size 1 or 2.
Thread: White or fine monofilament.
Eyes: Tie in small barbell eyes.
Tail: Tie in strands of copper or root beer flash material.
Body: Tie in copper or root bear Crystal Chenille and wrap forward to the hook eye, covering the barbell eyes.
Wing: Tie in strands of copper or root beer flash as a wing.
Head: Build a small head of thread, tie off and add head cement.

Hamilton Gold Spoon Fly | Captain Randy Hamilton

Spoon files are very effective throughout the Southeast and Gulf Coast region. Gold is a very productive color. This spoon design also incorporates rubber legs for added movement. Redfish and trout are especially partial to this small spoon-pattern design.

Hook: Any small stainless-steel hook, in sizes like 6 and smaller.
Eyes: Small bead-chain eyes, tied in at the rear of the hook on the bend.
Tail: Tie in six green/black-barred rubber legs at the base of the hook bend.
Body: The entire body of the pattern is crafted from Mylar and epoxy. Tie on a shaped body foundation of gold Mylar, and apply light coatings of epoxy. Rotate spoon until dry.
Weedguard: Tie in stiff monofilament at the hook eye.

Harvey's Half Eaten Bunker | Harvey Cooper

This pattern was designed to replicate small Atlantic menhaden that have been bitten in half by toothy gamefish. It works especially well in blitzes when remnants of the feeding frenzies float after the attacks.

Hook: Gamakatsu, Octopus sized to fly.
Thread: Flat-waxed nylon, white.
Entrails: Tie in shredded red Mylar flash over which is tied white Mylar flash. Whip finish and cut thread.
Body/Head: Create a template of the head. Tape template to 1/8-inch white foam and cut out pattern. Create a similar cutout pattern with pearl Sili-Skin. Fold the foam body in half. Color the middle third of foam with the olive marker. Color the backside of the foam with red. Coat the bottom of foam with epoxy. Position foam over the hook shank, making certain sure that both halves are aligned. Apply pressure until the epoxy sets. Apply a thin coat of epoxy to the top of the foam. Remove the backing from the Sili-Skin and overlay the foam body. As the epoxy begins to set the Sili-Skin will stay in place. Epoxy the silver flash lateral line.
Eyes: Affix 3-D mirage eyes and apply coat of epoxy.
Finish: Trim the Mylar flash with scissors.

Harvey's Little Lobster

Harvey Cooper | Inspired by the Rich Murphy Lobster

This pattern was designed to simulate a small lobster or crawfish.

Hook: Owner, #5317-158, sized to fly.
Thread: Danville flat-waxed nylon, tobacco.
Eyes: Tie in a 1/2-inch piece of foam cylinder on the outside of the hook. The foam should be positioned 1/4" above the bottom of the shank. Use figure-8 wraps to hold in place.
Antennae: Cut two three-inch lengths orange floating fly line and tie in positioned over the foam.
Rostrum: Tie in a small batch of olive bucktail on top of the antennae.
Weight: Tie in X-large dumbbells on top of the hook shank.
Claws: Cut a 3-inch piece of pearl E-Z Body small tubing. Color tubing with magic marker. Dab head cement on the pheasant body hackle stems before inserting the feathers into each end of the tubing. Whip finish each end. Palmer the orange and olive hackles the full length of the hook shank. Whip finish the thread and cut the thread. Trim the hackles above the hook shank as close as possible. Trim and hackles near the dumbbell to the same length. Trim the front hackles accordingly making certain the pattern rests in an upright manner.
Body/Carapace: Create templates of the body and tail. Cut two pieces of Sili-Skin twice the size of the templates and remove the backing. Color the right half of each piece with olive permanent marker. Fold left half over the right making sure there are no air pockets. Tape the templates to the colored Sili-Skin and cut to shape. Position the Sili-Skin tail on top of the hook eye. Once you know exactly where it should be placed make a slit in the material with an X-acto knife. Place a drop of crazy glue on top of the hackle, and insert the eye through the Sili-Skin. Lower the tail and press it against the hackle. Position the Sili-Skin body over the fly, and whip finish the thread creating the body segments.

Headless Horseman

Drew Chicone

This pattern was created for fishing late-spring snook and baby tarpon at the mouth of Florida's Caloosahatchee River and its tributaries. The fly is made entirely from Craft Fur. The flared head causes the fly to push water, animating movement. It is tied in tan or cream.

Hook: Owner Mosquito, sizes 2,1, 1/0.
Thread: Flat-waxed nylon.
Body: Start thread near the back of hook shank. Tie in and wrap four to eight turns of lead wire, .025-in diameter. Modify the number of lead wraps to match the water depth. Cover wire with a section of Craft Fur on top of hook and one on the bottom. Advance thread and tie in four sections of Craft Fur, one on the top, bottom and one on each side of the fly. The final application of Craft Fur is tied approximately 1/4-inch from clipped and, and flared at head. Pack flared tips back and build a small thread base to hold material in place. Color the thread and the uppermost front-facing fibers with a red permanent marker.

Hidalgo's Exterminator | Carlos Hidalgo

This fly design is a combination of two classic pattern. It is a Cockroach-style fly tied in the Black Death colors. It is good dirty or stained water tarpon fly. Tie it in the 1/0 version for small tarpon.

Hook: Gamakatsu SC-15 2H, size 1/0 to 3/0.
Thread: Black.
Tail: Tie in red Krystal Flash, flanked by four black neck hackles (curving out) on either side of the tail.
Body: Red Diamond Braid tied in and wound forward to form body.
Collar: Red dyed squirrel tail tied in around the hook at a point directly behind the head.
Head/Eyes: Build a head with thread and paint on white eyes with black pupils. Cover head with five-minute epoxy.

Hidalgo's Flashy Baby | Carlos Hidalgo

This imitation replicates a bay anchovy, glass minnow or other similar small baitfish. The fly is designed to stand out from the bait school.

Hook: Mustad 34007, size 4.
Thread: Olive.
Tail: Tie in a small clump of pearl Angel Hair.
Body: Tie in and wrap chartreuse Diamond Braid.
Wing: Tie in chartreuse Angel Hair, followed by a topping of dark green Angel Hair.
Head: Tie a length of Crystal Chenille or Cactus Chenille and wrap to form a head.
Eyes: Affix 3/8–inch yellow stick-on eyes, affixed with 5-minute epoxy.

Hidalgo's Ghost Shrimp | Carlos Hidalgo

This pattern was not designed to represent any specific type of shrimp but rather to convey the transparent and "ghostly" look of shrimp in the water. It has been used primarily as a skinny water bonefish fly in Biscayne Bay This fly can also be tied in a weighted version using small, gold bead chain eyes.

Hook: Mustad 34007, size 4.
Thread: Pale green.
Body: Tie in pearl Diamond Braid and wrap to form a body.
Wing: Tie in white calf tail, flanked by one thin ginger variant saddle hackle tip on each side. The hackle tips should be slightly longer than the calf tail.
Head: Using the thread build the head.

Hidalgo's Miami Whammy | Carlos Hidalgo

This is a very simple-to-tie and effective tan pattern for Biscayne Bay bonefish.

Hook: Mustad 34007, size 4.
Thread: Tan.
Body: Tie in one strand of tan Sparkle Yarn at the bend and wind toward the hook eye leaving enough room for the wing.
Wing: Tie in tan Craft Fur with gold Angel Hair on top, and two grizzly hackle tips on each side of the craft fur. The hackle should be approximately half the length of the fur.
Head: Build a head of thread, tie off and whip finish. Apply head cement.

Hidalgo's No Name Peacock Fly

Carlos Hidalgo

While this fly was originally designed for peacock bass in the freshwater lakes and canals of south Florida, it has also been a productive flats fly and has proven effective for baby tarpon, snook, sea trout, barracuda, jacks and ladyfish.

Hook: Mustad 34007, Size 2, 1/0, 3/0, and size 6 streamer hook.
Thread: Flourescent yellow.
Wing: The fly is tied as a hair wing. Tie in yellow bucktail, over which is tied orange Krystal Flash, topped off with green bucktail.
Throat: Tie in a sparse clump of red bucktail.
Head/Eyes: Using thread, build a head and paint on black with yellow eyes.
Finish: Cover eyes and head with 5-minute epoxy.

Hidalgo's Pink Eye Tarpon Fly

Carlos Hidalgo

This fly was developed in an attempt to create something new to show tough Florida Keys tarpon. It was designed to have good movement in the water, translucency, some flash and a prominent feature the fish could key in on—the big pink eyes.

Hook: Gamakatsu SC-15 2H, size 3/0.
Thread: Pale green.
Tail: Tie in a small bunch of badger fur, under fur and guard hairs included, followed by tan/UV Krystal Flash. Add additional badger fur tied on top of and on either side of the hook shank. The badger should completely surround the Krystal Flash.
Eyes: Attach 1/8th–inch pink plastic beads onto 50-pound monofilament eyestalks. The beads are glued onto the monofilament with five-minute epoxy then covered with a thin coat of epoxy.
Collar: Tie in raccoon fur, under fur and guard hair included, followed with a wide, webby tan/grizzly neck hackle.
Head: Build a moderate-sized head with thread. Whip finish and tie off.

Hidalgo's Red Med | Carlos Hidalgo

This fly was designed for redfish in Flamingo (Florida Bay) and incorporates many fish-attracting elements: favorite redfish colors of tan and brown, bright contrasting colors, flash, movement and a buggy look. Weighted eyes were added to get the fly to the bottom quickly and for a jigging effect when retrieved.

Hook: Mustad 34007, size 1/0.
Thread: Burnt orange.
Eyes: Tie in small, 5/32-ounce hourglass eyes or lead dumbbell eyes on the underside of the hook shank at a point slightly back of the hook eye.
Tail: Tie in two strands of chartreuse/silver-flake Sili Legs with ginger rabbit fur added on top.
Butt: Tie in and wind a short length of orange, short-fiber Crystal Chenille or similar material.
Underbody: Build with wraps of burnt orange thread.
Body: Cream Diamond Braid, wrapped and tied off behind the eyes.
Legs: Tie in two strands of chartreuse/silver-lake Sili Legs behind the eyes and on either side of body.
Wing: Tie in materials as follows: red squirrel tail, four strands of pearl Twisted Spectra Mylar Motion or Flashabou, approximately twelve strands of root beer Krystal Flash four strands of copper Krystal Flash) extending longer than the squirrel tail. Red fox fur (keeping the reddish brown under fur and guard hairs 1/2 the length of the squirrel tail).
Finish: Build head with thread, whip finish and tie off. Add head cement.

Hidalgo's Squirtin' Squid | Carlos Hidalgo

This fly was designed to reflect the color changes of squid and the way they expel ink. It is best fished with strips followed by pauses. When the retrieve is stopped in the water, the marabou flares, imitating the ejection of ink. The combination of chenille and braid convey the color-changing capabilities of squid.

Hook: Mustad 34001, size 1/0 to 3/0.
Thread: Tan or brown.
Articulated Tail/Ink: Tie in black marabou onto a piece of 16-pound Mason Hard monofilament. Saturate the thread wraps with head cement at least twice.
Mouth: Tie in tan/blue UV Krystal Flash, followed by a bump of several turns of tan Diamond Braid.
Tentacles: Tie in two ginger variant saddle hackles, surrounded by ten strands of amber/gold flake Sili-Legs. Hackles and legs should be tight so they flare out.
Body: Tie in one strand of cream/ginger variegated chenille, one strand of tan/olive variegated chenille and one strand of tan Diamond Braid. Braid strands together and wrap to form body.
Eyes: Affix 6 mm red/pink doll's eyes with 5-minute epoxy. Black/yellow or black/chartreuse colors can be substituted.

Hidalgo's Veil Threat | Carlos Hidalgo

This fly was tied to maximize reflective and transparent quality of materials.

Hook: Mustad 34007, size 1/0.
Thread: Blue.
Eyes: Tie in extra-small dumbbell eyes, painted white with black pupils.
Tail: Tie in pearl/UV Krystal Flash.
Body: Tie in tan Diamond Braid, wrap forward and around the eyes, and tie in at a point just in front of the eyes. Place a small amount of Ice Dub on the thread and dub in open spirals to the rear of the hook and back. Dub around the eyes.
Wing: Tie in tan/UV Krystal Flash. Whip Finish and cement.
Finish: Pick out the dubbing.

Hipps Soft-Body Diver | Anthony Hipps

This diver was originally developed as a freshwater bass pattern. It then evolved into saltwater fly for striped bass, bluefish, speckled trout, false albacore and redfish. The foam-bodied diver mimics the shape and action of the famous Dahlberg Diver, and has been fished effectively throughout North Carolina, Alabama and the Florida panhandle. The fly has proven much more durable than more traditional cork or balsawood popper bodies.

Hook: Mustad Signature CK74SSS or Mustad 34007, sizes 4 through 3/0.
Thread: Danville flat-waxed nylon, white.
Tail: Tie in synthetic or natural fibers, such as Arctic fox, and pearl and gold Angel Hair flash. Tie in two saddle hackles on each side of the hook shank. The tail should be at least 2 times longer than the body for best action.
Body: Stacked and tied layers of 2 mm thick closed-cell craft foam to form the bullet shaped diver head. Rectangular foam strips are stacked, glued and tied on the hook shank to form an underbody support structure sloping down toward the hook eye. A single layer of foam is folded over the underbody and trimmed to shape with scissors and tied down with light application of tying thread. After the paint dries, eyes (stick-on or painted) and markings are added with permanent markers. The diver body is dipped in water-based polyurethane gloss and placed on a slow rotary device to dry. Three applications of gloss are usually sufficient.
Collar: Cross-cut rabbit strip (orange on this fly) wrapped twice around the hook shank to form the collar.
Finish: Apply three-dimensional Scribbles fabric paint in color of choice purchased from a craft store. After the paint dries, eyes (stick-on or painted) and marking are added with permanent markers. The diver body is dipped in water-based polyurethane gloss and placed on a slow rotary device to dry. Three applications of gloss are usually sufficient.

Hipps' Soft-Bodied Popper | Anthony Hipps

This popper was originally developed as a freshwater bass pattern before evolving into a saltwater pattern for striped bass, bluefish, speckled trout, false albacore and redfish, and has been fished in North Carolina, Alabama and the Florida panhandle. This soft-bodied foam popper is very durable under most fishing situations.

Hook: Stainless-steel popper hook such as the Mustad Signature series CK74SSS, sizes 4 through 3/0. A straight-shanked hook such as the Mustad 34007 may also be used.
Thread: White Danville Flat Waxed Nylon or equivalent
Tail: Synthetic or natural fibers tied in. Typically, the tail is tied with white bucktail, and pearl Krystal Flash topped by pearl blue Angel Hair flash.
Popper Body: Stacked and tied layers of 2 mm-thick closed-cell craft foam, then painted with 3-dimensional Scribbles fabric paint. After the paint dries, eyes and marking are painted on with permanent markers. The popper body is dipped in water-based polyurethane gloss and placed on a slow rotary device to dry. Three applications of gloss are usually sufficient.

Homer Rhodes Tarpon Fly

Homer Rhodes | Tied by A.J. Forzano

This classic and versatile fly simply catches all varieties of fish. While originally designed for tarpon the fly is effective for snook in the mangroves, striped bass feeding on squid and all fish in between. The fly can be tied to match the size of bait and in any preferred color combinations.

Hook: Long-shank stainless-steel, size to match fly.
Thread: Red.
Tail: Two matched sets of inward-facing white hackles. Some variations splay the outside set of hackles. Several strands of flash are optional.
Body: Tie in one or more red hackles toward the rear of the hook and palmer forward, leaving about one-half the hook shank exposed. Wrap thread in tight winds forming a body extension along the hook shank. Tie off thread and coat body with cement.

Homosassa Deceiver | Oscar Feliu

This tarpon fly is a variation of Lefty's Deceiver.

Hook: O'Shaughnessy Style like Mustad S71SS, size 3/0 to 6/0.
Thread: Danville A plus, white.
Eyes: Affix molded 3-D, 3/8-inch, color of choice.
Tail: Tie in six white, wide feathers plus six strands of pearlescent Flashabou.
Wing: Tie in orange bucktail and orange flash on top.
Belly: Tie in white bucktail and Sea Fibers, plus strands of pearlescent Flashabou.
Head: Build a head with thread and epoxy head and eyes.

Interceptor

Craig Worthington/Tom Herrington
Historic Ocean Springs Saltwater Fly Fishing Club

Originally tied for small snappers that feed on crustaceans, this attractor shrimp pattern has also enticed small kings and trevally. The fly is tied in a manner that generates a lot of movement at slow retrieve speeds and is highly visible, making it quite productive throughout the region for a variety of gamefish.

Hook: 2/0 tarpon or equivalent.
Thread: Mono, fine/clear.
Tail: Tie in a small bunch of white marabou at the hook bend and around the entire hook shank.
Body/Wing: Move up the hook shank about 1/4 inch and tie in a clump of clear Supreme Hair around the hook. Move up an additional 1/4 inch and tie in pearl Krystal Flash around the hook. Move forward another equal distance on the shaft and tie in yellow Krystal Flash.
Eyes: Tie in tungsten barbell eyes, size medium/black approximately 1/4 inch from the hook eye. Whip finish.

Iron Man | Captain Marcia Foosaner

This pattern is a variation of a jig-head fly that is very effective for pompano. It has also taken other species in larger sizes. The smaller sizes are very easy to cast on light fly rods. The fly can also be tied with bunny strips or marabou, mixed with flash material.

Hook: Mustad 34007, size 1 or 2.
Thread: Any suitable thread.
Weight/Head: Slip a small jiggy-style head over the hook point and position it toward the hook eye. Put a small spot of Super Glue behind the eye of the hook and make a bulky wrap of thread that the head will sip over tightly. Add some glue inside the head to secure.
Body/Wing: Secure gold, wired eyelash ribbon at the bend of the hook and wrap thread forward. Begin to palmer the ribbon forward laying the lashes back as you wrap. Make an extra wrap up against the head. This will secure head against front of hook. Whip Finish.
Eyes: Apply stick-on eyes and coat eyes and head with epoxy.

JD's Flounder Fly

Jeff DuBinok | Tied by Lawrence Clemens

This fly was designed for summer flounder or fluke and attempts to replicate the attributes of a traditional fluke rig. The rabbit strip is a replacement for the squid or fish belly typically used by bait-fishermen. In addition to being an effective flounder fly this pattern has also worked well for large croakers, striped bass and bluefish.

Hook: Mustad 340011 or equivalent, size 2.
Thread: Flat-waxed nylon, orange or red.
Keel: Tie in lead fuse wire, size .30, as a keep on the underside of the hook shank. Use three or four lengths of wire to allow the hook point to ride up.
Tail: Tie in a four-inch length of white rabbit strip.
Collar: Tie in chartreuse Estaz. The collar will allow the bucktail wind to flare.
Wing: Tie in several bunches of chartreuse bucktail, encircling the entire hook shank.
Head: Form a head with thread, whip finish and apply head cement.

Jerkbait Fly | Captain Gus Brugger

This pattern was designed to mimic the features of jerkbait lures. It has caught almost every gamefish species that inhabits Florida's Indian River Lagoon as well as largemouth bass. It is especially productive when used over the shallow grass flats for seatrout and redfish. The use of rabbit strip gives this fly its strike-triggering action. It can be tied in a variety of colors and combinations.

Hook: Mustad 34007 hook, size, 2 to 2/0; 1/0 is best for 5-inch imitation.
Thread: Clear monofilament.
Weedguard: Tie in 4-inch piece of fluorocarbon 1/4" behind eye on top of shank and wrap with thread down top of hook to the halfway point of bend. Coat wraps with super glue.
Tail: Cut 1-inch piece of flex tube. Cut 5-inch piece of rabbit strip, trim fur off bottom 3/4-inch of rabbit strip. Slide bottom of rabbit strip through flex tube, leaving most of the trimmed strip extending out other side of tubing. Place strip/tubing on top of shank and tie in trimmed end of strip 1/4" behind eye of hook. Wrap thread toward bend and catch the beginning of the tube at the mid-point of shank and continue wrapping over the tubing with the rabbit strip inside until you reach the rear of the shank.
Body: Tie in Tinsel Chenille, Estaz, Cactus Chenille or similar body material at bend of hook. Apply super glue to thread wraps on hook shank and a light film on extended tubing. Wrap body material rearward over extended tubing then forward to eye of the hook. Tie off body material 1/4-inch behind eye. Bring weed guard forward and tie off behind eye, forming a loop type weed guard. Whip finish and super glue.
Eyes: Attach 3-D or doll eyes with your favorite adhesive directly onto the forward area of the body material.

Jim's Giant Killer | Captain Jim Hale

This fly was designed for large tarpon in areas of clear ocean-side flats. It also works well in the Florida Bay backcountry. The fly works well when stripped fast and allowed to sink slowly in front of moving fish.

Hook: Short-shank saltwater, 3/0.
Thread: Chartreuse and red flat-waxed nylon.
Weed Guard: Optional, tied in at rear of hook with 20-pound fluorocarbon.
Tail: Using chartreuse thread, tie in a three-inch section of chartreuse rabbit strip and attach it 2/3 of the way back on the hook. Tie in several strands of three-inch silver Krystal Flash in front of the rabbit strip. Cut thread and trim flash.
Body: Using red thread, tie in burnt orange marabou. Encircle the hook shaft with marabou as if tying a collar.
Head: Build an elongated head with thread, tie off and apply head cement.

Jim's Jumbo | Captain Jim Blackburn

This fly is designed as an articulated shrimp pattern. It is very effect for fish feeding on shrimp or crawdads, and has been productive for bonefish, tarpon, permit, snook, snapper, redfish and sea trout. Fly can be tied in tan, white, pink, chartreuse, brown, rust, olive and amber.

Hook: Any short saltwater hook, size 2/0, 6.
Thread: Thread of choice. Heavy thread for articulated tail.
Articulated Tail: Using a small size-6 hook tie on a tuft of marabou and Krystal Flash on top of the hook. Tie in V-Rib and wrap along shaft with flat side down. Wrap to hook eye and tie off. Cut thread and cut off hook at the bend using wire cutters.
Weight: Put hook in vise. Slide on brass bead and add additional weight with wire if desired.
Eyes: Tie in Larva Lace eyes in from of the bead. Burn the ends.
Weed Guard: Tie in a looped shaped section of monofilament to serve as a weed guard.
Body/Tail: Run a short piece of 15-pound spider wire, through the hook eye. Tie articulated tail tail to the hook at the bend. Cover the connection with a small amount of marabou and Krystal Flash. Tie in v-rib on the front hook and wrap to cover half the hook shank. Tie in mixed natural and colored bucktail to form the shellback and antennae. Tie in Estaz or Cactus Chenille and wrap to brass bead. Pull bucktail over Estaz and tie off. Finish with head cement.

J's Furry Friend | Captain Jim Hale

This fly is a variation of the famous Muddler Minnow. It has proven effective for snook, redfish, tarpon, sea trout and cobia. It can be tied in any number of color combinations.

Hook: Owner Mosquito, size 1/0 or 2/0.
Thread: Danville flat-waxed, chartreuse.
Tail: Wrap thread to eye and apply a drop of super glue. Tie in a length of marabou at the bend, approximately 1-1/2 to 2 inches in length. Apply several wraps under tail to minimize fouling. Apply barred marking to marabou with permanent marker.
Collar: Tie in a two-inch section of Zonker rabbit strip. Wrap strip forward around the shank, forming a thick but full body with the hair flowing toward the back. Add a few more thread wraps to secure and apply a drop of super glue. Leave adequate space for the head.
Head: Build a head by spinning deer hair and compacting tightly.
Weed Guard: Tie in 20-pound fluorocarbon forming a two-pronged weed guard. Apply a dab of glue.

Jumping Jack Flash | Captain Paul Dixon

This easy-to-tie fly is great for jacks and barracuda. The smaller version, a Flashy Pin Fish, is tied with barred tan marabou and is very effective for snook, tarpon and sea trout.

Hook: Gamakatsu SL 12 S, 2/0.
Thread: Clear heavy monofilament.
Tail: Tie in olive marabou at the hook bend blending in a few strands of Krystal Flash.
Body: Tie in medium, olive Palmer Chenille at the hook bend and wrap forward to a point behind the hook eye. For the smaller version the body can be built from strands of pearl Krystal Flash.
Eyes: Optional stick-on, prismatic eyes can be added.

Kanekalon Wig Greenie | Valerio A. Grendanin

This baitfish pattern is effective at imitating larger baits like the Atlantic thread herring or the poggie. The design takes advantage of the non-water-absorbent characteristics of Kanekalon Wig Hair. It generates enticing action while maintaining its shape. It can be fished with either a dead drift as an injured baitfish or stripped at varying speeds.

Hook: Owner Gorilla Light, 5107-141, 4/0 or 5/0.
Thread: Fine clear monofilament.
Body: Cut six- to eight-inch lengths of Kanekalon Wig Hair (white, yellow, light green, dark green or brown-olive) and blend with fine pearl shredded Mylar. Wrap a layer of thread around hook shank from eye to 1/8-inch of bend. Add a small amount of blended white wig hair at the bend and on top of the hook; tie down in the middle of the bunch. Fold forward facing end of bunch back and wrap thread in front of bunch, forcing hair back. Pulling both ends of the hair up, wrap about 5 turns of thread around the bunch over the hook shank. This is done only for the first bunch to help the hair stick straight up and not foul. Continue adding small bunches of hair, tying in the middle and folding back. Change and intermix different colors until you reach the eye.
Gills: At a point about 1/8-inch from the eye, add a small bunch of red wig hair to each side as gills.
Eyes: Affix 3-D Mirage Eyes, one to each side.
Finish: Epoxy head to a point just past the eyes.

Kanekalon Wig Herring | Valerio A. Grendanin

This fly is an excellent example of a baitfish pattern modification that is effective as a large bait imitation. Originally designed for striped bass in the Northeast, this fly has also proven effective for various gamefish throughout the range of the Southeast and Gulf Coast. The design takes advantage of the non-water-absorbent characteristics of Kanekalon Wig hair. It generates enticing action while maintaining its shape. It can be fished with either a dead drift as an injured baitfish or stripped at varying speeds.

Hook: Owner Gorilla Light, 5107-141, 4/0 or 5/0.
Thread: Fine clear monofilament.
Body: Cut 6- to 8-inch lengths of Kanekalon Wig Hair (blended white, pink, light blue and dark blue) and blend with fine pearl shredded Mylar. Wrap a layer of thread around hook shank from eye to 1/8-inch of bend. Add a small amount of blended white wig hair at the bend and on top of the hook; tie down in the middle of the bunch. Fold forward facing end of bunch back and wrap thread in front of bunch, forcing hair back. Pulling both ends of the hair up, wrap about five turns of thread around the bunch over the hook shank. This is done only for the first bunch to help keep hair sticking straight up and not fouling. Continue adding small bunches of hair, tying in the middle and folding back. Change and intermix different colors until you reach the eye.
Gills: At a point about 1/8-inch from the eye, add a small bunch of red wig hair to each side as gills.
Eyes: Affix stick-on eyes, one to each side.
Finish: Epoxy head to a point just past the eyes.

Kevin's Torpedo Fly | Kevin Cormier

When it comes to inshore flats, Heddon's Tiny Torpedo is tops among topwater lures. In keeping with the philosophy of matching the lure, Cormier modified Pete Cooper's popular perch-float popper by adding a propeller. It makes lots of noise when stripped in the water, and also when false casting. Cormier, an Army veteran who served in Iraq, compares the casting sound to that of an Apache helicopter.

Hook: Mustad 34007, size 1.
Body/Propeller: Cut the Styrofoam float in half, then cut a slit in the half lengthwise. Use the edge of sandpaper to widen the slit so it can pass onto a threaded hook. Slide the hook just barely inside the float and super glue in place. Use an airbrush or foam dipped in paint for the top of the body, and dowels of different sizes dipped in black or other color to make the eyes. Coat the body with transparent thirty-minute epoxy. When set, slide the prop past the hook point and to the body. Lean the fly in the vise downward so the prop stays close to the body and tie a thread ball. Then epoxy the thread ball; this will keep the prop in place.

Key Lime Fly | Drew Chicone

This baitfish pattern was originally designed for summer snook in the waters of southwest Florida. It has since appealed to a variety of gamefish.

Hook: Mustad 34007, sizes 2, 1, 1/0.
Thread: Chartreuse, 3/0.
Gills: Start the thread near the back of hook shank. Tie in a small amount of of red Wing-N-Flash.
Tail: Tie in a small section of lime green Wing-N-Flash, approximately 2 1/2 inches. Splay and tie in one chartreuse and one fluorescent grizzly neck hackle on each side of the hook.
Body: Tie in a section of chartreuse Neer Hair on top of the hackles, and a tan section underneath.
Cheeks: Tie in a sparse section of tan Neer Hair for cheeks.
Collar: Tie in and palmer one fluorescent chartreuse grizzly neck.
Head/Eyes: Wrap thread up the hook shank and then back to the collar. Continue wrapping forward creating a tapered head. Whip finish. Affix chartreuse doll eyes and epoxy all thread wraps.

Key's Floating Tarpon Toad | Dennis Ficco

Gary Merriman's original Tarpon Toad inspired this fly. It is a variation that allows the fly to remain up in the water column and float in front of laid-up fish, minimizing the potential for spooking.

Hook: Owner SSW or Gamakatsu Octopus 02412, size 2/0.
Thread: Flat waxed nylon.
Loop: Build a foundation of thread on hook shank, ending at the bend of hook. Attach a loop of 20-pound-test Mason hard monofilament as an anti-fouling device.
Tail: Tie in a three-inch piece of rabbit Zonker at the bend of the hook at a point above the monofilament.
Collar: Tear the barbs off both sides of a marabou quill stem. Tie the marabou barbs around the hook shank creating a collar in front of the Zonker strip.
Body: Cut five foam cylinders in one-inch strips. Attach the foam, Merkin-style, using crisscross thread wraps. Cover the entire hook shank. Trim the foam cylinders to shape, making the foam near the hook shorter than the foam near the hook bend.
Weed Guard: Attach 50-pound-test clear monofilament and apply head cement.

King Lepus | Tom Herrington

Historic Ocean Springs Saltwater Fly Fishing Club

This attractor pattern was adapted from the success of the Sunrise Double Lepus for cobia and tarpon. It is also known as the Big Eye Double Lepus and was designed as a larger fly for pelagic species such as kings, wahoo, sailfish and bull dolphin. A prominent feature of the fly is its oversized eyes.

Hook: Mustad 34011, size 3/0.
Thread: Danville flat waxed nylon, apple green.
Eyes (Step 1): Tie in tungsten flat-end barbell eyes one inch back from the hook eye.
Body: Wrap hook shaft down and back, alternating between closed and open wraps. Cut magnum-sized rabbit strips three times the length of the hook shank. Tie in the white strips first to form the belly region of the fly. Punch holes in the front and middle portions of the strips through which the hook can be threaded. This will allow for a snug and secure fit. Tie and whip finish. Tie in the dorsal chartreuse rabbit strip and whip finish. Apply a thin line of Fabric-Tac to the hairless sides of both strips. Align and press together firmly. Allow to dry.
Eyes (Step2): Using epoxy cement, apply large molded eyes to the eyestalks of the tungsten barbell eyes.
Flash: Tie in a 2-inch portion of chartreuse Krystal Flash over the chartreuse rabbit strip, and a 2-inch portion of red Krystal Flash over the white strip.
Head: Form a head with thread and whip finish.

Kinky Fiber Bend Back

Captain Gus Brugger | Originated by: Paul Van Reenen

This fly is patterned after a design by Paul Van Reenen. His best-known contribution to the fly-fishing world is the Polar Fibre Minnow. On frequent trips in the Indian River Lagoon this fly was his preferred pattern. It has since developed into a go-to baitfish imitation. The pattern has been used successfully on all inshore species, plus largemouth and peacock bass.

Hook: Mustad 34007 hook, size 4 - 5/0, 1/0 best for the flats, 3/0 for inlet and ocean.
Thread: Monofilament.
Body/Wing: With hook point facing up, tie in a dozen strands of Kinky Fibre or Slinky Fiber with or without flash already blended in. You can use one solid color or stack colors light to darker to more closely imitate a specific baitfish. It will take two bundles of fibers to form body and wing. To get the best results just catch the ends of the wing material with the thread and use as few wraps as possible. These wraps will eventually be super glued, so the thread is more or less holding the material in place.
Gills: Tie in a sparse amount of Fluorofibre or similar material for bleeding gill effect.
Eyes: Apply a drop of Goop to the back of 3-D eyes and apply directly to wing material just below and in front of the hook point, one eye on either side. Repeat on opposite side.

Chasing Red Tails

If there is one aspect of fly-fishing that I absolutely love it is casting to tailing redfish. My indoctrination to that form of angling took place in Pine Island Sound on the west coast of Florida. The experience all began as a flats skiff came to an abrupt halt 100 yards from an expansive sand flat. The skiff inched slowly toward thin water where my guide and I hoped redfish would be feeding. The sun was high providing the best visual opportunity to spot fish. Within minutes Ozzie pointed directly ahead of our path. I took a line of sight along the push-pole and spied the first glimmering tail of a mudding red. The puffs of sand were a dead giveaway to the fish's feeding behavior. I readied myself on the bow, stripping line from the reel and holding the brown-and-purple fly at the ready for a quick cast. We were soon within casting range and I dropped the small imitation crustacean immediately to the right of the fish's head, while it was preoccupied rooting in the sand for the next meal. The fish's snout went about business but it neither took the fly nor spooked. The redfish just moved away slowly. Despite seeing many other active tails on the flat we chose to pursue that specific fish, and I did get to make several more frustrating and fruitless presentations. After the last of those casts failed to elicit a strike I decided to leave the boat and wade. I always feel better when I am in the water rather than on it. I followed that redfish for about thirty minutes until it took a position that allowed me to make a number of close casts, trying all the while to be as stealthy as a heron. After many refusals, and for some reason known only to the fish, it finally decided to eat. One short strip prompted the solid take. Ozzie let out with a *whoop* as the red took off toward the deep edge of the flat. I held on and after an enjoyable tussle I slid my hand under the belly of a gratifying 30-inch Pine Island Sound redfish—the first of a few that we caught that morning and the first of long-term love affair with red drum throughout the Southeast and Gulf Coast.

I first fished that region of southwest Florida in the early 1990's and have been back many times since. The family-friendly resorts and pristine beaches of Sanibel and Captiva islands were the only places I found in the Sunshine State that could lure my wife and two young daughters away from the annual visits to Mickey's House. I had my fill of make-believe and wanted a nice Gulf of Mexico venue with a view and access to great fly-fishing. So I fibbed just a bit and told my daughters they might get to see some talking dolphins or perhaps even the real Ariel. It worked. Actually, they loved the Islands. Sanibel and Captiva are both splendid barrier islands that offer some of the best shelling in the world, with 250 types of shells available for the picking. The islands also form a natural aviary with 230 varieties of birds residing in a region that is home to such elusive creatures as the Florida panther. But what appealed to me most were the fifty species of fish that swim in these waters. That wealth of marine life opened up an entirely new world of fly-fishing. Once again, I was hooked harder than the fish.

High on that list of available species are the popular sport fish that attract avid anglers from points all across the country and the globe. The predominant species in season are: redfish, snook, sea trout, tarpon, jacks, ladyfish, grouper, cobia, tripletail, Spanish mackerel, pompano, permit, king mackerel, black drum and sheepshead. Over time I got to sample that entire offering. This region of Florida is indicative of many areas spread throughout the Southeast and Gulf Coast: great fishing and equally great places to visit. The beaches are Gulf-facing, providing direct access to endless miles of wade-able surf giving fly and light-tackle surf anglers access to an abundance of gamefish. The region's offshore opportunities are even more plentiful as are productive backwater areas and flats. For someone who enjoys prospecting with a long rod, these waters are a veritable paradise. I have been back to this region of Florida and the Gulf Coast many times since my first visit, usually with the intention of chasing redfish, sea trout, snook and the occasional tarpon. I am rarely disappointed.

Aside from the great beach snook fishing, this region of the country has given me some of my most memorable surf jaunts involving other tough critters like jack crevale. Big jacks are like performance-enhanced bluefish and can test the limits of light fly gear.

While roaming a stretch of a southern beach one morning immediately after dawn I happened upon a pod of daisy-chaining fish that had corralled small baitfish. The prey erupted from the water in a futile attempt to escape capture. I fished an eight-weight rigged with a small Clouser-style fly. One cast was all it took. As soon as the fly hit dead center of the circling fish the fly line went taut and I hung on for a joy ride that almost totally emptied the spool of Dacron backing. As the fight advanced I applied more pressure and turned the fish toward the beach. Eventually, it conceded and I landed a muscular twelve-pound jack. The fish in that pod ranged in size from twelve to fifteen pounds and they were supercharged. And best of all, the jacks were back in force at the same game the following morning, still willing to eat flies.

When I am not chasing red tails during my visits to the Southeast and Gulf Coast there is nothing I enjoy more than casting flies into the mangrove tangles in search of big snook. It is one of the most exciting ways to fish and demands a modicum of precision. The drill I enjoy most is to cast weedless flies right into the thick of things. During one of my last trips south I did just that in the mangroves of Matlacha. I was fishing with a local captain and fly tier. On the first day out with we motored to a mangrove island where the good captain set up about sixty or seventy feet from the trees. The first thing he said to me was, "Make a cast." Yet another one of those guide tests to see how close I could get to the mangroves so he would know how far out or close he needed to pole the boat. Not only did the fly hit the mark from seventy feet (some luck and some practice) but we immediately saw a large snook move toward the modified Deceiver and follow it out from the mangroves. The fish veered off but we now knew snook were in the zone. For four hours we poled in, out and around numerous mangrove islands, spotting many snook and the occasional redfish. We managed to fool a few into striking flies, including a couple of sizeable fish, but the real value of the day was that we were alone for most of the morning. At times it felt as if we were fishing in a wilderness zone. After one or two turns into the mangrove islands it was like being in another world. But the true highlight of the experience was the opportunity to talk about flies...all kinds of saltwater flies that have emerged over the decades from the creative minds of the Southeast and Gulf region's best fly-anglers and tiers. Red tails, snook and good conversation about the art of fly tying.

What more could I have asked for? Just one more cast. Just one more fish.

Krafty Seaducer | Captain Jim Blackburn

This easy-to-tie and versatile fly has been effective for most saltwater or freshwater gamefish feeding on small to mid-sized baitfish. It can be tied in a variety of color combinations.

Hook: Any short- or medium-shank saltwater hook, size 2/0 to 4.
Thread: Thread of choice.
Tail: Tie in a thread base on hook shank. Tie in Kraft Fur or other preferred synthetic material at the hook bend, 2 1/2 times the length of the hook shank.
Topping: Tie in strands of Krystal Flash.
Weed Guard: Tie in monofilament weed guard.
Body: Tie in Zonker rabbit strip and wrap toward the hook eye, leaving enough room to tie in an Estaz or Cactus Chenille Collar.
Finish: Build a head with thread and apply head cement.

Krystal Killer | Captain Paul Dixon

This fly design is representative of a generic crustacean pattern and is effective for all gamefish species that prey on shrimp.

Hook: Mustad 34007, size 2, 4 or 1.
Thread: Clear Monofilament.
Weight: Tie in black, gold or brass dumbbell eyes at a point immediately behind the hook eye and wind thread to the bend of the hook.
Nose/Feelers: Tie in pink marabou and either yak hair or synthetic polar bear hair. Tie in a few strands of Krystal Flash.
Eyes: Tie in large monofilament black eyes.
Legs: Tie in a pair of tan and gold flake Sili-Legs.
Body: Tie in large Krystal Hackle in bonefish tan color and palmer forward to the dumbbell eye. Whip finish.

Laid Up Tarpon Fly | Rick Ruoff

Tarpon feed heavily on crabs and shrimp near the surface. When these fish *lay-up* or float near the surface, presentations need to be accurate and delicate. Tarpon may be huge fish but even a small fly can be threatening form a poor presentation. This fly lands softly and hangs in the surface area where it can coax a strike from cautious fish. Give tarpon plenty of time to look at your offering.

Hook: Owner, 5280-121, size 2/0.
Thread: Black.
Tail: Tie in a clump of tan marabou and six strands of copper Krystal Flash and tie in three bleached grizzly hackles on each side of the tail.
Hackle: Tie in two large grizzly hackles and palmer forward leaving room for the leech yarn.
Body/Eyes: Tie in tan leech yarn and extra-large monofilament eyes. Wrap the leech yarn forward, figure-eight the eyes, secure thread and finish off.

Lefty's Bug | Bernard "Lefty" Kreh

This bug fly was developed many years ago. Lefty Kreh considers it one of the best all-around bug flies he has ever used. The bug offers very little air resistance and almost never fails in flight. It is tied in white and yellow.

Hook: Long-shank popper hook.
Thread: Any suitable thread.
Head: Cut a slight slit on the underside of the popper head. Mount head onto the shaft of the hook. The hook eye should be positioned flush with the base of the body. This will allow the body to sit above water. It will also allow for ease of pick-up on the back cast.
Tail: Tie in bucktail and a sparse amount of Krystal Flash. It is important to use materials that won't foul around the hook.
Collar: Tie in a small collar that butts up against the rear of the popper head.

Lefty's Deceiver | Bernard "Lefty" Kreh

Any book about fly patterns has to include the legendary Deceiver. This design is an effective pattern imitation for a wide variety of baitfish. It can be tied in numerous color combinations and either as a sparse or full fly. Furthermore, it can be tied large or small, weighted or un-weighted and short or long. It was first developed in the early 1960's for striped bass in the Chesapeake Bay and fast became one of the most popular pattern designs of all time. Due to its adaptability the pattern has evolved into a style of tying more so than simply just a fly pattern. It is one of the most imitated flies with multiple dozens of variations in use today worldwide.

Hook: Mustad 34007 or equivalent, sizes 4 to 3/0.
Thread: White, 3/0 or 6/0.
Tail: Six to twelve white saddle hackle feathers, with an equal number of pairs tied to each side of the hook shank.
Body: Either bare or wound silver Mylar Tinsel.
Collar: White bucktail tied in surrounding the hook shank, and extending beyond the bend of the hook.
Head: White thread.
Eyes: Black/Yellow.

Lenny's Almost Real Crab | Captain Lenny Moffo

This fly is a variation of Lenny's Real Crab but a little easier to tie. Both flies work well but this offers an additional tool in the box. When fishing for permit cast the fly very close to the fish—one to three feet. When permit are on the flats they are looking for food within close range.

Hook: Gamakatsu SC 15, size 2, 1, 1/0.
Thread: 3/0.
Tail: Tie in strands of Holographic Flashabou. Tie in splayed hackle feathers.
Eyes: Tie in the dumbbell eyes behind the eye of the hook.
Shell: Cut tan Velcro shell to size and hot glue it on the hook shank.
Legs: Hot glue flat rubber legs in place. Color for desired effect
Underbody: Apply 5-minute epoxy to bottom of crab and rotate until dry. Paint white.

Lenny's Bendback | Captain Lenny Moffo

This fly is a variation of the time-tested bend-back style. These flies are used because they are naturally weedless and they keel better when unweighted. The fly can be tied in any color or size. It is effective for most any gamefish.

Hook: Mustad 34007, size of choice. Place in vise and bend.
Thread: Monofilament, 3/0, flat waxed to finish head.
Body Ribbing: Tie in a swatch of Mylar followed by plastic body ribbing material.
Eyes: Tie on barbell type eyes.
Wing: Tie in bucktail wing, color of choice.
Topping: Tie in strands of peacock herl.
Head: Using flat waxed thread, build a head. Apply a light coating of epoxy.

Lenny's Big Boy | Captain Lenny Moffo

This fly resulted from a need for a large fly that was light enough to cast at sailfish. The design produced a pattern that could be cast just as far as a standard tarpon fly on a 12-weight outfit.

Hook: Sized to fly.
Head: 3/4-inch popper head, painted to color preference. Drill 1/8-inch hole through popper head and put on tube with super glue. Perform this step after materials are applied to tube.
Body/Tail: This fly is built in tube-fly fashion using a tube and tube-fly tool. Tie in white bucktail followed by silver Mylar. Next tie in white saddle hackle feathers followed by pink saddle hackle feathers. Then tie in additional white bucktail, followed again by silver Mylar. Lastly, add an additional set of pink saddle hackle feathers.

Lenny's Real Crab | Captain Lenny Moffo

Permit anglers are always searching for a better fly. This pattern was designed to replicate live blue claw-type crabs that are used by livebait fishermen in the Keys. It is tied in different sizes and weights to cover all fishing conditions. Always test sinking flies in water to make sure they descend correctly.

Hook: Gamakatsu SC 15, size 1 or 1/0.
Thread: Monofilament, 3/0.
Tail: Tie in strands of holographic Flashabou.
Weight: Flatten lead eyes and tie in at the middle of the hook shank and on the bottom so the hook rides up.
Shell: Cut Velcro in the shape of a crab shell and hot glue it to the hook shank between the hook point and eye. Color Velcro either olive or tan.
Legs: Prepare all the rubber legs and hot glue in place. Use an overhand knot to create the joint in the legs.
Underbody: Apply epoxy to the bottom of crab and rotate fly until dry. Paint bottom white and color legs as desired.

Lenny's Slammaroo Shrimp | Captain Lenny Moffo

This pattern was designed for bonefish, permit and small tarpon. It also works well for sea trout, pompano and other gamefish.

Hook: Mustad 34007, size 2.
Thread: Tan.
Tail Section: Tie in two tan mallard flank barbules. Add in two Sili-Legs. Tie in tan Polybear or similar synthetic material followed by two tan, small hackles. Tie on dumbbell eyes. Tie in two long hackles and palmer back to eyes.
Body: Tie in the vinyl rib, color of choice, then tie in Krystal Flash and wrap back to the eye. Follow by wrapping the vinyl rod over the Krystal Flash back to the eye of the hook.

Lenny's Tarpon Shrimp | Captain Lenny Moffo

This shrimp fly was designed for fussy laid-up tarpon. Work the fly nice and easy.

Hook: Gamakatsu SC 15, size 3/0.
Thread: Color to match.
Tail Section: Tie in tan Polybear and four to six strands of red or orange Krystal Flash. Tie in some additional Polybear. Using a brown marker add stripes to the Polybear. Tie in two tan grizzly feathers followed by two tan mallard flank barbules.
Eyes: Bend eyes outward and tie in place. Use glass beads on monofilament, coated with epoxy.
Collar: Tie in two or three large, tan feathers and palmer forward for collar. Wrap securely in place.
Body: Tie in tan Ultra Chenille, wrap forward and finish off.

Len's White Bait | Captain Lenny Moffo

This simple yet effective fly was designed for offshore fishing on reefs or wrecks when chumming with pilchards, threadfin herring, pinfish or other similar baitfish. The pattern does well on blackfin tuna, amberjack, cobia, dolphin, kingfish and other species.

Hook: Gamakatsu SC 15, 3/0.
Thread: White 3/0 mono, black flat waxed.
Tail/Wing: Tie in some silver Mylar flash and then a pinch of white bucktail, followed by an additional sparse clump of white bucktail. Next tie in olive bucktail, followed by a topping of peacock herl.
Throat: Tie in a red rabbit throat.
Head: Change thread and finish with black, flat waxed thread.
Eyes: Glue on mirror-type eyes, apply 5-minute epoxy and rotate until dry.

Lenny's Work Fly | Captain Lenny Moffo

This topwater design was patterned after the productive Top Water Tiger. It is a much simpler version of that fly with basic characteristics and no eye. It is considered a dependable work fly.

Hook: Gamakatsu SC 15, size 3/0.
Thread: Any suitable thread.
Tail: Tie in white bucktail, followed by silver holographic Mylar. Tie in seven or eight strands of peacock herl as a topping.
Head: All white 5/8-inch popper head. Drill hole and glue onto hook shank and apply markings with a black permanent marker.

Lepus Bug

Tom Herrington
Historic Ocean Springs Saltwater Fly Fishing Club

This fly was designed to blend the best motion attributes of rabbit strips and legs. It is a generic crustacean pattern and uses minimum flash for skittish bonefish and permit. The pattern has also proved effective for pompano, flounder, redfish, snook and sea trout.

Hook: Mustad 34007 or similar hook, size 2.
Thread: Danville flat waxed nylon, tan.
Eyes: Tie in tan or brown barbell eyes about 1/4" behind the hook eye.
Legs: Wrap thread to end of hook shank, tying in centipede (grizzly) brown and white legs every 1/4" or every 6-8 wraps. You should have 3 to 4 sets of legs tied in perpendicular to the hook shank. Brush head cement along the entire length of the shank.
Body: Tie in long tan Dan Bailey's flash chenille. Wrap thread forward to the hook eye and then wrap chenille up the hook shank to a point behind the barbell eyes. Pull chenille fibers back with care as you proceed so as not to foul the legs. Whip secure.
Carapace: Cut a length of brown and tan rabbit strip about three times the length of the hook shank. Punch a hole in the strip at a point a hook shank's length from the rear end. Thread strip onto hook, pulling to straighten. Apply a thick bead of Fabric-Tac glue onto the skin side portion of the strip that will be touching the chenille. Secure behind the hook eye with a whip finish. Split the end of the rabbit strip with a scissor for a length of about one inch.
Head: Build head with thread, whip finish and apply head cement.

Life Preserver Shark Fly | Captain John Hand

This is a simple and easy-to-tie shark fly.

Hook: Long shank, size 1/0 to 3/0.
Thread: Orange or white.
Eye: Tie in large Google Eyes flat to the hook shank.
Belly: Tie in white Polar Fibre on the underside of the hook shank, leaving a small tuft of exposed fibers extending behind the eyes.
Wing: Tie in orange Polar Fibre on top of hook shank and behind the eyes. Follow with Krystal Flash tied in behind the eyes to trail down both sides of hook.

Little Black Nasty | Capt. Nick Angelo

The Toad fly is popular pattern among tarpon fishermen. This fly is a modified version for redfish that utilizes bead-chain eyes or lead instead of monofilament eyes. Rubber Sili-Legs have been added to the fly to provide for additional action. The black body with accents of chartreuse act as an attractor for redfish. The fly can also be used for black drum on the west coast of Florida. This fly is designed for shallow water. If you are fishing tailing fish, position the fly as close to the fish as possible. If the fish are cruising through shallow sand holes, lead them just a few feet. Many times redfish will eat the fly on the fall. If the fish comes over and takes a look, give it just a short bump, but not too aggressively.

Hook: Gamakatsu B10S Stinger, size 2.
Thread: Flat-waxed nylon, chartreuse.
Tail: Tie in the thread at the bend of the hook and attach a 1-inch-long tuft of black marabou.
Legs: Fold three chartreuse/orange Sili-Legs in half, and tie them off in the middle to the top of the hook shank. Trim them so they are about as long as the piece of marabou.
Body: Tie in black fluffy hackle and palmer it from the hook bend, to the hook eye. Reverse the hook over so that the hook point is up. Take a 2-inch clump of black EP Fibers and figure-eight it to what is now the top of the hook shank. With EP fibers tied up the hook point will ride up. Continue this step forward 3 to 4 more times. You want to leave a little room for the eyes and weed guard.
Eyes: Flip the hook back over so the hook point is down again. Tie in the bead-chain eyes to the top of the hook.
Body Trim: Tie off the thread and remove the fly from the vise and trim the EP fibers into a crab-shaped body.
Eyes: Affix small bead-chain eyes with figure-eight wraps.
Weed Guard: Reattach the hook to the vise and tie in the doubled-over piece of mason for the 20-pound monofilament weed guard. Whip finish the fly and apply little Hard as Nails to the head.

Little Mullet | Captain Greg Poole

This fly was inspired by the Jimmy Nix Shinabou Mullet. It is a streamlined version of that fly that is easy to tie, easy to cast, durable and effective. The fly was designed for snook but it has taken most gamefish species in the Banana and Indian River lagoons.

Hook: Short-shank saltwater hook.
Thread: Flat waxed nylon.
Tail: Tie in FisHair with Flashabou on either side. The tail should be about two times the hook length.
Body: Make about ten wraps of .030 lead wire and cover with thread. Tie in and wrap one or two webby saddle hackles over the lead wire.
Topping: Tie in green and black Krystal Flash to match the length of the tail.
Cheeks: Tie in fluorescent red or orange Fluorofibre.
Head: Stack in a medium bunch of deer hair around the hook. Make a few wraps with the thread to flair hair slightly. Spin another small bunch of hair in front of the first and tie off at the eye. Trim the head to shape.
Eyes: Trim eye sockets with scissors. Glue in 3D Eyes with Goop.

L-R Fire Fly

Tied by Tom Herrington | Saltwater Fly Fishing Club
Style Origins Unknown

While the use of this versatile, easy-to-tie deep minnow pattern can be traced back to the 1960s in coastal Gulf states, and in freshwater for bass and bluegill, more modern versions of the fly are attributed to the Clouser Deep Minnow. Many variations of the deep minnow are a staple in the fly boxes of Gulf Coast fly-anglers—they are productive for a wide range of gamefish. This variation is especially effective for redfish. Natural or synthetic materials can be substituted as desired.

Hook: Mustad 34007 or similar. Small jig hooks can also be used. Size according to the species and bait.
Thread: Danville flat waxed nylon, red.
Eyes: Tie on gold barbell eyes on top of the hook shank about 1/4" from the hook eye. Any form of weighted, dual-eye will work.
Bottom Wing: With hook point facing upward, tie in a bunch of yellow bucktail at the eye and on the underside of the hook shank. Place the wing over and between the barbell eyes. Secure with thread wraps behind the barbell. Snug hair firmly enough to hold hair in place, while not allowing to flare.
Flash: Invert the hook and tie in pearl Krystal Flash.
Over Wing: Tie in a bunch of orange bucktail.
Head: Build a head with thread. Whip finish and apply head cement.

LSU Crab

Originated by Captain Greg Arnold
Tied by Joe McMahon, New Orleans Fly Fishers

This fly was developed for redfish in the coastal marshes of southeast Louisiana. This modification of the original design is tied with an all-purple body and tail that makes the fly readily visible to redfish in silt-laden marsh waters.

Hook: Mustad 34007, size 1 or 2.
Thread: 280 Denier, gold.
Eyes: Tie in dumbbell or bead-chain eyes.
Tail: Cut a thin segment of arctic fox and tie in at the and up the bend. Add in six to eight pieces of Krystal Flash below the tail and extending slightly beyond the tail.
Body: Tie sequentially segments of purple and gold EP 3-D Fibers to form the body. While figure-eight wraps can be used, a more desired V-like body shape can be achieved by first wrapping one side of the material with several wraps then pulling the material to the opposite side and securing with additional wraps. A single section of gold fibers is added for contrast one or two bands behind the eyes.
Finish: Trim the body to a crab-like shape, add the weed guard and build a small head.

M.S. Bonefish Arrowhead | Mike Sfakianos

This pattern was designed as a variation of a Mother of Epoxy fly. It is tied to offer more wiggle on the drop and is an effective bonefish fly. When tied in larger sizes it is equally effective for redfish.

Hook: Mustad 34007, size 2.
Thread: Flat waxed nylon, chartreuse.
Tail: Tie in tan Fly Fur, barred with a tan permanent marker.
Flash: Tie in strands of tan Krystal Flash.
Eyes: Tie in small silver bead-chain eyes on the underside of the hook shank and opposite the hook point.
Body Frame: Build a small body frame from pearl Mylar tubing. Fill in frame with EZ Shape Sparkle Body in tan. Apply a topcoat of 30-minute epoxy.
Weed Guard: Tie in and form a two-pronged weed guard with 30-pound fluorocarbon.

M.S. King Cuda | Mike Sfakianos

This fly is a variation of an older Florida barracuda pattern of unknown origin. Total fly length is approximately nine inches.

Hook: Mustad 34011, size 2/0.
Thread: Flat waxed nylon, blue.
Underwing: Tie in long strands of white Superhair at a point near the bend of the hook. The entire fly is tied toward the rear of hook.
Mid-Wing: Tie in long strands of chartreuse Superhair, slightly longer than the underwing.
Top-Wing: Tie in long strands of blue Superhair as long as the mid-wing.
Flash: Tie in strands of pearl/pink Flashabou on each side of the hook shank and as long as the mid and top wing materials.
Eyes: Affix orange 3D Hologram Eyes.
Finish: Build a base of thread up to a point behind the hook eye and then coat hook shank and eyes with 5-minute epoxy.

M.S. Mudminnow | Mike Sfakianos

This fly was designed as a shallow-water baitfish pattern for redfish, snook and speckled trout.

Hook: Gamakatsu SC15, size 2/0.
Thread: Fine monofilament.
Body/Wing: Tie in Mirror Image in mullet brown and cream. Form entire body and wing with material.
Flash: Tie in strands of mixed silver Polar Flash and gold Krystal Flash.
Head: Build a head from 30-minute epoxy.
Eyes: Affix stick-on silver/black eyes and coat with epoxy.
Weed Guard: Tie in and form a two-pronged weed guard using 30-pound fluorocarbon.
Finish: Use a tan permanent marker for adding stripes to the material.

M.S. Permit Crab | Mike Sfakianos

This pattern has proven to be a very effective permit fly. It sinks quickly and has a lot of motion. It was designed to work on both grass and sand/coral flats.

Hook: Gamakatsu SC15, size 2/0.
Thread: Flat waxed nylon, tan.
Eyes: Tie in medium dumbbell eyes.
Tail: Tie in a tuft of olive-barred marabou.
Claws: Tie in two grizzly saddle feathers as claws, one on each side of the shaft.
Flash: Tie in strands of root beer Krystal Flash.
Body: Build a segmented body with cream and tan Aunt Lydia's Sparkle Yarn. Tie in small batches of yarn with figure-eight wraps. The last segment should be just behind the eyes. If need be, trim to shape.
Weed Guard: Tie in and form a two-pronged weed guard using 30-pound fluorocarbon.

M.S. Pinfish | Mike Sfakianos

This easy-to-tie pinfish pattern is very effective for redfish, snook, sea trout, baby tarpon and jack crevalle.

Hook: Gamakatsu SC 15, size 2/0.
Thread: Fine monofilament.
Body/Wing: Tie in Mirror Image in mullet brown, neon yellow, light blue and white. The entire body and wing is tied from batches of this material.
Head/Eyes: Build a head with epoxy and affix gold, stick-on Hologram eyes.
Finish: Use a tan permanent marker pen for stripes and a black marker for spots.

M.S. Scorpion Crab | Mike Sfakianos

This design resulted from combining the attributes of other well-known patterns. The fly was originally created for bonefish but has since been adapted for permit and laid-up tarpon. It has been responsible for tournament wins in the middle to upper Keys.

Hook: Gamakatsu SC15, size 1.
Thread: Flat waxed nylon, chartreuse.
Eyes: Tie in medium, black bead-chain eyes.
Butt: Tie in a small piece of tan Estaz and make a wrap. This bump will serve to keep the tails separated.
Tail: Tie in two separate tails of tan Sparkle Yarn.
Body: Build a body with thread and segments of tan Fly Fur. Tie in the fur in small segmented bunches of fur, using figure-eight wraps. Tie in the last batch of fur immediately behind the eyes.
Weed Guard: Tie in and form a two-pronged weed guard from 30-pound-test monofilament.

Mackerel Clouser

Captain Dino Torino | Inspired by the Clouser Deep Minnow

This fly is crafted with all the materials tied in from the hook point back. The forward portion of the hook shank acts to prevent toothy fish like Spanish mackerel from biting through a leader.

Hook: Long shank, size 4/0.
Thread: Red flat waxed nylon.
Eyes: Tie in small barbell eyes on top of the hook shank at a point opposite the hook point.
Wing: Tie in clump of white Ultra Hair as a base followed by silver flash and an over-wing of chartreuse Ultra Hair slightly longer than the white hair.

Mad Tom | Scott Leon | Inspired by the Clouser Minnow

This variation of the Clouser Minnow was originally tied as a red-and-chartreuse cobia fly. It is an easy pattern to tie and may be modified for use in varying sizes and colors. Since its inception, the fly has taken a wide variety of Atlantic and Pacific species. The rabbit tail, combined with the large head, provides built-in action to this fly. It is especially effective in deeper water.

Hook: Gamakatsu SC15-2H, 3/0.
Thread: Danville, Chartreuse 6/0.
Eyes: Begin a wrap of thread about 1/3 down the hook shank from the eye, and make a bed for the eyes. Secure medium black brass eyes in place.
Tail: Secure a 3- to 4-inch-long chartreuse Zonker strip to a point on the hook shank behind the eyes. It is best to first measure the strip to determine where it will lay on the hook, and then cut a small insertion slot in the leather side of the strip. The hook point is inserted into this slot.
Wing: Tie in a small bundle of chartreuse bucktail.
Flash: Turning the fly over, add 6 to 8 strands of pearl Comes Alive or similar flash material.
Body: Tie in chartreuse kip tail.
Cheeks: Tie in one batch of chartreuse kip tail on each side of the hook.
Belly: Tie in a small batch of red bucktail on the underside of the shank.
Head: Tie in a medium bundle of bucktail as long as the bundle on the bottom of the fly to complete the head. Whip finish and cement or epoxy.

Mangrove Mauler | Jon Adams

This generic pattern can be tied in a variety of sizes and colors to replicate a wide range of small baitfish and crustaceans. It is tied most often in orange, chartreuse and white.

Hook: Mustad, 34007, size 1.
Thread: Fine monofilament.
Head: Small plastic bead inserted over the hook to the eye. Rendering the hook barbless facilitates this process.
Weed Guard: Tie in a section of stiff monofilament on the top of the shank at the hook bend.
Tail: Tie in a moderate tuft of marabou and several strands of Krystal Flash.
Body: Tie in Crystal Chenille and wrap forward to a point behind the head. Bring tag end of weed guard forward forming a loop and secure behind plastic bead head.
Eyes: Affix small stick-on eyes and lightly coat with epoxy.

Mardi Gras Mambeaux

Tom Herrington
Historic Ocean Springs Saltwater Fly Fishing Club

This pattern is the result of a challenge to produce a fly that would replicate the colors of Mardi Gras (purple, green and gold) and catch fish. The first attempt resulted in the Mardi Gras Mambeaux, a fly that has proven very effective on winter flounder in the bayous.

Hook: Mustad 34007, size 2.
Thread: Danville flat waxed nylon, red.
Eyes: Tie in gold barbell eyes 1/4 inch from the eye.
Flash: Cut a 5- to 6-inch hunk of gold Krystal Flash and tie in at the tail, leaving about 1 inch for the tail. Whip finish to secure in place. Wrap the remaining flash to the eyes, all the thread wraps on the hook and secure in place at the eye.
Legs/Gills: At the eyes, wrap the flash over and between the barbell eyestalks and under the hook, securing the flash behind the eyes. The remaining flash (now about 1" long or the length of the hook shank) is splayed under the hook, appearing to be gills or legs.
Mid Wing/Dorsal: Measure and tie in first the green, then the purple bucktail at and behind the hook eye, each about twice the hook shank in length.

Mardi Gras Momma | Captain Rich Waldner

This fly design results in a very flashy Clouser-style fly that appeals to Louisiana redfish and trout. The fly is slim, easy to cast and sinks quickly. When stripped and paused on the retrieve this fly moves up and down and motivates strikes.

Hook: Mustad Signature Series Stainless Steel, size 2. Hook is bent slightly downward at the eye.
Thread: Any suitable thread.
Eyes: Tie on barbell eyes, coat with epoxy and sprinkle on glitter.
Wing: Coat hook with epoxy and sprinkle on glitter. Tie in bucktail or calf tail as a wing and Krystal Flash.
Finish: Apply a final coat of epoxy on the eyes.

Mighty Mullet | Captain Chris Newsome

This fly is designed to imitate mullet. It is tied with a cylindrical body that is very durable. The fly is effective for a wide variety of gamefish species throughout the Southeast and other regions of the country.

Hook: Mustad C68SSS, TMC 600SP, size 1 to 4/0.
Thread: UTC monofilament .006.
Preparation: Make a blend of Slinky Fiber and Angel Hair in desired colors.
Tail/Body: Add portions of hair near the bend of hook to form the tail and body of the fly.
Head: To form the cylindrical head, stack clumps of material on the top and bottom of the hook shank, working toward the eye. Trim to achieve desired profile.
Eyes: Secure plastic eyes with Fletch-Tite Platinum glue then apply Zap-A-Dap glue.

Mike LaFleur's Charlie

Mike LaFleur | Red Stick Fly Fishers

This fly is a variation of the Pink Charlie. It was designed to meet three criteria: easy to tie; durability; and it catches fish. The fly is also tied in chartreuse for dirty water, and a black version for clear water.

Hook: Mustad 34007, size 2 or Signature C71S SS Circle Streamer Hook, size 2.
Thread: 3/0 light pink.
Eyes: Tie in 1/50-ounce lead eyes. Coat the eye wraps with Zap-A-Gap and let dry.
Body: Tie in pearl long-flash Crystal Chenille and wrap tightly toward the eyes.
Wing: Invert the fly and tie in a bunch of pink Fly Fur or Craft Fur. The length of the wind is twice the shaft length. Tie off the fur ahead of the lead eyes and in back of the hook eye.
Head: Build a conical head with the thread, whip finish and apply head cement or Hard as Nails.

Mike's Mylar Mullet | Mike Conner

This streamer is considered a solid "bread-and-butter" imitation of small Spanish sardines and finger mullet. It suspends well in current. The pattern has caught numerous species of gamefish but the all-white version is a very effective snook fly under dock and bridge lights. The fly is also tied in brown and gold for stained waters.

Hook: Standard length, 1/0 or 2/0.
Thread: Red, 3/0.
Wing: Wind a thread base from hook eye to bend and tie in a 3-inch wing of fine white bucktail. Tie in a few strands of fine pearl flash material to each side of wing. Add a dab of cement to tie-in spot.
Body: Tie in a 5- to 6-inch strand of Hackle Flash and palmer the strand forward to the hook eye, covering the hook shank. Stroke fibers back toward bend as you proceed. At hook eye snip excess Hackle Flash, whip finish and tie off.
Eyes: Affix stick-on eyes with Goop or similar adhesive.

Mikkleson Hard Body Crab | Glen Mikkleson

Crab flies are very effective for large bonefish and permit. This is a very easy crab fly that involves little actual tying. It can be tied in tan, olive, gray and clear, and must be fished patiently.

Hook: 34007, sizes 4 to 1/0. Bend eye and 1/5 of shank down slightly. This allows the hook to ride up.
Thread: A thread. Tie in a base over entire hook and coat with liquid acrylic.
Body: Press a small ball of clear liquid acrylic caulking over the hook shank and form into a flat disk shape perpendicular to the hook bend.
Eyes: Melt 30-pound mono and paint the tips with black nail polish. Insert the eyes into the edge of the disk on one side.
Claws: Snip the stems from 2 hen feathers just back from the tip. Trim the fibers on either side of the stem, forming the shape of a claw. Glue the claws to the bottom, extending out from the eyes. Apply another coat of liquid acrylic.
Legs: Glue in 4 strands of Sili-Legs over the claws, extending out to either side behind the claws.
Weight: Glue a disk of lead tape to the underside, half the size of the crab body and covering the legs.
Finish: Let cure for a day or two, then coat the bottom with 30-minute epoxy and color the top with nail polish. If desired, mottle or speckle the back and claws with Sharpie markers.

Mikkleson Rainbait | Glen Mikkleson

The fly is very similar to the Surf Candy designed by Bob Popovics and is best used when rainbait is present. Craft Fur is used for consistency. It is a very effective fly for false albacore and other members of the small tuna and mackerel families. Sometimes in the mayhem of a blitz it might be difficult to hook-up. When that happens, cast the fly into the mix and use a "no-retrieve", just keeping the line slack.

Hook: Gamakatsu SL11-3H, TMC 800S, Eagle Claw 254, regular or short shank, sizes 4 to 8.
Belly: Tie in silver Mylar Braid and bind it to the underside of the shank. Build up a belly underneath by folding and binding the Mylar braid in layers under the shank.
Underbody: Tie in 6 strands of pearl Flashabou. Wrap the silver braid over the underbody. Wrap pearl Flashabou over the silver.
Wing: Tie in a small clump of Craft Fur at the head, a length of 2 to 2 1/2 inches. Tie in a mixture of silver, pearl and pearl/lavender Krystal Flash slightly shorter than the Craft Fur. Tie in another clump of Craft Fur on top.

Head: Whip finish and paint the head with pearl and gold nail polish.
Finish: Soak wing in the body area with liquid acrylic and make certain it adheres to the body as it dries. After the acrylic dries, brush on two coats of 30-minute epoxy.
Eyes/Gills: Silver stick-on eyes, size 2 and bits of red Flashabou are set into the first coat of epoxy after 20 minutes.

Mikkleson Soft Body Shrimp | Glen Mikkleson

This pattern is quite similar to other shrimp flies yet this design uses foam on the back to keep the flies riding upright. Elements of this fly were influenced by a pattern of Bob Sater. This fly can also be tied weighted with the hook riding up and in a variety of colors. It is best fished in dead-drift fashion.

Hook: Mustad 34011, size 4 to 10.
Thread: A thread.
Antennae: Tie in antennae of Krystal Flash. Two will be as long as the shank and two will be half that length.
Mouthparts: Tie in mouthparts of marabou half the length of the short antennae.
Eyes: Tie in burnt 30-pound monofilament eyes on either side of the marabou, curve outward and extend half the length of the marabou.
Thorax/Rib/Abdomen: Dub a small amount of Pseudo Seal and Angora goat fur and tie in the saddle hackle. Dub along the shank to form a thick thorax. Tie in 4-pound mono for the rib. Palmer hackle over thorax and dub the abdomen down the rest of the shank, tapering it thinner toward the eye.
Shellback: Crinkle clear pearl wrapping film by twisting it and sticking it to the foam. Cut to a shape about 1 1/4 times the length of the shank. Color the back, edges, under the tail and under the tip of the nose with a Sharpie marker. Place a drop of CA glue on the top front of the thorax. Tie in shellback at its tail joint at the end of the abdomen, hold down front end and let glue set. Bind the shellback down with 4-pound mono. Rib from the back of the thorax to tail.
Finish: Whip finish at the eye and coat the entire back, under the tail and the whip finish with liquid acrylic. After the acrylic has dried, touch-up color and add speckles to the shellback.

Mini Diablo | Alan Caolo

Big bonefish can be very difficult to fool, and they often prefer big prey. The number of small swimming crabs he consistently observed darting along the shoreline led Alan to adapt a proven striped bass crab pattern—the Green Diablo—to southern flats fishing. The fly was downsized and its coloration changed to brown (a common color of tropical prey), and switched from lead to bead chain for weighting. The result was the Mini Diablo, which has become a very successful fly for big bonefish.

Hook: TMC 811S, size 4, barb flattened.
Thread: Brown Danville's flat waxed nylon.
Eyes: Secure medium, bead-chain eyes to the back of the hook shank, close to the eye of the hook. Wrap thread to cover the shank to a position over the barb and coat the eyes with bronze nail polish.
Legs: Secure two Sili-Legs to the back of the hook, across from the barb (about a hook's length long, 1/2 the length of the finished fly).
Tail: Attach a chocolate brown schlappen feather (about 1" wide) just ahead of the tail-legs attachment and palmer it with four or five tight turns and secure and cut. Carefully back-wrap this hackle with a few thread turns so it lays back, flaring evenly over the bend of the hook.
Body: Attach a second chocolate brown schlappen feather just ahead of the flared tail, and secure the chenille to the hook over that feather attachment. Wrap the chenille to the eyes and over-wrap them with one turn, secure head. Palmer forward the second schlappen feather over the chenille with five or six wraps to just behind the eyes, secure with thread, and cut. Secure the thread ahead of the eyes, trim and cement. The body schlappen fibers should now be trimmed off the top of the fly only to give it a flat, crablike profile; leave long side and bottom fibers as is.

Moonshiner Minnow | Drew Chicone

This pattern was originally designed for night-fishing dock lights for summer snook. It has also proven productive in larger sizes in the clear water off the beaches of Sanibel and Captiva, Florida.

Hook: TMC 811s, size 6, 4.
Thread: Clear monofilament.
Tail: Tie in a clump of cream marabou about one hook length long.
Body: Cut a piece of Mylar cord about 1 1/2 inches long and remove the core. Fray one end of the Mylar about 1/4-inch and fold around the hook shank. Wrap Mylar around marabou, leaving frayed end exposed. Tie in the clear vinyl rib at the same point as the marabou and Mylar. Wrap rib forward to create the body and tie off.
Head: Wrap Mylar to create the head and whip finish.
Eyes: Affix 1/8-inch hologram eyes and epoxy head.

Mousy Trout Special | Erwin "Scooter" Gaines

This spotted sea trout fly was originally adapted from an East Coast weakfish pattern. The fly has a relatively large profile built on a small protected hidden hook. It is fished exactly as one would fish a weighted Clouser Deep Minnow.

Hook: Mustad 34007 #2 stainless-steel hook or similar. It can also be tied on a circle hook.
Thread: Danville flat waxed nylon, white.
Eyes: Tie in barbell eyes (yellow, black pupils) as you would for a traditional Clouser.
Body: Tie in and wrap a body of small, hot pink chenille up to the eyes. Secure in place and trim excess material.
Gills: Turn the fly over and tie in about 10 to 20 strands of red synthetic hair immediately in front of and under the eyes. Trim the gills about half way up the chenille body so the red and pink colors blend.
Wing: Tie in a sparse portion of white bucktail on top of the eyes using crisscross wraps. The bucktail should not fan out.
Flash: Tie in a sparse clump of pearl Tinker Bell Hair.
Wing: Tie in a small portion of chartreuse buck tail on top of the flash and at a point immediately in front of the eyes. Trim the flash back so it blends with the other material.
Head: Build a head with thread, whip finish and apply Hard-as-Nails or any other hard cement.

Mr. Mantis | Captain Chris Newsome

This fly was designed to imitate the mantis shrimp.

Hook: Mustad S71S SS, size 4.
Thread: UTC monofilament, .006 or equivalent.
Weight: Attach lead dumbbell at the hook eye.
Feelers: At the hook bend, tie in several strands of midge flash for feelers.
Mouth: Tie in a clump of orange Craft Fur for "mouth" and trim closely to hook bend.
Eyes: Tie in mono eyes extending to the rear of the hook.
Legs: Create the walking legs by palmering a neck hackle.
Claws: Tie in two short neck hackles to create the claws.
Body/Carapace: Work toward the hook eye, by adding clumps of Craft Fur and palmering neck hackle. Once the hook eye is reached, trim the neck hackle to create swimming legs and trim the Craft Fur to create the carapace of the mantis shrimp.
Weed Guard: Tie in a two-pronged monofilament weed guard at the hook eye.

Mud Bunny | Captain Randy Hamilton

This generic pattern is effective for all species that eat small crabs and crustaceans.

Hook: Mustad 34007, size 1.
Thread: Black.
Eyes: Tie in barbell eyes, red with black pupils.
Tail: Tie in two small barred grizzly hackles and a small tuft of brown rabbit fur.
Body: Tie in both a barred grizzly hackle and a strip of rabbit fur and palmer both forward to the barbell eyes.
Head: Build a small head with thread, tie off and add head cement.

Murdich's Minnow | Bill Murdich

This fly was originally designed as a mullet imitation for snook, redfish and sea trout. The large head, collar and inherent wiggle of the fly make it a very enticing pattern. It is also very effective as a subsurface freshwater fly for largemouth bass and pike.

Hook: Mustad 3407, sizes 4/0 to 2.
Thread: While 3/0 Danville Monocord or UNI-thread.
Wing: Tie in alternating sparse bunches of white bucktail and silver Flashabou along the length of the hook shank. Tie each section directly on top of the previous one, the Flashabou should be slightly longer than the bucktail. End with three sections of bucktail and two of Flashabou.
Topping: Tie in a large bunch of ocean green Flashabou along the hook length, slightly longer than the Flashabou in wing.
Collar: Attach white Body-Fur in front of hook bend, making three or four wraps. Tie in ocean green Flashabou on top of Body-Fur.
Body: Attach white Estaz Grande directly in front of the Body-Fur and wrap forward toward the hook eye. Wraps must be close together.
Head: The layers of bucktail and Flashabou tied along the length of hook serve as the foundation for the head. Trim the Estaz body into a blunt, bullet shape.
Eyes: Glue 3/8-inch silver or white 3-D molded eyes.
Finish: Coat thread wraps with head cement.

Murdich's Wiggler | Bill Murdich

This successful pattern has taken more than forty species of gamefish from both saltwater and freshwater, and has accounted for seven IGFA tippet class records. Tying it properly requires attention to detail. The fly is tied primarily in black and white. The white version can be colored with a marking pen to any desired color. Other popular colors are root beer, tan and chartreuse.

Hook: Mustad 34011, size 2 or Dai-Riki 700B, size 4.
Thread: White 3/0 Danville monocord or UNI-Thread.
Preparation: You must first bend the Mustad hook shank at an angle of about 25 degrees. Bend hook at mid-shank bringing the eye toward the hook point. The Dai-Riki is already bent.
Weight: Wrap the hook shank with approximately 18 turns of .035 wire, leaving 1/8-inch space between last wrap and hook eye.
Tail: Tie in pearl SparkleFlash, Polar Flash or Flashabou where the hook bend begins.
Body: Tie in Estaz Grande or large Cactus Chenille at the bend of the hook. Create smooth, tight body with thread over the wire wraps. Wrap body material forward and tie off behind the hook eye.
Trimming: The key to this fly is to trim the body as thinly as possible without making it too skinny from side-to-side. Using curved scissors, cut a deep groove down the center of the top and bottom of the fly, and expand the center grooves to the outer sides of the fly. Taper the fly to shape and trim fibers as needed.

Mutant Gurgler

Captain Rich Santos | Inspired by Jack Gartside's Gurgler

This Gurgler variation is very effective for spotted sea trout and snook in South Florida. Redfish have also responded well to the pattern, as have most other gamefish that are attracted to top-water lures. The easy-to-tie fly is tied with foam extending only halfway down the hook shank from the hook eye. The fly is best fished at dawn to early morning and during dusk periods when there are flat, calm conditions.

Hook: Gamakatsu SP11-3L3H , size 1.
Thread: Red Danville's 210 Denier Flat Waxed Nylon
Weed Guard 1: Tie in two 3-inch-long pieces of the 16-pound hard Mason 1/3 of the way around the hook bend.
Tail: Place and tie on a small amount of chartreuse bucktail approximately 1-1/2 inches long. Then place about four to six strands of Krystal Flash over the bucktail, following with a small amount of hot pink bucktail. You can also add a small short piece of hot pink deer hair on the front top part of the bucktail and splayed upward with the tread tension.
Body/Head: Cut a strip of sheet foam 3-4 inches long and 3/8-inch wide. Lay one end down on top of the shank near the hook eye. Wrap the foam strip toward the hook bend. The wraps should be firm. You want approximately 1/8-inch thickness of compressed foam and thread on the shank. Tie on a piece of chartreuse Estaz Grande at the hook bend over the wrapped foam. Palmer the Estaz around the hook shank up to the hook eye and tie off. Fold over the tag end of the foam strip on top of the Estaz-covered shank and tightly wrap-tie it a few times so the foam end splays upward. Bring the thread bobbin in front of the foam face and trim to approximately 3/8-inch high.
Throat: Tie on a small amount of red Flashabou at the throat and trim to 1/4 inch.
Weed Guard 2: Carry the two tag ends of monofilament weed guards around the hook bend and tie down at the hook eye. Remove from vise if necessary to adjust the weed guard properly.
Finish: Super Glue the foam head in a 90-degree position against the foam back.

No Mur-See Streamer | Bill Murdich

This fly was designed to incorporate five key elements that trigger fish to strike. The red marabou mimics the flared gills of a wounded fish. The silver Flashabou transmits the same flash as a struggling fish. The big eye gives a predator a target to key in on. The peacock herl back intensifies natural counter shading and the white bucktail provides a natural base color for the fly. The fly was originally tied for snook but is also a superb pattern for redfish feeding on sardines and big sea trout.

Hook: Mustad 3407, size 2/0.
Thread: Red 3/0 Danville monocord or UNI-Thread.
Tail: Tie in alternating sparse bunches of white bucktail. The flash should be slightly longer than the bucktail.
Body: Attach silver Mylar tinsel in front of the hook bend and wrap forward within 1/4 inch of the hook eye.
Wing/Belly: Tie in white bucktail and silver Flashabou on top of the Mylar body (repeating the procedure for the tail), and below the hook shank to form the belly.
Collar: Tie in two Woolly Bugger marabou tips on each side.
Topping: Tie in ten to twelve strands of peacock herl on top of the fly. Head cement the thread wraps.
Eyes: Affix 6mm or 3/8-inch 3-D molded eyes using a thick gel adhesive.

Noisy Deep Minnow | Captain Chris Newsome

The Noisy Deep Minnow is a variation of the classic Clouser Deep Minnow, but incorporates a hidden glass rattle. This pattern excels in murky water conditions where the noise of the clicking rattle allows fish to home in on the fly. Different sized rattles can be used to give off varying frequencies of noise. Fish this fly with sharp strips to work the rattle. It is effective for speckled trout, flounder, croaker, striped bass, black drum, puppy drum and redfish.

Hook: Mustad S71SSS or equivalent standard-shank hook, size, 1-2/0.
Thread: Danville Flat Wax—210 denier.
Body: Push rattle (micro to large) inside medium Mylar tubing and close the tubing with thread. Tie in the tubing/rattle approximately 1/3 of the way up the hook bend and then tie the basic Clouser pattern incorporating bucktail, Flashabou, Krystal Flash and grizzly saddle hackles. The color preferences are either vivid fire tiger or dark black over purple with generous amounts of flash.
Eyes: Waspi Real Eyes Plus.

Nuclear Ballyhoo | Drew Chicone

This fly was designed for nighttime barracuda using glow-in-the-dark materials and a concealed stinger hook to remedy short strikes.

Hook: Mustad 34011, size 1/0 and Owner Mosquito 5177-111, size 1/0.
Thread: White flat-waxed nylon.
Body/Gills: Double about ten inches of 86# stainless-steel wire. Pass it around the shank and through the eye of the stinger hook and tie in place. Cut a six-inch piece of Mylar tubing and remove the center core. Fray about one inch of the tubing and insert the wire through the tubing, frayed fibers hanging past the hook. At free end of wire make a 90-degree bend. Start thread at the eye of the main hook and pass the bend of the wire through the eye. Bend tag ends of wire parallel with the hook shank and tie in back to hook point. Tie in red Krystal Flash at the hook point for gills. Mix and tie in gold and green tinsel the same length as the Mylar tubing. Tie in yellow glow-in-the-dark Flashabou and chartreuse/pearl Flashabou Accent, slightly shorter than the tinsel. On top, tie in green glow-in-the-dark Flashabou and pearly blue, the same length as the yellow.
Head: Wrap thread forward to the hook eye and build a tapered head. Tie off and whip finish. Color top of head and nose with an aqua-colored permanent marker.
Eyes: Affix 5mm orange Doll Eyes and epoxy both head and eyes to the eye of the hook.

Oscar's Action Bait | Oscar Feliu

This generic baitfish incorporates an articulated tail section for greater action.

Hook: Mustad C47S D, size 3/0.
Thread: Danville A Plus, white.
Articulated Tail: Insert a streamer-style hook into vise. Tie on a tuft of chartreuse marabou and flash material. Thread on pearl body material and tie off at hook eye and slightly over the ends of the marabou tuft. Cut off hook at the bend.
Main Fly: Insert hook and tie in a small wire loop that will function as a connection point for the articulated tail. Insert through wire loop and secure wire along shank with thread.
Body: Tie in an underbody of white Sea Fibers and flash blend. Add additional white fibers to top of hook shank.
Wing: Tie in chartreuse Sea Fibers and flash blend.
Topping: Tie in black or dark colored Sea Fibers on top.
Eyes: Affix eyes to small plastic plates and cover with a coating of epoxy.

Oscar's Eels | Oscar Feliu

This generic eel pattern can be tied in a variety of colors to replicate small eels.

Hook: Mustad S74S SS, size 4 and 6.
Thread: Monocord, 3/0, color to match.
Belly: Tie in white Crystal Chenille trimmed tight to shank.
Ribbing: Tie in brass or copper light wire and wind forward over belly.
Tail/Wing: Tie in squirrel or rabbit strip over body, olive or brown.
Flash: Tie in four strands of Krystal Flash or Flashabou.
Eyes: Tie on small, black barbell eyes.
Weed Guard: Tie in 30-pound hard monofilament.
Finish: Epoxy to cover from the eyes to behind the hook eye.

Oscar's Mini Pin-Fish | Oscar Feliu

This fly was designed as a miniature pinfish fly. It is a versatile fly and can be modified to replicate other small baitfish as well.

Hook: Mustad Circle, size 1 or 2.
Thread: Monocord 3/0, white.
Tail: Tie in four or six small chartreuse barred feathers and four strands of pearlescent Flashabou.
Skirt: Tie in white calf tail hair.
Top Wing: Tie in chartreuse Sea Fibers mixed with green/pearl flash.
Bottom Wing: Tie in white Sea Fibers mixed with white pearl flash.
Eyes: Small molded eyes affixed to plastic translucent gill covers.
Finish: Color the fibers with a permanent marker to resemble pinfish coloration. Apply a coating of epoxy to the head and eyes.

Oscar's Needlefish | Oscar Feliu

This needlefish pattern is effective for many gamefish throughout the Southeast and Gulf Coast. The fly is tied on the back one-third of the hook.

Hook: Mustad C47S D, size 3/0 to 1.
Thread: Danville A plus or monocord 3/0, white.
Tail: Mix and tie in eight strands of olive Flashabou and a clump of olive Super Hair. Materials should be approximately four inches long.
Under Tail: Tie in mixed pearl flash and white Super Hair, approximately 2 1/2-inches long.
Body: For bottom portion tie in white arctic fox. For top portion, tie in olive arctic fox.
Eyes: Affix 5/32 orange or chartreuse molded eyes.
Finish: Build a long tapered head and apply head cement.

Oscar's Pilchard | Oscar Feliu

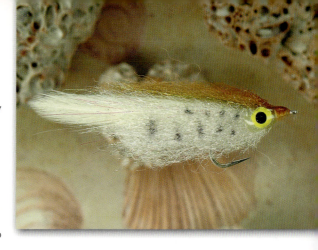

This fly was designed to replicate the pilchard as well as other baitfish that inhabit the edges of beaches. Snook, pompano and redfish, and many other predatory fish, target this species of bait.

Hook: Mustad C70S D or C74S D, sizes 6 and 4.
Thread: Monocord 3/0, white.
Tail: Tie in four white feathers flanked by pearl flash material.
Skirt: Tie in sparse clumps of white calf tail hairs.
Top Wing: Tie in strands of white and colored Sea Fibers with mixed pearl flash. Coloration of top wing should be tan for this fly.
Bottom Wing: Tie in strands of white Sea Fibers mixed with pearl flash. Apply black barred markings to flanks.
Eyes: 7mm molded eyes affixed to plastic tags.
Head/Finish: Build a head of thread. Cover head and eyes with a coating of epoxy.

Oscar's Pin-Fish | Oscar Feliu

This fly was designed to replicate pinfish and allows for color variations to match habitat and water conditions.

Hook: Mustad Circle, size 3/0.
Thread: Monocord 3/0, white.
Tail: Tie in four or six chartreuse barred feathers and four strands of pearlescent Flashabou.
Skirt: Tie in white calf tail hair.
Top Wing: Tie in chartreuse Sea Fibers mixed with green/pearl flash.
Bottom Wing: Tie in white Sea Fibers mixed with white pearl flash.
Eyes: 3/16 mm molded eyes affixed to plastic translucent gill covers.
Finish: Color the fibers with a permanent marker to resemble pinfish coloration. Apply a coating of epoxy to the head and eyes.

Palmetto Crab | Enrico Puglisi

This pattern is designed to replicate small crustaceans. It is an effective and easy-to-tie crab fly that can be tied in a number of productive colors: cream, olive and tan.

Hook: Wide-gap saltwater hook matched to size of fly, size 1/0.
Thread: Waxed, chartreuse.
Weight: Tie in a set of small barbells.
Eyes: Tie in a pair of EP Crab Eyes on the top of the hook shank at the bend. Hook rides point up.
Tail: Tie in a tuft of brown marabou.
Claws: Tie in a pair of EP Crab Claws at the rear of the hook.
Body/Legs: Glue in one precut EP Crab Body. Glue in three sets of knotted Sili-Legs spaced along the body form. Glue in the second half of the shell.

Pink Cactus Charlie

Tied by: Tom Herrington
Historic Ocean Springs Saltwater Fly Fishers
Inspired by: Kyle Moppert original

A variation of the highly effective Crazy Charlie, Dr. Rod Fields is credited with this specific pattern modification. The original design incorporated smaller red barbell eyes and Craft Fur, while this variation utilizes Long Flash chenille. It is an easy-to-tie fly, and is very effective for schooling summer "specks" as well as other inshore and flats species.

Hook: Mustad 34007 or similar, size 2.
Thread: Danville flat waxed nylon, pink.
Eyes: Tie in large barbell eyes (pearl with black pupils) about 1/4 of an inch from hook eye.
Body: Tie in Dan Bailey's pearl Long Flash Chenille, wrapping to the base of the eyes while gently pulling back filaments to prevent over-wrapping. Secure with a whip finish.
Wing: Tie in pink calf tail or kip tail. The length of the wing should be about three times the length of the hook shank.
Veil: Spread an equal length of pearl Krystal Flash evenly over the calf or kip tail as a veil.
Head: Build a head with thread and finish with a coating of head cement.

Polar Minnow | Captain Doug Sinclair

This Polar Fibre synthetic-hair fly is a solid performer for many Southeast and Gulf Coast gamefish. Its effectiveness on many species of gamefish is attributed in part to the synthetic-hair blend and the resultant subtle presentation.

Hook: Gamakatsu or Tiemco, size 1.
Thread: Black.
Throat: Tie in a small tuft of orange synthetic-hair material.
Lower Wing: Tie in a length of orange Polar Fibre synthetic hair.
Flash: Tie in strands of gold flash material.
Upper Wing: Tie a wing of black synthetic-hair material.
Eyes: Affix black eyes.
Head: Using dabs of epoxy to build a small triangular head and allow to dry.

Pomp Fly

Tom Herrington | Historic Ocean Springs Saltwater Fly Fishing Club

Designed for pompano, this attractor pattern was responsible for the Mississippi state record of that species. Patterned after the colors of the successful Fire Fly, this version utilizes materials that create the effect of enhanced motion.

Hook: Mustad 34007, size 2.
Thread: Danville flat waxed nylon, red.
Eyes: Tie in barbell eyes (yellow or white with black pupils) on top of the hook shank about 1/4 inch from the hook eye.
Tail: Tie in a section of yellow fluorescent marabou about three times the length of the hook shank.
Body: Tie in red Dan Bailey's Cactus Chenille at the base of the marabou and wrap toward the hook eye about half way up the shank.
Collar: Tie in either red hackle or long fiber red Estaz and wrap to the hook eye.
Head: Build a head with thread. Whip finish and apply head cement.

Pretender | Captain Mike Starke

The Pretender was developed to replicate a wide variety of baitfish. Designed to be lighter and more buoyant, the fly should suspend and remain in the strike zone longer. It is especially effective when fished slower with short, rapid and erratic strips, followed by intermittent pauses, and can be fished with floating, intermediate and sinking lines. While originally designed for striped bass in the Northeast, the pattern has proven productive for a wide range of gamefish throughout the Southeast and Gulf Coast.

Hook: Mustad 34011 long-shank, size 1/0 to 4/0.
Thread: White flat waxed nylon.
Tail: Tie a medium bunch of white bucktail at the rear of the hook shank, topped with 4 to 6 strands of Flashabou. Fold the flash back over itself, extending the flash about 1/2 inch past the bucktail to form a flash tail. Tie in six long white saddle hackles.
Body: Tie on a length of large pearl Mylar piping or Ultra-Flex tubing about 1/2 inch before the eye of the hook. Whip finish and cut thread. Pull the piping back over itself and the hook shank so that the piping extends to the end of the hook. Rattle optional.
Wing/Beard: Re-attach the thread just behind the eye. Tie in a small bunch of white bucktail as a beard on the bottom of the hook shank so that the hairs extend slightly past the hook point. Loosely tie a bunch of white bucktail on top of the hook shank, and then roll slightly between the fingers to allow some hair to drop down along the sides, mimicking fins. Complete the wing of the fly by tying on successive layers of white bucktail.
Flashtop: Add a top of aqua rainbow Sparkle Flash.
Head/Eyes: Whip finish and coat with a thin layer of 5-minute epoxy. Affix Mylar stick-on eyes and apply a second coat of epoxy.

Prince of Tides

Tied by Captain Steve Bailey | Originated by Flip Pallot

This fly is a modification of an original pattern by Flip Pallot. It was first tied on a long-shank hook with lead eyes and in bend-back style with no body. This variation is a dressed-up version with a regular-style wing. It has proved to be an exceptional pattern for tarpon.

Hook: Any suitable hook. Original was tied on a Mustad 34011.
Thread: Danville flat-waxed nylon, brown.
Underbody: Tie in two strands of black Flashabou, wound on together.
Overbody: Formed with 30-pound monofilament.
Wing: Tie in clumps of white, dark green and brown bucktail.
Flash: Tie in copper Flashabou and gold Krystal Flash, positioned between the green and brown bucktail.
Eyes: Painted, black on yellow, then coated with epoxy.

Rattlin' Minnow | Jon Cave

This fly was designed in the early 1980s and utilizes a rattle capsule to enhance its overall effectiveness. The design appeals to a fish's sense of hearing that often plays a significant role in its feeding habits, and it can be tied in a standard upright position or in an inverted weedless position. This pattern is tied to replicate a generic minnow-type bait and is productive for a varied range of gamefish.

Hook: Mustad 34011 or equivalent, size 1/0.
Tread: Flat waxed nylon to match over-wing.
Tail: Strands of Mylar tubing.
Body: Large Mylar tubing over rattle capsule. After capsule is fastened to the hook shank with thread, adhesive-backed lead Zonker tape is wrapped around the capsule to give the body shape and to weight the fly so that the hook rides upright.
Gills: Six to eight strands or red Flashabou or Accent Flash.
Wing: Dark bucktail over light-colored bucktail. Six to eight strands of Accent Flash are tied between the layers of bucktail.
Eyes: Painted or stick-on.

Rattlin' Mullet | Jon Cave

This fly was designed as another in the Cave series of rattle flies. It was also first tied in the early 1980s and utilizes a rattle capsule to enhance its overall effectiveness. The design appeals to a fish's sense of hearing that often plays a significant role in feeding habits. It can be tied in a standard upright position or in an inverted weedless position. This pattern is replicates a mullet and is productive for a number of varied gamefish species.

Hook: Mustad 34011 or equivalent, size 2-2/0.
Thread: White flat waxed nylon.
Tail/Rattle: Tie in brown bucktail over rainbow Accent Flash over white bucktail. The entire tail is tied around a rattle capsule.
Body/Head: White deer-body hair spun around the hook shank with brown and natural deer hair stacked on top to give a mottled mullet-like effect.
Eyes: Affix 7mm hollow doll eyes.

Red Back Minnow | Captain Doug Sinclair

This is another in a series of synthetic Polar Fiber flies tied in a proven color combination. The fly is a solid performer for many Southeast and Gulf Coast gamefish. Its effectiveness is in part attributed to the subtle and seductive action of Polar Fiber.

Hook: Gamakatsu or Tiemco, size 1.
Thread: Black.
Throat: Tie in a small tuft of orange synthetic-hair material.
Lower Wing: Tie in a length of white Polar Fiber.
Flash: Tie in strands of silver flash material.
Upper Wing: Tie a wing of red Polar Fiber, dotted with black markings.
Topping: Tie in a small tuft of black Polar Fiber.
Eyes: Affix black eyes.
Head: Using dabs of epoxy, build a small triangular head and allow to dry.

Redbone Special | Captain Paul Dixon

This versatile pattern is great for big Keys bonefish and redfish that feed on large shrimp which can reach a size of five inches. The fly can be tied large or small to match the prevailing size of the local shrimp.

Hook: Mustad 34007, size 1.
Thread: Color to match or complement body color.
Eyes: Tie in brass or copper eyes at a point near the hook eye.
Feelers: Tie in a clump of calf tail and a few strands of Krystal Flash.
Claws: Tie in two barred hackles, splayed to replicate claws.
Eyes: Tie in large, red or black, EP Monofilament eyes at the hook bend.
Body: Tie in tan or orange Metz Wingbrite Body Fur at the hook bend and wrap forward; trim to size. Whip finish.

Redgetter | John Baker

This fly was designed for tailing redfish. It has developed into a go-to fiddler crab imitation for some guides in the Low Country of South Carolina and Georgia. The pattern can be tied in black, golden tan and redfish orange.

Hook: Standard saltwater hook, size 2.
Thread: Matched to body color.
Eyes: Tie in gold Dazl Eyes on the underside of the hook shank, at a point behind the hook eye.
Tail: Tie in a length of rabbit strip.
Body: Build a body Larva Lace Polybear by tying in small clumps of fibers in a figure-eight pattern.

Redfish Candy | Angelo Tirico

This fly was designed specifically for tailing redfish. Despite its simplicity, fish charge this fly with reckless abandon. It's a very durable pattern.

Hook: Mustad 3407, Size 4.
Thread: Danville flat waxed nylon.
Body: Tie in bead-chain eyes approximately mid hook using figure-eight wraps. Extend thread wraps about 1/8 inch past the eyes. Secure in place gold Sparkle Braid, and wrap the braid towards the hook eye. Make several figure eight wraps around the bead chain eyes to form the body shape. Secure Sparkle Braid 1/8 -inch past the bead-chain eyes, wrapping towards hook eye. Whip finish and cut thread. Using epoxy, coat the Sparkle Braid and bead-chain eyes forming a teardrop body with a bump extending opposite the hook bend. The body lays flat on the side of the hook shank.
Wing: To form the wing, tie in six strands of Sili-Legs extending 1/2 inch past the hook bend. Then tie in 1/8 inch clump of fox fur. Wrap three times around the base of fur to elevate it along the side of the body.
Weed Guard/Eyes: Secure 40-pound fluorocarbon weed guard with figure-eight wraps and burn the tips to create eyes.

Redfish SP Crab | Enrico Puglisi

This pattern was specifically developed for Gulf Coast redfish. It is a durable and effective fly that has proved especially productive for bull reds. It can be tied in any of the productive crab colors.

Hook: Wide-gap saltwater hook matched to size of fly, size 1-8.
Thread: Waxed, chartreuse.
Eyes: Tie in lead barbell eyes on the top of the hook shank. Hook rides point-up.
Tail/Claws: Tie in two lengths of EP Fibers knotted at the base. The knots help keep the claws splayed. Tie in flash material.
Eyes: Tie in a pair of EP Crab Eyes.
Body: Tie in a small tuft of orange marabou or EP Fibers at the base of the hook bend and on the underside of the hook shank below the barb. Tie in small bunches of EP Fibers across the underside of the hook shank with figure-eight thread wraps. Build a body progressively with additional bunches or EP Fibers and flash to a point behind the lead barbells.
Weedguard: Tie in a section of stiff monofilament and form a two-pronged weed guard. Tie off, whip finish and add cement.

Richard's Rattle Crab | Richard Schmidt

This fly is similar to the Crabe Voyant but incorporates the use of a rattle for fish-attracting sound. It too was inspired by Del's Merkin crab, and was originally tied for large Biloxi Marsh redfish. It has since proven effective for a wide array of gamefish including striped bass, snook, large sea trout, weakfish, flounder and pompano.

Hook: Mustad 34007, size 2-2/0.
Thread: Danville flat waxed nylon.
Tail: Tie in tan or light brown marabou and pearl Krystal Flash.
Mid-Body 1: Cut 1/8-inch to 3/16-inch gold Mylar tubing twice the length of the hook and tie in tip of Mylar tubing on top of the hook at the bend. Allow to hang loosely.
Main Body: Tie in brown Sparkle Yarn employing the Merkin body method. Brush out fibers.
Eyes: Tie in barbell eyes 1/8" from the hook eye.
Rattle: Insert rattle into tube and bring forward to a point between the hook eye and over the barbell eyes. Tie down and whip finish.
Mid-Body 2: Work the Mylar tubing over the end of the hook and hook eye and over the barbell eyes. Tie down and whip finish. Pick out the gold Mylar, allowing it to flare to the hook point and out to the body.
Finish: Whip finish at head and apply head cement.

Rich's Holographic Deer Hair Clouser

Captain Rich Santos | Inspired by Bob Clouser Deep Minnow

This fly is a modified version of the original Clouser Deep Minnow. The pattern is most effective on redfish, spotted sea trout and flounder in northeast Florida. It is designed to push water with its wide silhouette and shows up well in stained water due to its flashiness and dark color. The color and profile replicate a small four-inch baitfish like mullet. It's best fished with an erratic strip motion in stained water in two to five feet of water with a floating line.

Hook: Mustad 34007 SS size, 2 or Mustad C47S D Shrimp, size 1.
Thread: Red Danville's 210 Denier Flat Waxed Nylon.
Eyes: Tie on medium dumbbell Wapsi Fly Eyes, metallic red.
Belly: Tie on approx. 2 1/2 inches of Flash N Slinky under belly at back of eyes and cross material over eyes and wrap-tie down between eyes and hook eye.
Flash: Tie on 12-15 strands of Holographic Flash fibers 1/4 inch to 1/2 inch longer than Flash N Slinky underbelly. Stagger length of the flash fibers. Tie on eight strands of black Krystal Flash fibers over Holographic Flash in the same lengths.
Wing: Tie on approx. 1/8-inch thickness of black bucktail the same length as underbelly over the black Krystal Flash.
Head: Tie in 1/4-inch-wide clump of black deer hair about 1/8 inch from hook eye with tips facing back on top of bucktail. Tie 3-4 times around and splay out the deer hair just enough to stand out at an almost 90-degree angle. Fold hair ends backward and bring thread wrap in front and tie off. Trim head round with tapered effect.
Weed Guard: Optional.

Rich's Silent Crab | Captain Rich Santos

This stealthy, light-landing fly was designed to imitate the black-brown fiddler crabs that inhabit the flooding spartina grass in northeast Florida during the warmer months. It was tied for the tailing and cruising redfish on the grass flats. It has also proven to be successful in the backwater mud flats and creeks.

Hook: Tiemco 777SP, size 6. Slightly bend a shallow curve in the hook shank.
Thread: Black Danville's 210 Denier flat waxed nylon.
Weight: Tie on a short piece of .025 lead wire and wrap around shank toward the hook eye about 8-10 turns. Thread wrap the lead wire and coat with Hard as Nails or similar cement.
Weed Guard 1: Tie in two three-inch-long pieces of the 16-pound. hard Mason monofilament 1/3 of the way around the hook bend.
Tail/Claw: Then tie on a one-inch short piece of orange Angler's Choice Polybear Fiber over the mono. Point in a downward position toward the hook point.

Body: Flatten black Cascade Glimmer Braid to an oval shape with a pair of flat-nose pliers. Tie one end of the braid over the tail and trim. Use a couple drops of super glue to secure. Tie on two or three grizzly hackles or natural Cree feathers just inside where the Glimmer Braid is tied. Palmer the hackles around the shank up to where you started near the hook eye and tie off. Then tie the tag end of the Glimmer Braid over the hackle to the hook eye. As you do this fold the hackle in a downward angle toward the hook point and adjust the Glimmer Braid so it has the right profile. Trim the hackle to the desired shape.
Weed Guard 2: Then carry the two tag ends of monofilament weed guards around the hook bend and tie down at the hook eye. Remove from vise if necessary to adjust the weed guard properly.
Legs: Attach four sets of double-stranded Sili-Legs through the glimmer braid. This is done by using a bobbin threader and held in place by knotting one end of the Sili-Legs after its been pulled through the braid body.
Eyes: Cut two pieces of 50-pound monofilament and burn the ends to look like crab eyes. Feed through the edges of the braid body on two sides and secure with super glue. Trim excess mono that sticks out from braid body. Color eyes black with Sharpie marker.

Rod's Crafty Speck Fly

Tom Herrington | Historic Ocean Springs Saltwater Fly Fishing Club

This fly originated from a request for a speckled-trout fly to replicate baitfish like finger mullet. Crafted in vibrant colors and with materials that offer movement in potholes and currents, the fly is tied with the hook facing up for fishing in deep grass and mangroves. It is also an effective fly for snook.

Hook: Mustad 34007, size 2 through 2/0.
Thread: Danville flat waxed nylon, green or pink.
Belly: Tie in a bunch of white calf tail, two to three times the length of the hook shank. Tie in on the bottom of the hook shank.
Mid-Body: Tie in a clump of pink Craft Fur, four times the length of the hook shank. Tie in fur on the shank side opposite the calf tail.
Flash: Tie in several strands of flash on top of the green fur or blend with fur before tying in body.
Dorsal: Tie in a bunch of green Craft Fur on top of and slightly ahead of the pink fur.
Topping: Tie in several strands of peacock herl.
Head: Form a head with the thread and whip finish.
Eyes: Apply molded or stick-on eyes and apply epoxy to the eyes and head.

Russell's Mussel

Ron Russell | Tied by Lawrence Clemens

This simple dubbed fly is tied as a piece of clam or mussel. Its design is attributed to Ron Russell of the Virginia Coastal Fly anglers. The fly is effective for spadefish that show up annually in late spring and in the area of islands, towers and wrecks of the Chesapeake Bay. The fly is often fished in a chum slick of cut clam. The fly can be tied in any number of colors to match the feeding temperament of spadefish. Red also performs well.

Hook: Any suitable hook, size 2.
Thread: Monofilament, fine.
Body: Densely dub tan dubbing material, folding toward the rear of the hook as you dub around the hook shank. Gently tease the body with a bodkin to achieve the irregular shape of a piece of clam.
Collar: Dub a collar with orange dubbing material. Pick out the fibers with a bodkin to form an irregular shape.

Rz's Bunny Deceiver | Captain Roan zumFelde

The fly has its origins in a Jim Grace Snook Fly and the Deceiver. This version is tied with grizzly hackles and cross-cut bunny hair. It is tied in two sizes and is fished in the canals of the "Glades" and along beaches. The pattern replicates a small black-lined chub and a finger mullet. This has been an effective fly for a wide array of Southeastern fish species, as well as various Alaskan gamefish. A weed guard is optional.

Hook: Mustad 3407 or Big Game Light, size 1/0 or 2.
Thread: Red.
Tail: Tie in four grizzly hackles married together and tied down the back of the hook extending approximately two inches behind the hook bend.
Flash: Advance thread 3/4 of the hook and tie in approximately ten strands of rainbow Polar Flash, running down the hook and on either side of the hackles. Snip flash to vary the tip length.
Body: Tie in white crosscut rabbit strip, palmer forward about three times around the hook and tie off.
Topping: Tie in six strands of peacock herl on top of the body. Using the back of scissors, shape the herl over the hackles and rabbit-strip body.
Head: Wrap thread to form a cone-shaped head.
Eyes: Glue on either yellow prismatic or holographic eyes.
Finish: Build a final head with epoxy.

Rz's Bunny Ducer | Roan zumFelde

This fly was designed to push a lot of water, wiggle when retrieved, and suspend when stopped. A key to the fly's success is attributed to the marriage of palmered chenille and crosscut rabbit. It has proven an effective fly for tarpon, either inshore laid-up fish or cruising beach tarpon. It is also a terrific snook fly in size 1/0 and can be tied in various sizes and colors, purple being the favored color. In addition to tarpon and snook the fly has also worked well on redfish, and little tarpon in the backwaters of Naples and the Ten Thousand Islands.

Hook: Mustad Signature Big Game Light Hook, 1/0 to 3/0.
Thread: Black.
Loop: To reduce fouling tie in a 30-pound-test monofilament loop extending 1/4 inch off the back of the hook.
Body/Tail: Tie in medium, purple bunny Zonker strip on top of the mono loop. Also tie in an equal length of purple Palmer Chenille. On top of the bunny strip tie in six to eight strands of rainbow Polar Flash extending back approximately the same length as the bunny strip. Next tie in two splayed, purple saddle hackles down either side of the bunny strip. The saddles should be slightly shorter than the bunny strip. Palmer both the rabbit strip and the chenille forward approximately four to six wraps and tie off just behind the hook eye.
Eyes: Glue holographic eyes on so that half of the eye is on the thread and half on the bunny. Apply epoxy behind the eyes and allow to soak into the bunny fur.

Rz's Hammerhead Jerk Bait | Roan zumFelde

This fly was developed to be fished in the mangrove roots and retrieved like a soft plastic jerk bait. The pattern has accounted for numerous big snook. The fly has also proven very effective for largemouth bass in heavy cover, as well as numerous other species. This versatile pattern is tied in three hook sizes and in five colors, including tan, chartreuse, gray, purple and the favored all-white.

Hook: Mustad Signature Big Game Light, 1/0—3/0.
Thread: White.
Loop: Tie in a base of thread back to the bend of the hook and tie in a loop of stiff monofilament as a weed guard.
Tail: Tie in a white rabbit Zonker strip extending back about three inches from the bend of the hook.
Flash: Tie in approximately ten strands of pearl Polar Flash extending back the length of the tail. Trim tips to varying lengths.
Body: Tie in a white crosscut bunny strip and an equal length of pearl Palmer Chenille at the last tie-in point. Marry the two materials and palmer forward approximately 3 to 6 elongated wraps. Do not allow materials to bunch up.
Foam Head: Finish wrapping thread as a base for the foam head. Tie in a piece of white foam approximately 1/2 inch wide by 1 inch long. Poke a small hole in the middle of foam and insert eye of hook through hole. Move foam onto hook through the hole you made and dab a small amount of glue on thread wraps. Pull up bottom piece of foam and close thread over on top of it to lock into place. Push top piece of foam down and lock in with thread. Make a half dozen wraps tightening down the foam to produce a collar over front part of rabbit, tie off thread.
Eyes/Head: Glue on red holographic eyes on the tips of foam wings and lightly epoxy over the head and the eyes.

Rz's Mangrove Slider | Roan zumFelde

This pattern was inspired by the Dahlberg Diver and designed for casting into the mangroves for snook and redfish. The prototype for this fly resulted from a collaboration with Don Ingram. The fly exhibits an erratic motion when stripped and creates an attracting bubble trail in the water. It can be skipped under the mangroves without hanging up in the roots. This versatile pattern is effective for numerous species of gamefish, especially snook, redfish and largemouth bass. It is tied in six colors with the favorite being yellow and brown.

Hook: Mustad Signature Big Game Light, 1/0.
Thread: Yellow.
Tail: Tie in two large full plumes of yellow marabou at the bend of the hook, extending approximately two inches behind the hook bend. Tie in splayed two grizzly hackles on either side of the marabou and extending back the same length.
Flash: Tie in ten to twelve strands of gold Flashabou extending back slightly past the marabou. Apply a spot of glue.
Body: Tie in and spin the first clump of rust brown deer hair so that the tips extend back over marabou and hackles. Tie in a second clump of rust brown deer hair and spin. Trim to shape.
Collar: Tie in and spin a clump of red deer hair for collar. Tie in and spin a clump of yellow deer hair.
Finish: Trim bottom of fly flat with razor blade and tie in the 30-pound monofilament weed guard. Tie off thread and apply head cement.

Rz's Sparkle Shrimp | Roan zumFelde

This fly was designed to mimic a shrimp and be light enough so as not to spook fish in very shallow water. It was originally fished on the flats of Pine Island and Estero. A key to the fly's effectiveness is the positioning of the hackles and deer hair on the tail to enhance movement of the fly. This is a shrimp imitation that should be stripped slowly and with a hopping effect. It is tied in four colors: root beer, crystal, pink and chartreuse. The pattern has proven productive for snook, redfish and large trout. It has also taken bonefish in the Bahamas, Turks & Caicos, and the Keys.

Hook: Mustad 3407 or Big Game Light, size 2.
Thread: Fluorescent orange.
Tail: Start thread on shaft opposite the point of the hook and work back past bend creating an orange base of thread. Clip a few strands of brown bucktail mixed with white bucktail strands, about ten or fifteen strands in total. Tie strands onto bend of hook to the bend-length, about 2-inches. Tie in approximately ten strands of rainbow Flashabou on top of the bucktail and slightly forward onto the hook. Clip the ends at various lengths from the same size as the buck tail to about 1 inch long. Move thread to top of bend of the hook and tie in four orange grizzly hackles, two on each side and splayed, extending to a point about two inches off the back of hook.
Body/Eyes: Tie in medium root beer Estaz to the point where the hackles are tied in. Advance thread to where you will tie in the yellow dumbbell eyes. Leave about 1/4 inch of space in front of the eyes. The fly should ride inverted with the point facing upward. Wrap the Estaz around the hook, packed tightly, and pull it back each time you make a wrap so it lays back. Wrap to the eyes and tie off.
Finish: Make a thread base up to eye of hook and over eyes, add V weed guard if desired at this time. Glue thread wraps.

Rz's Tarpon Slayer | Roan zumFelde

Versions of this fly have been tied for quite some time. This particular pattern was inspired by Stewart's baitfish and Whitlock's baitfish flies. Badger hackles and multi-colored marabou have been key to the fly's effectiveness. The fly was originally tied to mimic a sand bream or mojarra minnow found on the beaches and flats all along the west coast of Florida. The fly is tied for both tarpon and snook in two sizes and six color combinations. This particular combination of colors is favored in the off-colored waters in the Everglades for Snook.

Hook: Owner SSW 4/0 or AKI for tarpon; Mustad 3407, 1/0 for snook.
Thread: Black.
Body/Tail: All materials are tied in behind the point of the hook. Start thread at point of hook and wrap a base back to bend of hook. Tie in one full plume of ginger marabou extending about 1 to 2 inches off back of hook. On either side of the marabou tie in three splayed rust brown badger hackles. Hackles should extend back at least 2 inches behind first tuft of marabou. Tie in 5 or 6 strands of tan Flashabou Accent down each side of hackles. Next tie in three whole plumes of rust or burnt orange marabou and measure them so they lay on top of the first plume of marabou and extend an equal length off the back of the hook. Allow the marabou to drape slightly over the hackles. Clip about eight strands of pearl Flashabou and tie in directly on top of last plumes of marabou, allowing them to drape over the top of the marabou and extend back almost as long as the hackles.
Back: Tie in a full plume of black marabou directly on the top of the fly. This batch of marabou should be almost as long as all the other tufts of marabou.
Head/Eyes: Finish head with black thread tapered down toward hook eye. Affix yellow prismatic eyes with glue and cover with a thin coating of epoxy.

Samson Mantis Shrimp | Jack Samson

This mantis shrimp is a relatively new pattern. The fly is fished most effectively by casting ahead of a fish, allowing it to sink several feet, and then retrieving quickly with one-foot long strips. It has proven effective on sea trout, redfish and large bonefish.

Hook: Eagle Claw 413, size 1/0.
Thread: Clear mono.
Clubs/Pincers: Tie in black, extra-small dumbbell eyes on outside of hook at the bend.
Tail: Tie a loop of chenille to the hook eye. Wind chenille and saddle hackle from eye back to the dumbbell.
Body: Wrap body area with mono thread, then palmer the hackle in the direction of the wrap.
Back: Attach and tie in suitable greenish skin material to back.
Mouth: Tie in green hackle fibers as mouth parts.
Antennae: Six strands of Betts Tailing Fibers.
Eyes: 1/8-inch stick-on molded eyes, yellow with black pupils.

Sanibel Special | Catch Cormier

Blind Pass between Sanibel and Captiva, Florida, was once a snook fisherman's heaven. The very first rattle flies had great success there. With the aid of Captain Steve Bailey, Catch designed a fly that combined elements of a Rattle Rouser, Charlie, and several popular snook flies, which are usually pearl or white. While it's been a proven killer for snook under lights, this fly has been very special for many other species in clear water, day or night.

Hook: Mustad 34007 stainless hook, size 2.
Body: Cut two sections of pearl Mylar tubing, each 1 1/2" long. Lay one section of Mylar along top of hook. This will create the Mylar body and tail. Secure the Mylar at the bend of hook, and then knot off (whip finish preferred). Slide glass rattle, 16mm long, into the Mylar, and then secure the front end of the Mylar with thread, sealing off the rattle.
Wing/Tail: Flip hook over, and lay the second section of Mylar on bottom of hook. This will create the wing. Make sure the ends of both sections are even. Tie off the wing section in front of eyes, and finish the head with a whip finish. Apply a couple of drops head cement to the lower half of the wing, then pinch it so the cement locks into the Mylar. This will keep the lower end from unraveling. Next, unravel the upper end of the wing, and also the tail. Finally, take a fine brush and apply thirty-minute epoxy to the body and head.

Sea Pup | Captain Lenny Moffo

This fly was originally used for snook and offshore and wreck-type fishing. Then it was tried on tarpon and has since developed into a very effective tarpon fly. Favorite colors are chartreuse, purple/black and tan, and white for snook. The pattern is also productive for many other species of gamefish.

Hook: Gamakatsu SC 15, 3/0.
Thread: 3/0.
Anti-Foul Guard: Tie in a piece of 12- or 15-pound monofilament and loop to form guard.
Tail: Tie in strands of holographic Flashabou and a magnum rabbit strip.
Eyes: Tie in plastic doll eyes.
Body: Tie in a regular rabbit strip and palmer up to the eyes.
Throat: Tie in small clump of rabbit.
Head: Finish head by tying in a section of Ultra Chenille and wrapping around eyes to form head.

Sea Rat | Lou Tabory

This fly is a hybrid of the Tabory Snake Fly and the Tabory Slab Fly. Designed as a generic pattern, it is effective, easy to tie, and is very productive for tarpon and snook. The fly imitates the profile of a mullet and other medium to large sized bait. When fished along the mangroves, employ an intermediate line and allow the fly to settle; hang near the roots before retrieving. Vary retrieve to mimic the movements of the particular baitfish. Select colors to match particular bait.

Hook: Mustad 34007, 1/0 to 3/0 or Tiemco 600SP or Daiichi 2546.
Thread: Match to head.
Tail: Six to eight saddle hackles tied at the hook's bend. Add some flash if preferred.
Wing: Tie several sections of marabou just ahead of the saddle hackle about half way back from the hook's eye.
Eyes: Tie in pewter eyes on the hook shank, splitting the distance from the marabou to the hook's eye.
Body Collar: Between the marabou and the eyes, spin deer-hair body hair to achieve a good flare. Point the tapered ends toward the rear of the fly. Trim hair around the eyes and taper to the back, leaving some longer hairs over the marabou.
Head: Wrap chenille around eyes and taper to the hook's eye. Collar and head should resemble a rat's head.

Seaducer | Homer Rhodes

This is an all-time favorite fly pattern. It was introduced in the 1940s as the Streamer Fly, a pattern designed for snook. It later became known as the Seaducer and has been used for many types of saltwater and freshwater gamefish. It is a very effective fly for many species of gamefish, especially when tied in red and white. The fly is both delicate and deadly since it can be presented to wary fish like snook, yet it has a seductive appeal that drives most other fish crazy. When fishing deep, try adding a set of barbell eyes to give an already enticing action a boost. In addition to the red and white version, try tying the Seaducer in blended yellow, green and chartreuse.

Hook: Stainless steel of choice, size to vary.
Thread: Red.
Tail: Tie-in two to three sets of matched white hackle.
Body: Tie in one or two large red hackles and palmer forward leaving enough room to shape an elongated head.
Head: Shape head with thread, whip finish and apply head cement.

Seatrout Bug | Captain Paul Strauss

The inspiration for this fly was weighted flies that mimic jigs but have a more substantial body and imitate crustaceans more closely. From that, the Seatrout Bug was developed. It is a versatile fly that can be tied in many sizes and weights, and can be used in very shallow water or deep grass flats. The fly rests with the hook point up so there is no need for a weed guard. This effective pattern has caught seatrout, pompano, flounder, jacks, ladyfish, bluefish and Spanish mackerel. The fly works best when allowed to sink slowly over grass beds and retrieved in short hops that simulate the movement of shrimp or other crustaceans.

Hook: Mustad, SS, size 1 or red Owner hook, size 1.
Thread: Matched to body.
Eyes: Tie-in either 1/36- or 1/24-ounce Eyes in red and yellow or black and yellow. Apply a few drops of epoxy on the eye thread.
Tail: Cover the hook shank with a thread base, and then tie-in hackle feathers splayed style.
Body: Starting behind the lead eyes, tie in medium root beer chenille for 1/2 the body. Tie in and wrap a few turns of small fluorescent orange chenille to finish the body.

Shad Dart Fly

Leigh West | Charlie Chapman

This fly resembles the popular Shad Dart commonly used by spin-fishermen. It is tied flashy by using pearl Mylar tubing for the body, and allowing some of the Mylar to unravel and trail behind the hook. Fish this fly in areas with current, on or just off the bottom. Allow the fly line to swing down current and retrieve the fly using short, quick strips.

Hook: Mustad 9672 or other 1X to 2X long freshwater streamer hook, #6. Pinch down barb.
Thread: Red floss or flat-waxed nylon.
Body: Cut a piece of pearl Mylar tubing about 4 inches long and remove the core string. Tie in, leaving about 1/2 inch of the Mylar tubing trailing behind the hook; Sparkle Braid or pearl Flashabou over wrapped with clear monofilament or medium vinyl rib. Wrap the Mylar forward around the shank to create a body, secure the Mylar behind the eyes with a few wraps of thread and trim away the excess.
Eyes: Wrap thread forward, and tie in the extra-small lead or brass dumbbell eyes approximately 1/4-inch behind the hook. Coat the exposed thread with head cement.
Wing: Tie in 10 strands of pearl Krystal Flash about 4 inches long; tie in the strands at the middle of their length and just behind the eyes. Fold the forward-facing half of the strands over and around the eyes so that they now point back, and secure them with a few wraps of thread. Cut the Krystal Flash skirt to about the same length as the trailing Mylar.
Head: Wrap the thread so that it is now in front of the eyes. Cut a 3-inch-long piece of chenille and secure one end to the hook. Using the chenille (hot color of choice), build up a small symmetrical head around the eyes and hook shank, secure the loose end, trim the excess chenille and finish the fly with a few whip finishes or half hitches. Coat the thread with head cement.

Sickle | Bill Murdich

This fly was developed as a subsurface version of the Top Sickle. The combination of head, collar and curly tail results in a compact fly that pushes water and creates vibration. The fly is especially effective in dingy or off-colored water, or for low-light conditions. The pattern has proven productive for snook, spotted sea trout and redfish, as well as jack crevalle and ladyfish.

Hook: Mustad 3407, size 2/0.
Thread: Medium brown Danville 3/0 monocord or UNI-Thread.
Weight: A large cone head is optional.
Tail: Attach a large, pumpkin/black flake Wapsi Fly Tail directly in front of the hook bend.
Collar: Tie in root beer Body-Fur on top of wraps that secure the tail, making three or four close wraps forward. Tie in gold Flashabou collar topping on top of Body-Fur, trimming flash slightly longer than fur.
Stripe: Attach a piece of gold Saltwater Flashabou on each side of the hook.
Body: Tie in root beer Estaz Grande on wrap to the hook eye. Trim the body into a blunt, bullet shape. Pull each piece of Saltwater Flashabou forward along the midline of the body and tie off at the hook eye.
Eyes: Glue 1/4-inch gold 3-D Molded Eyes on each side of the fly.
Finish: Coat the thread wraps with head cement.

Simple Shrimp

Captain John Hand

This is a classic, simple guides' fly, one that is effective and can be tied quickly. This pattern is designed to replicate shrimp.

Hook: Mustad 34007, size 4 or 6.
Thread: Clear, fine monofilament.
Body: Tie in thread from mid-shank back to hook bend. Tie in olive or root beer Estaz at the bend of the hook, then wrap back 3/4 to the hook eye. Wrap Estaz on 3/4 of the shank and tie down.
Weight: Wrap small lead wire behind hook eye and wrap thread over wire to secure.
Eyes/Wing: Turn hook over. Tie in long-stem monofilament eyes, followed by brown, tan or olive marabou, and olive or Everglades EP Fibers. The materials should be tied in about 1/4 way down hook shank from the eye.

Slab Fly | Lou Tabory

This fly was designed to match the wider profile of large baitfish that have a wide, flat, slab-like side. It can be tied to match a variety of white baits and pilchards. Fished on an intermediate or sinking line, the fly flutters slightly or rolls during the retrieve, and will track straight with a fast retrieve. It has proven effective on sandy beaches. Long pulls and pauses during the retrieve make the fly swim like a crippled baitfish.

Hook: Mustad 34007, 1/0 to 4/0 or Tiemco 600SP.
Thread: White.
Tail: Layered long bucktail or marabou, with some flash mixed in, three to six inches long. Make the tail wide from the side to suggest a large, flat-sided baitfish. Colors can vary to match particular baitfish.
Eyes: Either glass or pewter, keeping the eye near the hook shank, about one-third of the shank length from the hook's eye.
Head/Shoulders: Spin deer-body hair to form a large, flat-sided head. Hair is trimmed flush to the eye on both sides, leaving the top and bottom tapered longer to the tail.

Snake Fly | Lou Tabory

This fly was developed in the late 1970's to simulate the Eric Leiser Angus Fly. While originally fished for large Alaska rainbow trout, this pattern has emerged as an excellent tarpon fly. Its effectiveness is attributed to its buoyancy, action and adaptability. Varying the amount of materials used, this fly can replicate many slim to medium bodied baitfish. Fished with an intermediate line, the fly either noses up after each pull of the retrieve or it suspends in the water column. This is a very productive night pattern when fished on a floating line. The more successful colors are black, white, chartreuse, olive or blends of light olive or purple over white.

Hook: Mustad 34007 or 34011, size 2 to 2/0 or Daiichi 2546.
Thread: Black.
Tail: Ostrich herl or saddle hackle, tied about 1 1/2 to 11/4 inches long.
Wing: Two sections of marabou tied about halfway between the bend and the eye, leaving room for the head. Flash can be added between the marabou and tail.
Head: Spin and flare deer-hair body hairs. Use fat hairs for best results. Trim head flat on bottom, rounding the top. Leave some hair long for color. Head size and shape will vary with size and bulk of fly. The action and density of this fly depends on its head size.

Soft-Top | Captain Mike Starke

This fly was designed to take fish on or near the surface. The pattern utilizes soft closed-cell foam to form the head and top of the fly, giving the fly sufficient buoyancy and a soft lifelike feel. The Soft-Top can be tied with bucktail or Ultra Hair in a variety of colors to mimic a wide variety of baitfish. The imitation is effective for sea trout, Spanish mackerel, bonito, little tunny, redfish, snook and tarpon.

Hook: Mustad 34011 SS, sizes 2/0 to 4/0.
Thread: Danville's white flat waxed nylon, 1/0.
Tail: Tie a medium bunch of white bucktail at the rear of the hook shank, topped with 4 to 6 strands of pearl Flashabou. Fold the flash back over itself, making certain to extend the ends about 1/2 inch past the bucktail to form a flash tail.
Body: Tie on a length of large Mylar piping or tubing about 1/2 inch before the eye of the hook. Whip finish and cut the thread. Pull the piping back over itself and the hook shank, extending the piping to the bend of the hook. Re-attach the thread behind the eye of the hook.
Beard: Tie in a small bunch of white bucktail as a beard on the bottom of the hook shank. Allow the hairs to extend slightly past the hook point for more lifelike movement.
Wing: Complete the wing by tying on sparse and successive layers of purple, gray and white bucktail.
Flash Top: Add black rainbow Sparkle Flash on top.
Head: Cut a piece of soft foam for the head. Coat the underside with Super Glue. Center the foam, fold around the head and squeeze together.
Eyes: Mylar silver stick-on eyes.
Markings: Color the top of the head with a Sharpie pen. Use a red pen for gills.

Spring-Fall Half & Half

Paul Schwack, Jr.
Inspired by Bob Clouser and Lefty Kreh

This fly is a variation of the renowned Half & Half design by Bob Clouser and Lefty Kreh. The hybrid pattern modification evolved to take advantage of the best attributes of the Deceiver and Deep Minnow. It is effective for a wide range of gamefish throughout the Southeast and Gulf Coast.

Hook: SC15, 1/0 -3/0.
Thread: Monocord, white.
Eyes: Start by tying the eyes to the hook and work the thread to the bend. Use eyes appropriate for the hook size.
Tail: Tie-in a split tail of white saddle hackles, 3 or 4 feathers per side.
Body: Wrap a body of pearl Bodi Braid forward and tie off.
Wing: Invert the hook and tie-in a mix of about 6 hairs each of yellow, pink and purple bucktail. Mix in 4 or 5 strands of pearl Flashabou and add about 12 hairs of turquoise bucktail.
Top: Tie-in a small bunch of light gray bucktail.

Stealth Muddler | Tom Tripi

This unique Muddler variation was designed for redfish and brackish-water largemouth bass. The pattern is best fished on a 12-foot leader for optimal action. It can be tied weedless, if required. The best color combination for use as a searching pattern is all natural browns and tans—a preferred color combination that motivates bass to strike is olive with gold and red accents.

Hook: Any standard-shank salt-water hook or wide-gap bass hook.
Thread: Red Danville Plus.
Tail: Wrap hook with thread creating a foundation and build a tail with three stacked colors of bucktail. White is always on the bottom, a darker color is on the top. Tie-in a few strands of red Krystal Flash or similar flashy material on each side of the tail and between the layers of bucktail. Tie-in one or two long grizzly or similar saddle hackles, curved-side out. Black lace hackles dyed chartreuse are used in this colored version of the fly. Use a toothpick and dot acrylic paint along center of the hackle. Bright colors work best.
Body: Wrap body with the Sparkle Chenille and palmer a saddle hackle to a point just behind the eye. Tie-in bucktail and Krystal Flash on top of hook, just behind eye and dot with super glue. Clip off materials just behind eye to form a flat surface on top of hook shank. Stack a clump of deer body hair on the flat surface just formed, spin the deer hair on top of the hook only, pull hair back and repeat about three times until flat surface is filled with spun deer hair; shave the spun deer hair with a razor into a triangular shape, dot the wraps under the hook shank with super glue; then glue eyes on each side of cut surface.
Head: Tie-in and build a head of bucktail, Krystal Flash and spun deer-body hair.
Eyes: Your choice of stick-on eyes, sealed with super glue.

Stone Crab | Jack Samson

A modification of the older Jack's Fighting Crab, this is an excellent bonefish and permit pattern. It works well on other Southeast and Gulf Coast gamefish that feed on crabs. When fishing this fly, allow it to sink to the bottom and then retrieve with 6-inch strips.

Hook: Gamakatsu SC 15, size 4. Prepare the hook by slightly opening the bend to increase the gap. The fly is tied/constructed with the hook on a lateral plane rather than with the hook point down.
Thread: Olive.
Body: Stick one Velcro sticky-back coin, 5/8 inch, on the hook shank. Glue split shot or small section weighting material to the underside.
Legs: Lay in thin rubber band or Sili-legs.
Eyes: Lay in monofilament eyes; melt 100-pound mono.
Claws: Medium-wide rubber bands, knotted and tips painted.
Glue: Pour on Zap-A-Gap or Krazy Glue on the hook shank and underside of the Velcro coin to prevent turning.
Upper Body: Place a second Velcro coin on top of the first and squeeze together.
Finish: Color the crab green with a marking pen or leave the tan coloration.

Stu Apte Tarpon Fly

Originated by Stu Apte | Tied by A.J. Forzano

This classic tarpon fly, originated by one of the sport's legendary anglers, is also effective for many other species of gamefish. Size and color can vary to match prevalent baitfish.

Hook: Stainless steel to match size, typically 1/0 to 3/0.
Thread: Flat waxed nylon, hot orange.
Wing: Tie in one pair of wide, bright orange hackle feathers followed with a pair of bright yellow hackle feathers tied one on either side of the orange hackles. The hackle feathers are tied in the classic version splayed outward. All feathers are tied on to the rear of the hook shank at a point approximately opposite the hook point.
Collar: Tie in one bright orange hackle feather and one bright yellow hackle. Palmer each feather forward to form the collar, leaving adequate room for the elongated head.
Head: Form a head with the tying thread, and then apply a coat of head cement.

Stuck Up Bunny | Captain Chris Newsome

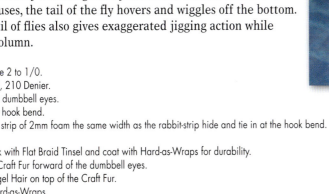

This design incorporates the addition of a foam strip to the tail end of a nose-weighted fly creating unique action. The foam makes the tail end of the fly float upward while the weight of the dumbbell eyes cause the nose of the fly to sink downward. By bouncing the fly across the bottom with short strips followed by pauses, the tail of the fly hovers and wiggles off the bottom. Foam added to the tail of flies also gives exaggerated jigging action while stripped mid-water column.

Hook: Eagle Claw 413, size 2 to 1/0.
Thread: Danville flat-waxed, 210 Denier.
Eyes: Tie in Wapsi Eye Balz dumbbell eyes.
Tail: Tie in rabbit strip at the hook bend.
Foam/Underbody: Cut a strip of 2mm foam the same width as the rabbit-strip hide and tie in at the hook bend. Glue the foam to the hide with Super Glue. Palmer a schlappen feather at the hook bend.
Body: Wrap the hook shank with Flat Braid Tinsel and coat with Hard-as-Wraps for durability.
Gills: Tie in a clump of red Craft Fur forward of the dumbbell eyes.
Wing: Tie in a clump of Angel Hair on top of the Craft Fur.
Finish: Coat thread with Hard-as-Wraps.

Stuck Up Deep Minnow | Captain Chris Newsome

The Stuck Up Deep Minnow is a variation of the Clouser Deep Minnow with the addition of a foam strip that extends towards the tail of the fly. The floatation makes the tail end of the fly buoyant counterbalancing the weight of the dumbbell eyes. The fly is designed to bounce across the bottom with short strips followed by long pauses. The fly excels during the pause because the foam strip induces a unique motion where the tail of the fly rises and hovers off the bottom. Use this fly is in cold-water conditions where fish are semi-dormant and an extra-slow presentation is required. It has proven effective for flounder, speckled trout, red drum and croaker.

Hook: Mustad S71SSS or equivalent standard-shank hook, size 1-2/0.
Thread: Danville flat wax, 210 denier.
Body: Tie-in 2mm foam strip at the hook bend and then tie the basic Clouser pattern using bucktail and Flashabou. The foam strip is cut from a 2mm-thick foam sheet. The dimensions of the strip can vary based on size of the fly. For size 1 to 2/0 flies, use a strip 3/16 inches wide and 1 1/2 times the length of the hook. Attach the foam strip at the bend of the hook shank so that strip is angled slightly up.
Eyes: Waspi Real Eyes Plus.

Sunrise Lepus

Tom Herrington/Reed Guice
Historic Ocean Springs Saltwater Fly Fishing Club

This durable, easy-to-tie fly is constructed of bonded rabbit strips for more body depth and action. It is especially effective for cobia and tarpon as well as large snook, jack crevalle and redfish. This pattern was used to take the Mississippi state fly-rod record cobia—a fish weighing in excess of 41 pounds.

Hook: Mustad 34007 or similar hook, size 2 through 6/0.
Thread: Danville flat waxed nylon, bright orange.
Body/Wing: Wrap thread from hook eye to end of shank. Tie-in barred red and yellow rabbit strip behind the hook eye and down the hook approximately 1/4-inch. Let strip hang in place. Measure a length of a second rabbit strip and punch hole in the strip so it can be threaded onto the hook shank. Slide the strip over hook point, pulling tightly. Both strips should be threaded and aligned with leather sides facing each other. Run a small bead of Fabric-Tac glue down the leather side of each strip, pressing together firmly.
Collar: Tie in orange saddle hackle immediately ahead of the tie-in point of the rabbit strips. Palmer to the hook eye. Secure with a whip finish.
Head: Build a head with thread and apply head cement.

Surface Shrimp | Captain Chris Newsome

This shrimp design incorporates a foam carapace that allows the fly to float.

Hook: Mustad S74S SS, Size 2 to 2/0.
Thread: UTS monofilament, .006.
Weed Guard: Tie in 20-pound monofilament along the bend of the hook to be used as a looped weed guard.
Legs: Create the walking legs by palmering a neck hackle at the bend in the hook shank.
Feelers: Create feelers by adding a small clump of bucktail on top of the palmered neck hackle.
Eyes: Add the mono eyes so that they extend off the rear of the hook.
Antennae: Add the antennae by tying in two strands of crystal mirror flash.
Carapace/Underbody: Cut the carapace for the shrimp fly out of sheet foam. The sheet-foam carapace should include a tail and pointed head to replicate the shape of a shrimp. The total length should allow for the tail to extend off from the hook eye and the head to extend off from the rear of the hook. For the underbody of the fly, tie in medium chenille at the rear of the hook. For the swimming legs of the fly, tie in a neck hackle at the rear of the hook. Tie in the foam carapace at the rear of the hook.
Body Segments: Wrap the chenille and neck hackle forward and secure the foam carapace with wraps of thread along the way to create the segmented body of the shrimp. Cut and secure the chenille and neck hackle once the hook eye is reached. Trim the palmered neck hackle barbs to create the short swimming legs of a shrimp.
Finish: At the hook eye, tie in the loose end of mono to complete the looped weed guard.

Tarpon Bunny | Enrico Puglisi

This variation of the highly effective EP Tarpon Streamer embodies dual tails of rabbit strip and a shaped, triangular EP fiber head. The four-inch orange version of this fly has proven especially effective.

Hook: Gamakatsu CS 15, size 3/0 or 2/0.
Thread: Mono, .004.
Tail: Tie in two lengths of orange rabbit-fur strips, skin side down.
Body: Using black EP fibers build a layered body and wing by tying the fibers on the shank in successive layers. Begin at a point approximately half way down the hook shank and tie-in the fibers on the top and bottom of the shank. Layer fibers as you tie. Add in a small amount of fine pearl Magic Flash.
Head: Tie in EP fibers and stack tight, building a small triangular head.
Eyes: Affix black on yellow, 6mm plastic eyes.
Finish: Apply markings to tips of rabbit-fur strips with a permanent marker.

Tarpon Crab | Enrico Puglisi

Tarpon and crabs go perfectly together. This fly design has become increasingly popular and effective. It can be tied with extended and knotted EP fibers as claws or with rabbit-fur strips. While it is tied in many different color patterns, tan, purple/orange and olive have proven very productive.

Hook: Gamakatsu CS 15, size 3/0.
Thread: Mono, .004.
Claws: Tie in a set of purple EP Crab Claws or rabbit-fur strips.
Eyes: Tie in a pair of EP Crab Eyes on top of the hook shank at the hook bend.
Legs: Tie in four rubber legs, purple with orange tips.
Body: Using purple EP fibers build a layered body and wing by tying the fibers on the shank in successive layers. Begin at a point approximately at the hook bend tie forward toward the eye. Lay in fiber bunches as you tie. About half way down the body tie in a V-shaped wedge of orange EP fibers. Continue adding purple bunches of fibers. Tie off thread and whip finish. Cut and shape the body into a triangular form.

Tarpon Shrimp Fly | Captain Nick Angelo

Shrimp-style patterns are very popular for tarpon. This fly is a modified shrimp design used for "laid up" or feeding tarpon. The fly is often used where there is floating grass, and the fish are beneath it, waiting to grab a meal off the surface. The fly resembles food with its natural coloration, and the undulating trait of marabou is very effective. Try to present the fly a few feet in front of or to the side of feeding tarpon, and slowly drag the fly in front of the fish. Once a tarpon appears keyed on the fly, keep teasing it by the fly moving the fly forward slowly. If you see the tarpon eat, remember to keep stripping the fly until the line gets tight. When the line is tight, strike.

Hook: Owner Aki, 2/0.
Thread: Flat-waxed nylon, tan.
Tail: Tie-in brown marabou about two inches in length.
Flash: Fold over and tie in three lengths of copper Krystal Flash. The flash should extend 1/2 inch beyond the marabou.
Eyes: Tie-in the monofilament EP shrimp eyes, making them about an inch in length.
Body: Tie-in ginger rabbit strip, and palmer it around the hook. Tie-in the brown saddle hackle and then the tan chenille. Palmer the chenille forward around the shank until you reach the eye of the hook. Palmer the hackle forward through the chenille. Secure the hackle and chenille and whip-finish the fly.
Finish: Make a number of finishing wraps with thread and apply Hard as Nails.

Tarpon Tantalizer | Captain Paul Dixon

This fly is effective for hard-to-feed ocean tarpon. It can be tied in a variety of colors.

Hook: Gamakatsu SL12S, 2/0 or 1/0.
Thread: Chartreuse, 2/0.
Tail: Tie-in one tail hackle flat-wing style, color of choice.
Body: Tie-in a small length of Krystal Chenille and a hackle feather. Wind the chenille to a point immediately behind the hook eye and then follow by winding the hackle forward to the same point. Whip finish. Add a dab of head cement to the base of the tail. This will prevent it from wrapping around the hook when casting.

Tarpon Toad | Gary Merriman

The design of this fly allows for keeping it in front of tarpon for extended visibility since it does not sink as fast as other patterns. It is based upon the Harry Spears bonefish pattern, the Tasty Toad, and has successfully scored numerous Keys Tarpon Tournament victories. It is fished with a variety of stripping techniques depending on the reaction of tarpon. The pattern has also proven effective for other species of gamefish and can be tied in many sizes and colors.

Hook: Owner 5180.
Thread: UTC 140, 3/0.
Fouling Guard: Tie in a small looped section of stiff monofilament.
Tail: Tie-in length of 1/8-inch Zonker strip, tied fur side down. Add strands of Krystal Flash.
Collar: Tie-in a marabou as a collar.
Head: Tie-in a crab-style head using approximately five to six strips of floating poly yarn. When fly is complete, trim poly yarn to shape.
Eyes: Tie-in a set of monofilament eyes and finish off thread.

Tarpon Toy | Captain Lenny Moffo

This fly originated as a result of using a rabbit strip rather than bucktail or squirrel tail as a collar on a tarpon fly. It worked well and the fly has proven very effective.

Hook: Gamakatsu SC 15, size 3/0.
Thread: Monofilament, flat waxed.
Platform: Tie in brown bucktail.
Flash: Tie in Flashabou at the rear of the hook.
Tail: Tie-in large neck hackles, splayed.
Collar: Tie-in rabbit strip and palmer forward.
Head: Build classic elongated tarpon-fly head. Use the flat waxed thread for the head.
Eyes: Affix eyes of choice and apply a light coating of epoxy to the head and eyes.

Terminator Crab | Captain Rich Waldner

This crab fly was designed to be cast easily, with less bulk than traditional crab patterns, yet retain the desire crab-like profile. The fly also incorporates flash that Louisiana bull red and black drum respond well to.

Hook: Mustad Signature Series stainless steel, size 1/0.
Thread: Any suitable thread.
Eyes: Tie-in barbell eyes on the topside of the hook shank so the hook rides point up.
Tail: Tie-in strands of Unique Hair and Krystal Flash, colors of choice.
Body: Build a body by tying in five separate bundles of Unique Hair using figure-eight wraps. Trim the hair to shape and coat the body with Devcon 2-Ton Epoxy. Add sprinkles of glitter material to the outer edges of the body, forming an outline. This epoxy has a 30-minute working time with a two-hour setting time.
Weedguard: Install a 25-pound monofilament weedguard.
Finish: Epoxy the barbell eyes and head area.

The Big Ugly

Tom Herrington
Historic Ocean Springs Saltwater Fly Fishing Club

This fly was designed to enhance inherent action and sound. It is a hybrid tie of a large Zonker or Rattle Rouser, effective on king mackerel and other large offshore gamefish, especially around oilrigs. The fly can be fished without much stripping, just allow it to move and undulate in the current with periodic twitches. The pattern can also be tied in smaller sizes and different colors for other species of fish.

Hook: Mustad 34011, size 3/0.
Thread: Danville flat waxed nylon, hot orange.
Eyes: Tie in large red dumbbell eyes 1/2 inch from the eye and wrap the entire hook shank.
Body: Tie in gold Mylar tubing (1 1/2 times the length of the hook shank) tightly along the shank and wrap thread back to the eyes.
Rattle: Insert a large glass rattle into the tubing and secure the rear-facing end behind the hook. Epoxy entire Mylar tube. Let dry.
Tentacles: Tie in 4 to 6 silicone gold to hot-orange-tip legs behind the eyes. The legs should be the length of the hook.
Dorsal: Measure a hook length of orange rabbit strip and punch a hole through the forward portion of the skin. Push the rabbit strip down the Mylar, pulling it tightly. Secure at the hook eye.
Head: Build a head with thread. Whip finish and add head cement.

The Birds | Glenn Mikkleson

This is a hybrid pattern that performs well in shallow water and flats situations where fish feed on a variety of crustaceans. It is especially effective for species like redfish and striped bass. Two preferred color combinations are copper/brown and olive/grizzly.

Hook: SS, size 1/0, 1.
Thread: Color to match body.
Eyes: Tie-in gold barbell eyes on the top of the hook shank leaving enough room for a head. Fly rides hook point up.
Body/Wings: The entire fly is tied at a point behind the hook eye, leaving enough room for a small head. The hook shank is left bare. Tie in a base of bucktail and strands of Krystal Flash. Tie-in splayed two matched sets of hackles (four total hackles).
Head: Build a small head with thread and apply a coating of epoxy covering the head and the barbell eyes.

The Bloodline Clouser | Captain George Beckwith, Jr.

This fly is a variation of the Clouser Deep Minnow. It incorporates a "bloodline" to enhance contrast. Its best attracting qualities occur when tied with three colors. Pink, red and chartreuse are favored colors and allow the fly to stand out. Black, brown, red and yellow are best for dirty water.

Hook: Mustad 34007, size to match fly.
Thread: Chartreuse.
Eyes: Barbell eyes, silver or gold.
Body/Wing: Tie this fly in standard Clouser fashion, adding the "bloodline" feather or hair as a mid-line in the fly. White bucktail is used for the underbelly and a darker shade of hair for the topping. Flash is added to the wings as desired.

The Fabulous Floyd | Drew Chicone

This shrimp-style fly was designed for bonefish on the grass flats of Florida and the Bahamas. It was named for Floyd M. Dean and is tied in pink, tan or white.

Hook: Any stainless steel, sizes 2, 4, 6. Hook bent slightly upward.
Thread: Pink 3/0 or color to match body color.
Weight: Tie in a double piece of .025 lead wire on the underside of the hook.
Antennae: Tie-in two strands of pink Krystal Flash slightly down the bend of the hook.
Eyes: Tie-in 20-pound monofilament eyes on top of the antennae.
Body/Legs: Tie-in tips of salmon-colored marabou plume just past the eyes leaving the entire plume attached. At the same tie-in point, tie-in the tip of another marabou plume and palmer it two wraps for legs. Tie off and clip excess. Advance thread to hook eye. Palmer first plume toward the hook eye, covering the wire to create the body. Tie off.
Tail: Leave a 1/4-inch section of plume on top of the hook as tail.
Shell: Puncture the clear scud back with hook at a point about two-thirds its length and wrap, tying in the scud back for the shell. Whip finish behind the legs.

The Ficco Furbee | Dennis Ficco

This fly blends techniques developed by Enrico Puglisi with materials and colors used in Henry Cowen's Baitfish patterns. The key ingredient in this design is the use of rabbit. The fly has proven effective for dolphin, striped bass, sea trout, false albacore, Spanish mackerel and peacock bass.

Hook: Gamakatsu SP11-3L-3H, size 1/0.
Thread: Danville fine monofilament.
Loop: Attach a rearward loop of 50-pound-test monofilament.
Weight/Body: Tie-in and wind lead-free wire around the hook shank and cover the wire up to the hook eye with flat pearl Body Braid.
Upper Body: Tie-in four or five small clumps of white Flash & Slinky Kinky Fiber on the top portion of the fly, ending 1/2 inch back from the hook eye.
Lower Body: Trim to size a white rabbit Zonker strip and pierce the skin with the hook point, leaving two inches or more beyond the hook bend. Push the end of the Zonker strip through the monofilament loop to prevent fouling. Tie down the rabbit 1/2 inch back from the hook eye on the lower portion of the fly.
Throat: Tie-in strands of hot pink Fluorofibre in front of the Zonker.
Finish/Eyes: Tie-in additional Flash & Slinky on top and white Flash & Slinky on the bottom of fly. Trim fly to desired profile and affix 3-D Molded Eyes with glue.
Optional: A rattle can be inserted into body if desired.

The Glades Toad

Matti Majorin | Inspired by the Gary Merriman Toad

This smaller and lighter variation of the original Toad is best used for smaller tarpon and can be tied in a broad pattern of colors. Three color variations are shown: orange, minnow, gray and tan. Tied with the inclusion of a very small amount of Angel Hair, these patterns are best suited when waters are slightly off-color, in the backcountry or even after a few windy days. For laid-up tarpon, cast low, aim for the "lips" and just twitch. The pattern can motivate explosive strikes.

Hook: Tiemco 600s Owner Mosquito Hook/Owner Aki hooks, sizes 1/0—2/0.
Thread: Danville's Flat Wax nylon to match fly colors.
Tail: Marabou Blood sparse.
Tail Flash: A few Angel Hair fibers mixed in, typically blue or green.
Collar: Grizzly marabou feathers; use softest feathers with the most breathing movement. Two or three feathers should cover entire shank and circumference of fly.
Body: McFlylon figure-eight wrapped along shank Merkin-style. Add a few strands of Angel Hair to McFlylon fibers. Angel Hair should be very sparse. Body should be trimmed to a narrow profile.
Eyes: Small or medium black mono eyes, tied figure-eight near hook eye.

The Mean Green Weenie | Captain Russ Shirley

This fly was originally designed for the Tampa Bay area, Chassahowitzka, Bayport and Boca Grande. It was patterned after the Chaz the Yellow Weenie fly and has proven effective over darker grass bottom areas.

Hook: Mustad 3407 SS size 3/0 or Owner 4/0.
Thread: Green flat-waxed nylon.
Tail: Tie in a 20-pound hard-nylon loop on top of the hook, near the rear. Divide six equally sized green or grizzly cock saddle hackles. Face each bunch outwards and high-tie on top of hook above the hook's barb. Coat feathers from tie-in spot back for approximately one inch with Flexament or Softex. This keeps feather wrapping to a minimum.
Collar: Once coated feathers are dry, add a sparse green squirrel tail collar.
Head/Eyes: Build-up a head with thread, affix Mylar stick-on eyes and coat with epoxy; turn until dry.

The Mohawk | Tom Tripi

This fly was designed specifically for redfish and brackish-water largemouth bass. The Mohawk has developed into a very productive and durable pattern that can be tied in any color combination or used with a gold or silver body. All materials for this fly are tied on the down-bending curve of the hook shank.

Hook: Mustad 34007, size 2 to 3/0, 2x to 4x-long, or a light wire, wide-gap worm hook for a lighter version that nearly floats as it is retrieved.
Thread: Danville Plus or similar thread, in a color scheme of other materials.
Tail: Tie in Flashabou, 3-inch fibers of Krystal Flash, hen hackle flared out and marabou, all in a color scheme of choice.
Body/Wing: Wrap hook shank with thread from the eye to the start of the bend as a foundation for the body. Apply a small amount of super glue to the wraps. Slip 3/4-inch-wide gold Mylar tubing that has been hot-pressed flat onto the hook shank, from the eye back towards the bend, covering just the edge of the tail materials. Tie in a 1/4-inch-wide Zonker rabbit strip upside down, securing at a point behind the eye and at a point near the top of the hook bend. Lift the rabbit strip slightly and apply a dot of super glue under the strip to secure it to the Mylar.
Legs: An optional pair of rubber legs can be tied near the front portion of the Mylar body for additional action.
Eyes: Tie in red or pearl dumbbell eyes at the rear point of the Mylar body, on the curve of the hook bend.

The Savannah Fly | Captain Scott Wagner

This fly was created to replicate the appeal of a gold spoon for redfish on the mud flats, and in dirty or clear water. Although primarily tied for reds this fly has enjoyed success with trout, stripers, false albacore, ladyfish, flounder and snook. It is a versatile and easy-to-tie pattern.

Hook: Style and size of choice.
Thread: White.
Tail: A substantial clump of supple gold flash material tied in immediately ahead of the hook bend.
Body: Root beer Krystal Flash tied in near the hook bend and wound forward to a point immediately behind the hook eye.
Head: Build a small head with thread, tie off and finish.

The Sluggo Fly | Captain Dino Torino

As the name implies this fly was designed to replicate the highly productive Slug-Go plastic baits that are effective for many inshore and offshore gamefish species. This feathered facsimile is easy to tie and produces results.

Hook: Mustad 34011, long-shank, size 4/0.
Thread: White flat waxed nylon or monocord.
Tail: Tie-in long length of white or chartreuse bucktail, followed by two white saddle hackles tied in and splayed outward on either side of the bucktail.
Body: White foam under large pearl EZ Body. The EZ Body is inserted over the hook shank. Cover the body with a light coating of Softex.
Lip: White foam tied in and trimmed to shape.

Flies to Take to Heaven

By Angelo Peluso

Oh no, is this it?
Surrounded by all great fish...
Without the right fly!

That haiku is entitled "Hell Hole" and reflects one of my greatest fears. I wrote it a while back for a haiku contest while contemplating what fishing in the hereafter might be like. It won! So I guess there are other fly-fishermen out there who feel the same as I do. When my judgment day comes and I have the chance to meet my maker at the pearly gates, I wonder if I will have the right saltwater flies with me to use throughout all eternity?

A Thousand Flies... Over the course of researching and writing three fly-fishing books, two of which are fly patterns books, I've had the good fortune of talking with literally hundreds of fly-fishing guides, captains, and professional and amateur fly-tiers from Maine to the Texas Gulf Coast. I've interviewed some of the best fly-fishing and fly-tying talent on this planet and I've examined literally 1,400-plus flies, including the best saltwater flies this side of heaven. Some of those patterns were original designs but most were innovative modifications of tried and true designs, each in its own way a marvelous creation. Those patterns got me thinking about the flies I've seen, tied and fished over the years in saltwater and freshwater that might be the ones I take with me into eternal angling bliss. I debated putting aside some of my own personal go-to creations that have served me well over the years, but decided against that. I also contemplated two dozen of my favorite working patterns tied by others I've come to know over the years, but decided against that as well. I also pondered taking a pile of patterns from this book. I thought long and hard about this dilemma but no matter which flies I felt I might like to take along on that heavenly ride, only a select handful continually floated to the top of my list. In many respects, these flies are classic, household names—and for good reason. They catch tons of fish anywhere they are fished and they have endured the test of time. While many of my own productive ties are variations and modifications of these patterns I decided to go with the un-altered originals. But for all practical purposes and with a bit of tweaking of size and color, any of these patterns will be extremely effective on most gamefish throughout the Southeast and Gulf Coast. So here are my choices for the flies I will place in a fly box that will take the grand journey with me—a baker's dozen plus one I wouldn't be caught dead without.

Lefty's Deceiver

One of the greatest highlights of my angling career was a note I received from fly-fishing legend, Lefty Kreh, offering kind words on my book, *Saltwater Flies of the Northeast.* His note gave me an excuse to call him to extend my thanks for the gracious comments. I mentioned to Lefty that one of the things I want included as part of the fishing gear I take with me to the hereafter is an adequate supply of Lefty's Deceivers, in all sizes and colors. I told him I couldn't imagine entering The Gates without them. Truth be told, there is simply no better style of fly on earth than the Kreh creation. In Lefty's own words, the Deceiver is a "style of pattern," rather than a singular fly. It is versatile, adaptable and just about every fish that swims loves it. When pressed to choose but one fly they could count on in a pinch, many saltwater fly-anglers across the globe select the venerable Lefty's Deceiver or some fitting variation. The fly is time-tested and remarkably effective. As a pattern, it has accounted for more fish than any other fly design in the era of modern fly-fishing. It is simply one of the greatest patterns of all time. Most of us who fish the Deceiver have tweaked it a bit to suit our own preferences and needs, and that is the true beauty of the fly—it lends itself to tinkering.

Clouser Deep Minnow

Bob Clouser originally created his world-famous *minnow* for smallmouth bass in his home water, the Susquehanna River in Pennsylvania. The pattern's reputation grew exponentially as its success grew, measured not only in terms of numbers of fish caught but also in the diversity of species succumbing to its effective design. Like the Deceiver, the Clouser has

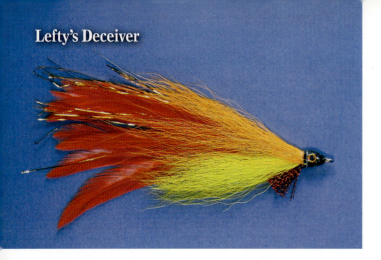
Lefty's Deceiver

Clouser Deep Minnow

Half and Half

Crease Fly

taken most all fish it has been cast to, both in freshwater and saltwater. In many respects—and as is the case with most all truly great flies—there is simplicity in its design. Fundamentally, the fly is an upside-down hair pattern with a wing, some flash and a pair of barbell eyes set like those of a predecessor, the Crazy Charlie. But the genius is in the design and the way in which the components are assembled. It is one of those flies that makes you say, "Now, why didn't I think of that?" The Clouser, as it has come to be known, is a very versatile fly, adaptable to size, color and profile preferences. While there is actually one original and specific tying recipe for the fly, it has proven successful in many modified forms.

Half and Half

When one considers the enormous success of both the Deceiver and the Clouser, it only stands to reason that a hybrid of the two flies would double your productivity.

The fly gets its name because it is tied half as a Deceiver and half as a Clouser, utilizing the best attributes of both patterns. Interestingly, it was both Kreh and Clouser that first fused their original flies into the new crossbreed pattern. Like its parent flies, the Half and Half is so effective, it too has spawned an entire genre of flies patterned off its design. While purely an impressionistic fly pattern, the hybrid leaves plenty of room for creative tinkering to suit various fishing conditions. Personally, I like to tie mine heavily weighted—with oversized dumbbell eyes—so that it can be used as a dredging pattern when fish lay deep in currents or simply near the bottom in a neutral mood. Tied in larger sizes, this is a terrific big-fish fly.

Crease Fly

The world renowned Crease Fly is the creative genius of Captain Joe Blados. While all tiers strive to produce flies that are new and different, in reality, very few ever accomplish that goal. Most *new* flies are typically designs that represent variations of existing and proven patterns. But every once in a long while, we witness true innovation in the art of fly-tying, a fly design or technique that is so unique it changes the way we fish, and fundamentally changes the sport. One such innovative design technique led Joe Blados to create the Crease Fly, a pattern intended to mimic the profile of prolific immature menhaden, otherwise known as peanut bunker. While originally conceived for the inshore fishery of the North Fork of Long Island, this fly has an established track record and devotees wherever it has been fished around the globe. It has become a staple in the fly box of many Southeast and Gulf Coast anglers to replicate small, wide-bodied baitfish. I have witnessed the range of the Crease Fly's effectiveness from silver salmon in Alaska to the surface-feeding gamefish of the Yucatan Peninsula and all stops in between, both in saltwater and fresh. It is also a very effective offshore pattern. The Crease Fly can be fished on the surface, under the surface, fast, slow and any speed in between, and it simply drives fish crazy. I am going to have to pack extras of this fly because Saint Peter is going to want one soon after he sees what it can do!

Mikkleson Epoxy Baitfish

Glen Mikkleson is one of the best fly-tiers in the universe when it comes to patterns crafted with epoxy or acrylics. He has made tying epoxy flies an art form. The generic Mikkleson Epoxy Baitfish is one of the best small to mid-sized baitfish patterns ever designed for gamefish anywhere on the planet. It is a very versatile fly, and when tied properly, it is well balanced, foul resistant, and extremely durable. It can handle its fair share of toothy critters as well. There are plenty of imitations of this fly on the market but none come close to the effectiveness of Mikkleson's original. The fly's design suggests any number of small to medium-size baitfish that are prevalent throughout the coastal Unites States. The pattern can be tied in numerous color combinations and is extremely effective for a wide range of gamefish species that prey upon white bait and rain bait.

Mikkleson Epoxy Baitfish

Ray's Fly

Perfection through simplicity of design is the best way to describe Ray's Fly, a creation of Ray Bondorew. This extremely versatile and effective pattern is ideal for replicating a wide assortment of small to mid-sized baitfish. The fly's origins extend back to the rocky shoreline of Narragansett, Rhode Island. The primary driver behind the fly's design was a desire to match the olive, yellow, pearl and dark back coloration of the Atlantic silverside. Ray's Fly is one of the most effective Atlantic silverside patterns of all time. I am often surprised that even seasoned fly-anglers are not familiar with this Rhody phenomenon. When dressed sparsely, it performs exceptionally well as a slender baitfish imitation. If I have room in my fly wallet, I might also sneak in another of Bondorew's flies: the Bondorew Bucktail. This outstanding performer is often used in tandem with Ray's Fly, making for a very effective combination.

Ray's Fly

Brooks Blonde

Joe Brooks' hair-wing streamer fly has stood the test of time and has been the basis upon which many other "hair" flies have been crafted. It is a classic fly pattern and one of the first true saltwater flies to emerge during the 1950s. While the original tie has accounted for many varied species of freshwater and saltwater fish, the pattern lends itself well to numerous variations and enhancements. Very simply tied, the fly sports a tail, and wing of bucktail combined with a body of silver tinsel. The head is typically built with black thread. It can be tied in most any color combination and size but the original versions were tied as the Platinum Blonde, Honey Blonde, Black Blonde, Strawberry Blonde and Argentine Blonde. Fished with a greased-line technique, the fly drifts with the current while mending the line; this pattern will yield results for salmon, trout and steelhead.

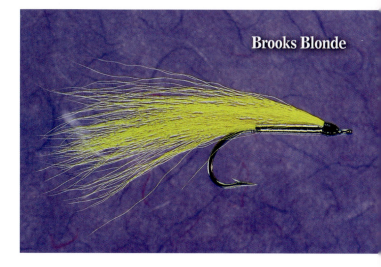

Brooks Blonde

Flatwing

The origins of this fabulous fly are attributed in part to the coloration of Ray's Fly and the flat-wing tying concepts of New England's Ken Abrames and Bill Peabody. The combination of those two features resulted in a fly that can replicate an array of baitfish and be tied in any number of productive sizes. The fly fishes and casts exceptionally well and the flat-wing hackle design adds an illusion of body mass when viewed from a fish's upward-looking perspective. The fly is a favorite among striped bass anglers and it is a wonderful pattern to experiment with, varying size and color to match prevalent baitfish. This is also a great pattern to swing in currents using greased line mending techniques. The fly has a significant amount of intrinsic movement, making its design most appealing to gamefish.

Flatwing

Tabory Snake Fly

The heavenly fly angler needs at least one eel-like pattern in his or her arsenal. None is better suited to that task than Lou Tabory's Snake Fly. The pattern was developed in the late 1970s to simulate the Leiser Angus Fly. The effectiveness of the fly is attributed to its buoyancy, action and

Tabory Snake Fly

Loving Bass Fly

Seaducer

Jiggy

adaptability. By varying the amount of materials used, the fly can be tied slim- to medium- to full-bodied, to match the profile of the available bait. It can be fished on a floating or sinking line. The more effective colors are black, white chartreuse, olive or an assortment of blended colors. This is a great fly for big fish seeking a big meal and it works equally well fished seductively on the surface. Variation of this fly are effective for tarpon. And if you happen to get detoured "downstairs", it will work well with the serpents!

Loving Bass Fly

Tom Loving created this classic fly some time around 1922 for both brackish water largemouth bass and striped bass. Not only is it still an effective largemouth fly but it is also a very productive pattern for many Northeast, Southeast and Gulf Coast gamefish. Tom Loving was one of the true pioneers of saltwater fly-fishing. The Loving Bass fly is a design that has bridged many generations of saltwater fly-anglers. Any fly that has endured throughout all those years and remains as effective as the day it was first tied certainly deserves a spot in any fly wallet.

Seaducer

This is one of my all-time favorite fly patterns. It is the creation of Homer Rhodes and was introduced in the 1940s as the Streamer Fly, a pattern designed for snook. It later became known as the Seaducer and has been used for many types of saltwater and freshwater gamefish. It is a very effective striped bass fly, especially when tied in red and white and fished in rips where squid are present. I refer to the fly as being delicate and deadly since it can be presented to wary fish like snook, yet it has a seductive appeal that drives most other fish crazy. When fishing deep, I like to add a set of barbell eyes that give an already enticing action some additional jigging motions. In addition to the red-and-white version, I like tying the Seaducer in blended yellow, green and chartreuse.

An all-black tie is a terrific nighttime fly.

Jiggy

Very few lures are as consistently effective as a bucktail jig. The Jiggy was created by world-renowned fly angler and fly-tier, Bob Popovics, as a fly version of a small jig. The Jiggy is another of those pattern styles that is often modified and varied for no other reason than it reliably catches fish. It is another example of a simple yet durable and effective tie. The weighted head of the Jiggy enables it to be fished in the lower portions of the water column and depending on depth, close to or right on the bottom. Pauses in strips allow the fly to flutter and move like a jig. The fly presents a slim profile and can tied in a range of bait sizes and colors. Bounced along the bottom, few fish can resist the temptation to strike the Jiggy.

Marabou Bunny

One of the most effective flies that I have ever fished anywhere I've traveled is a hybrid pattern that blends the best features of marabou and bunny, two tantalizing and seductive fly-tying materials. My arsenal of flies is replete with an array of colorful flies tied either material or a combination of both. I would not venture to a tidal coho stream without a sampling of each style of fly and at least several hybrid patterns in multiple colors. The effectiveness of a marabou and bunny combo pattern is legendary. In my own experiences the range of gamefish taken on that style of fly runs the gamut: bonefish, redfish, snook and tarpon to striped bass, sea trout, weakfish, bonito, Spanish mackerel, salmon and small tunas. Within the

fly-fishing community this combo pattern seems to have developed naturally without any one single tier credited with the creation. For avid fly-anglers and tiers it really doesn't take too much of a leap of faith to marry bunny and marabou. They are perfect together.

Gibbs Bucktail (Streamer)

Harold Gibbs created his now famous streamer to replicate the Atlantic silversides, a choice menu item for Northeast gamefish. The origins of the fly date back to approximately 1946. Originally tied with a white goat hair wing and blue swan feathers for flanks the fly was later modified by Gibbs using more resilient bucktail. Overtime the pattern was varied even further to match peanut bunker (juvenile menhaden) and immature alewives. It can also serve to replicate many species of small baitfish indigenous to the Southeast and Gulf Coast. The Gibbs streamer has not only accounted for its fair share of striped bass but numerous other species as well. Given its design simplicity and materials, modification to color and length enable the fly to be tied in a manner to match a wide variety of baitfish. The Gibbs Streamer was such a prominent fly of the time that the Mustad Hook Company was motivated to produce a hook specifically designed to complement its features. This is another terrific pattern to swing in currents for bright salmon.

So there you have it, my personal heavenly selection of some classic and some modern flies. Hopefully, I will continue using them right here on earth for a long time to come. I am sure I will also smuggle in a few packages of flies from this book as well.

Marabou Bunny

Gibbs Bucktail (Streamer)

Tidal Shrimp | Captain Edward Wasicki

This fly was originally developed for striped bass feeding in tidal creeks flowing from salt ponds and marshes. The pattern is effective as a grass-shrimp pattern for many southeast gamefish.

Hook: Mustad 3407, size 2.
Thread: Tan monocord.
Eyes: Tie-in small, black plastic eyes.
Body/Tail: Tie-in a section of translucent tan Crystal Chenille at the rear of the hook. Tie in a bunch of pearl Krystal Flash over the chenille, leaving a small segment of fibers extending behind the hook point as a tail.
Carapace/Body: Wind the chenille forward and tie off at a point behind the eyes. Trim chenille on top of hook shank. Bring the strands of flash forward over the top of the chenille forming a carapace, and extend to a point forward of the eyes. Tie off with several wraps of thread. Apply head cement.

Tomoka Mullet Fly

Captain Doug Sinclair | Inspired by Ken Bay

This fly has been a work in progress and is very effective for jacks and bluefish. Tied with a red and/or green head combination the pattern becomes a very productive snook fly.

Hook: Mustad 34007, size 1/0 or 2/0.
Thread: Size G, gray, with red used to finish fly.
Tail: Tie-in a pair of long white saddle hackles, splayed, followed by a pair of splayed barred hackles. Tie-in strands of pearl Krystal Flash.
Body/Head: Stack and spin deer hair for the body and head, leaving strands of hair extending beyond the midsection. The body is a blend of several colors: tan, chartreuse and brown. The head is red with a pink collar. Shape the body and head to size.
Eyes: Affix eyes with adhesive or epoxy into slots formed in the head.

Top Sickle | Bill Murdich

This pattern is a version of a top-water lure used for largemouth bass. It has also proved successful for a variety of inshore saltwater species. The fly is unique in that the surface commotion occurs at the rear of the fly instead of at the front. The fly is tied in white, tan, chartreuse, orange and black.

Hook: Mustad 34011, size 1/0.
Thread: White 3/0 Danville monocord or UNI-Thread.
Tail: Attach a large Wapsi Fly Tail, white with silver flake.
Body: Beginning at bend of hook, tie in white Crystal Chenille and wind it half way up the hook shank toward the hook eye, forming the rear half of the body. Tie off and cut excess. Tie-in red Crystal Chenille at the point where the white ends. Wind forward to the hook eye. Stop about 1/4-inch before the eye and tie off.
Top: Cut strip of gray foam about 1/2 inch wide. Trim point at one end. This end is attached to the hook. Tie in the foam with the point facing to the rear, and the long end of the strip extending in front of the fly.
Bottom: With hook point now facing up prepare a strip of white foam and tie-in to match the gray. Tie-off thread and cut. Transfer thread to bend of hook. Pull gray foam strip all the way back to hook bend and secure with thread. Repeat process with white foam.
Eyes: Glue on 3/8-inch silver or white 3-D Molded Eyes or 7.5 mm Plastic Eyes (with stem).
Finish: Coat the thread wraps with head cement.

Top Water Tiger | Captain Lenny Moffo

This topwater design was patterned after productive artificial lures finished with fire tiger coloration. The fly is light and easy to cast and it is a more decorative version of Lenny's Work Fly.

Hook: Gamakatsu SC 15, size 3/0.
Thread: Any suitable thread.
Tail: Tie-in orange bucktail, followed by holographic Mylar. Tie-in a clump of chartreuse bucktail.
Flanks: Tie-in one barred chartreuse saddle hackle on either side of the tail.
Topping: Tie-in several strands of peacock herl followed by a tuft of chartreuse marabou.
Head: All-white 5/8-inch popper head. Drill hole, glue onto hook shank and apply markings with a black permanent marker.
Eyes: Affix preferred eyes with five-minute epoxy.
Finish: Color the mouth section of the head and add black markings.

Trilobal Crab | Captain Billy Trimble

The inspiration for this pattern was a spoon fly. Trilobal Hackle was incorporated into the design to achieve that effect. It was originally tied to replicate small mud and baby blue crabs and in a manner that was easy to tie, easy to cast and allowed the fly to remain somewhat weedless. The fly is very effective on redfish; they spin around it and sip it down. Drop the fly in the proximity of reds and allow it to fall. Fish usually pick it up on the drop. Strip to get the fish's attention, then let the fly fall.

Hook: Tiemco 811S, size 6, 4, 2.
Thread: UTC 210, color to match cone head.
Head: Mash down the barb and slip cone onto the hook.
Legs: Cover the hook shank with thread to the mid-point of the bend and then bring thread back to the bend. Take three strands of small or medium Centipede Legs folded around the thread then tied on top of the hook shank. Stretch legs and tie down to mid-point of hook bend, bringing thread back up to the top of bend.
Tail: For a trailing claw fold in a small clump of synthetic fibers (Puglisi, Slinky, Polar) and tie down to mid-point of hook bend.
Body: Tie-in a strand of holographic Trilobal Hackles (3/4 or 11/4 matched to fly size) followed by two saddle hackles. Palmer hackle forward, tie off at cone and trim tips. Palmer Trilobal Hackle forward to cone; tie off and trim.
Wing: Invert fly and tie in a small clump of deer hair (color to match fly), with the tips just covering the hook point. Spin the hair around the hook shank causing them to flare. Fill in under the cone head.
Finish: Whip finish and trim and deer-hair butts down to the height of cone. Trim hackle fibers and Trilobal fibers off the top of the fly. Apply cement.

Trout Slammer | Captain Doug Sinclair

This fly is also known as a Cactus Clouser, since it was patterned off the Deep Clouser Minnow. It is an easy-to-tie fly that is very effective for seatrout.

Hook: Mustad 34007, size 2.
Eyes: Small barbells, black over red.
Platform: Tie-in fine brown deer-hair fibers as a base.
Tail: Tie-in white bucktail over which is tied a blend of pearl and red Krystal Flash.
Body: Tie-in a length of pearl Crystal Chenille at the hook bend and wind toward the hook eye.
Head: Continue to wind the chenille over the eyes in figure-eight fashion and build a small head with thread. Tie off and whip finish.

U.V. Copperhead | Captain Randy Hamilton

This fly is a flashy version of a Clouser-style minnow. It incorporates flash into body, tail and wing. It is effective for a number of gamefish species found in southwest Florida and elsewhere.

Hook: Mustad 34007, Size 1/0 and 1.
Thread: White or fine clear monofilament.
Eyes: Medium dumbbell eyes.
Tail: Tie in strands of mixed pearl and pink Krystal Flash and Flashabou.
Body: Tie in white Crystal Chenille and wrap forward to the eyes, making a few wraps around the eyes.
Wing: Tie in additional strands of pearl and pink Krystal Flash and Flashabou.
Head: Build a head with thread. Tie off and add head cement.

Ubiquitous

Tied by Tom Herrington
Historic Ocean Springs Saltwater Fly Fishing Club
Style origins unknown

While the use of this versatile, easy-to-tie deep minnow pattern can be traced back to the 1960s in coastal Gulf States, and in freshwater for bass and bluegill, more modern versions of the fly are attributed to the Clouser Deep Minnow. Many variations of the Deep Minnow are a staple in the fly boxes of Gulf Coast fly-anglers—they are productive for a wide range of gamefish. This variation is one of the most often-used color combinations. It is very effective for Spanish mackerel.

Hook: Mustad 34007 or similar. Small jig hooks can also be used. Size according to the species and bait.
Thread: Danville flat waxed nylon, chartreuse.
Eyes: Tie-on chartreuse dumbbell eyes on top of the hook shank about 1/4" from the hook eye. Any form of weighted dual-eye will work.
Bottom Wing: With hook point facing upward, tie-in a bunch of white Super Hair at the eye and on the underside of the hook shank. Place the wing over and between the barbell eyes. Secure with thread wraps behind the barbell. Snug hair firmly enough to hold hair in place. Do not allow to flare.
Flash: Invert the hook and tie-in pearl Krystal Flash.
Over Wing: Tie-in a bunch of chartreuse Super Hair.
Head: Build a head with thread. Whip finish and apply head cement.

UFO Crab | Captain Ron Kowalyk

This fly was designed as a saltwater variation of the Woolly Worm. It is effective for redfish, pompano, sea trout and jacks.

Hook: Billy Pate Tarpon Hook, size 1 to 3/0.
Thread: Olive or tan.
Weight: Large, gold conehead. Render hook barbless to facilitate sliding the head on.
Tail: Tie-in a blend of white or tan bucktail and pearl and copper or gold Krystal Flash.
Body: Tie-in a green, black, gray or tan grizzly hackle, and champagne Icicle Chenille. Wrap the chenille forward forming the body and tie off.
Markings: Using a permanent magic marker add some brown, green or black barred markings.
Weed Guard: Using 40- or 50-pound monofilament form a double prong-style weed guard.

UFO Green Thing | Captain Ron Kowalyk

This fly was designed for dark, tannic water and is productive for tarpon, snook, sea trout and redfish. This is a simple-to-tie yet effective pattern that allows for easy adaptation.

Hook: Billy Pate Tarpon Hook, 1/0 to 3/0.
Thread: Green.
Weight: Large, gold conehead. Render hook barbless to facilitate sliding the head on.
Tail: Tie in a blend of chartreuse bucktail and pearl, copper or gold Krystal Flash. Detail the fibers with a purple magic marker, especially for tarpon.
Body: Tie in a green hackle and green Icicle Chenille. Wrap the chenille forward forming the body and tie off.
Markings: Using a permanent marker add brown, green or black detailing, such as dots, bars and stripes.

UFO Minnow | Captain Ron Kowalyk

This fly was also designed as a saltwater variation of the Woolly Worm. It is effective for snook, redfish, pompano, sea trout and jacks, and intends to mimic small baitfish.

Hook: Billy Pate Tarpon Hook 1/0, 2/0
Thread: Red or green.
Weight: Large, gold conehead. Render hook, barbless to facilitate sliding the head on.
Tail: Tie in a blend of white bucktail and pearl/copper or gold Krystal Flash.
Body: Tie in a green, black or gray grizzly hackle, and white Icicle Chenille. Wrap the chenille forward forming the body and tie off.
Markings: Using a permanent marker, add brown, green or black detailing, such as dots, bars and stripes.

UFO Shrimp | Captain Ron Kowalyk

This fly was designed as a saltwater variation of Woolly Worm style flies. It is effective for redfish, pompano, sea trout and jacks.

Hook: Billy Pate Tarpon Hook, size 1 to 2/0.
Thread: Olive or pink.
Weight: Large, gold conehead. Render hook barbless to facilitate sliding the head on.
Tail: Tie-in a blend of pink, white or tan bucktail and pearl/copper or gold Krystal Flash.
Body: Tie-in a green, black, gray or tan grizzly hackle, and pink Icicle Chenille. Wrap the chenille forward forming the body and tie off.
Markings: Using a permanent magic marker add some brown, green or black barred markings.
Weed Guard: Using 40- or 50-pound monofilament form a double prong-style weed guard.

Ultra Bait | Ben Furimsky

This easy-to-tie fly is effective for false albacore, bonito, Spanish mackerel, sea trout and stripers. Tied in various sizes it can replicate various small baitfish and rain bait.

Hook: Gamakatsu SC15 or Eagle Claw LO54.
Thread: White, 3/0.
Tail: Tie-in six to eight strands of pearl Krystal Flash on the top of the hook shank.
Belly: Tie-in a clump of clear Ultra Hair on the bottom of the hook shank.
Back: Tie-in a clump of tan Ultra Hair as a top layer of hair.
Flash: Tie-in strands of pearl and silver Angel Hair.
Eyes: Affix stick-on eyes.

Ultra Hair Spread Fly | Captain Dino Torino

This fly was designed to replicate any number of wide-bodied baits. Colors can vary to more closely resemble prevalent bait.

Hook: Stainless steel, 2/0 through 4/0.
Thread: Red flat waxed nylon.
Underwing: Tie-in a long bunch of white Ultra Hair. To build a more dense body, tie-in a double length of hair, equal lengths, one extending out over the eye and the other straight back; fold the portion extended over the eye back over the hook shank.
Middle Wing: Tie-in an additional white Ultra Hair.
Top Wing: The top wing can vary in color: fluorescent chartreuse, pink, olive or blue Ultra Hair.
Lateral Line: Tie-in several strands of pearl Hobbs Glimmer Flash on either side of the fly.
Head/Eyes: Build a head with thread and affix 3/8 to 5/16 3D molded eyes.
Finish: Apply epoxy to head for durability. Trim fly to desired shape.

Val's Floating/Suspending Shrimp

Valerio A. Grendanin

This fly was originally designed for striped bass in the Northeast but works equally as well for sea trout and redfish feeding on shrimp that are close to the surface or in very shallow water.

Hook: Mustad, 34007, size 2.
Thread: Fine clear monofilament.
Body 1: Cut from 1/8 inch foam sheet (color of choice) into a shrimp-like shape. Lead wire may be added at this stage for the suspending version of the fly. Six or eight wraps of .025 wire is a good starting point.
Mouth Parts: Tie-in marabou fluff, extending 1/4 inch past the bend of hook.
Eyes: Add eyes of hairbrush bristle, with dark tip and clear stem. Burnt monofilament eyes may be substituted. Place eyes on top of hook shank, extending 1/4 inch past start of hook bend. Bend eyes back to each side so they are at approximately 45 degrees to the hook shank.
Legs: Starting at bend of hook, tie in one hackle and palmer to 1/8 inch of eye. Tie down and trim top and sides flush.
Body 2: Place foam shape over trimmed hackle, so narrow tail portion of shape is positioned just behind eye and tie down. Wrap thread at an angle back and under foam body and between hackle, about 1/8 inch toward the bend of the hook. Wrap one turn over foam forming a segment. Repeat this until the body is segmented four times. Wrap back toward eye in the same manner. Wrap a few turns of thread over narrow tail section, then under tail.
Weedguard: Add optional weed guard.
Finish: Epoxy threads under tail.

Vernon's Cape Fear Crab | Captain Seth Vernon

This variation of the Merkin Crab is very effective on tailing reds in the grass. It is best fished from May through November on flood-tide grass flats. Retrieve with slow strips and an occasional twitch, creeping fly line through fingers on line hand. It can also be tied in blue and cream to replicate a blue crab.

Hook: Gamakatsu SL11 3H, size 1.
Thread: Chartreuse.
Tail: Tie-in a small clump arctic fox and strands of Krystal Flash and a pair of splayed, tan grizzly hackles.
Eyes: Tie-in a pair of EP Crab Eyes at the bottom of the hook bend.
Body: Tie-in small clumps of Aunt Lydia's Craft yarn, alternating between tan and green.
Legs: Tie-in a pair of round, white rubber legs after every other piece of yarn for a total of three pairs of legs.
Weight/Weed Guard: Tie-in an aluminum dumbbell behind the eye and on the underside of the hook shank. Tie-in 25-pound-test Mason monofilament weed guard. Tie off and whip finish.

Vernon's Cape Fur Shrimp | Captain Seth Vernon

This fly is a variation of a pattern originated by Chris Weber. It is designed for fishing mildly stained water where redfish feed on shrimp. It is an excellent searching pattern along grass edges and oyster points, and when sight-fishing. Retrieve the fly in short, erratic 2- to 4-inch strips, that allow the rattle to engage and "click".

Hook: Gamakatsu SC 15, size 2 or 1.
Thread: Brown, 3/0.
Body 1: Prepare the medium, gold Mylar tubing by removing the inner stuffing. Cut a four-inch strip of tubing and tie in at the base of the hook shank.
Eyes: Tie-in small bead-chain eyes on the underside of the hook shank opposite the hook point.
Body 2: Tie-in copper Krystal Flash and bring the thread forward to a point behind the hook eye. Palmer the flash forward around the hook shank.
Rattle: Insert the rattle into the Mylar tubing and tie off at the hook shank, allowing the tubing to ride over the bead-chain eyes. Leave enough of the "frayed" Mylar tubing as a small tail.
Wing: Tie-in tan Craft Fur under rust Craft Fur and add several strands of flash material. Build a small head with thread and whip finish. Add bars to the Craft Fur using a brown Sharpie.

Vernon's Jalapeno Popper | Captain Seth Vernon

This Gurgler-like fly was designed for redfish in any habitat where they feed on the surface. The pattern is simple, effective and does not require hard strips to achieve a pop or gurgle. The fly is great for redfish, sea trout and snook as well as small tarpon.

Hook: Tiemco 411S, size 3/0.
Thread: Chartreuse.
Tail: Tie in green Craft Fur and strands of chartreuse Krystal Flash.
Body: Cut a rectangular strip of Locofoam approximately 2 1/4 inches long. Taper the belly of the strip approximately 40 degrees. Tie-in foam on the topside of the hook shank at the bend. Leave in place. Tie-in chartreuse Estaz and a chartreuse grizzly hackle. Palmer forward the Estaz followed by the hackle and tie in behind the hook eye. Fold the foam body forward and tie-in at a point behind the hook eye. Add bars and color with a brown Sharpie.
Weed Guard: Tie in 25 pound mason monofilament as weed guard.

Vernon's Killer Kwan | Captain Seth Vernon

This fly is a variation of Pat Dorsey's Kwan. It is a versatile pattern for tailing and cruising redfish and those holding in deeper water. The fly can also be fished in the grass. It replicates a shrimp, crab or mud minnow.

Hook: Gamakatsu SL 113H, size 1 or 2.
Thread: Brown.
Tail: Tie in rust Craft Fur and gold Krystal Flash. Tie-in brown schlappen and make three palmered wraps.
Body/Legs: Tie-in Aunt Lydia's tan Craft Yarn then rust with figure-eight wraps. Repeat that process until a crab-like body is formed. About 3/4 of the way toward the hook eye tie-in three pair of Fire Tip Sili-Legs, then add another two strips of Craft Yarn.
Eyes/Weed Guard: Tie in large, bead chain eyes and 25-pound Mason monofilament as a weed guard.

Vernon's Salty Shrimp | Captain Seth Vernon

This fly was inspired by early Homer Rhodes Shrimp and Seaducer patterns. It fishes weedless in the upper to middle portion of the water column when targeting cruising or schooling redfish. The fly's coloration and retrieve works to imitate minnows and shrimp.

Hook: Gamakatsu SC15, size 1, 1/0.
Thread: Brown.
Tail: Tie-in two matched pairs of tan grizzly feathers and strands of UV/tan Krystal Flash.
Eyes: Tie-in a pain of EP monofilament eyes.
Body: Tie-in the tips of three to four tan grizzly hackles and palmer forward. Tie-in and build a small head of thread.

Wahoo Lepus

Tom Herrington | Historic Ocean Springs Saltwater Fly Fishing Club

This fly was designed specifically for wahoo; it replicates the purple and black colors of successful wahoo lures. Dominant features of this fly are the extra-large glow-in-the-dark molded eyes and the dual rabbit strips glued together. The combination of these attributes creates a noticeable fly with excellent inherent movement.

Hook: Mustad 340011, size 3/0.
Thread: Danville flat waxed nylon, black.
Eye Stalks: Tie-in tungsten flat-end barbell eyes approximately one inch back from the hook eye. The flat side of the barbells will serve as attachment points for the larger eyes.
Body: Wrap hook shaft to bend and then back again. Cut magnum-sized black and purple rabbit strips three times the length of the hook shank. Tie-in the purple strip on the bottom of the shank and after punching a hole in the strip, and thread the hook through the hole. Secure the strip tight and up behind the hook eye. Tie-in and whip finish.
Dorsal: Tie-in the black rabbit strip as a dorsal section. Apply a thin line of Fabri-Tac to the skin side of both strips. Align strips from end-to-end and press together firmly, forming one solid profile.
Eyes: Using epoxy, apply large molded glow-in-the-dark eyes to the flat sides of the barbell eyes. Allow to dry.
Head: Build a head with thread. Whip finish and apply head cement.

Waldner Spoon Fly | Captain Rich Waldner

This spoon fly originated from a need for a design that would sink faster and have more action than standard Mylar spoons. It is a refinement of the Florida epoxy spoon. The spoon is very durable; one Fly Spoon accounted for seventy Louisiana redfish. It is also effective for black drum, sheepshead, flounder and speckled trout.

Hook: Mustad Signature Series stainless steel, size 2.
Body: Bend hook and form a frame with copper wire. Form the body into the frame using Devcon 2-Ton Epoxy. This epoxy has a 30-minute working time and sets in two hours. Initially apply a light coat of epoxy and dust with glitter material. The glitter should be applied to both sides of the spoon. Slowly build bulk to the spoon with applications.
Weed Guard/Eyes: Install the 40-pound monofilament weed guards and paint-on eyes. Apply a final top coat of epoxy.

Weedless Gurgler

Angelo Tirico | Inspired by Jack Gartside

This fly is a modification of the Gartside Gurgler. It works to attract fish via a seductive bubble trail. Ideally, it is fished in one to three feet of water over thick grass. The fly casts well, virtually weedless and lands softly, rarely spooking fish in shallow water.

Hook: Mustad 34011, size 1/0.
Thread: Danville flat waxed nylon.
Tail: Tie in extra select white Craft Fur at the bend of hook.
Body: Tie in large, pearl Cactus Chenille at the bend and advance to within 1/8 inch of the hook eye. Whip finish and cut thread. Prepare 1/4-inch white foam by cutting 1/2-inch strip about 1 inch larger than the hook. At one end cut a "v" into the strip. Attach thread at hook bend and invert the hook. Slide foam with the V on either side of the hook bend, extending past the hook point. Secure rear of foam with five to eight wraps and whip finish. Cut thread and soak wraps with head cement. Lift up foam and attach thread at hook eye. Secure foam with five to eight wraps. Bend excess foam at a right angle to body and wrap the thread to form a head under the foam. Trim foam head to a rounded shape.

Weighted Grass Crab | Captain Gordon Churchill

This fly is a variation of the Grass Crab. It was inspired by the design of the Borski Chernobyl Crab, and was crafted to suggest life rather than imitate it. Dumbbell eyes are added to this version for fishing over sand or mud bottoms up to approximately a foot in depth. The fly is productive for redfish; bonefish and other fish that feed on crabs or shrimp will eat it as well.

Hook: Standard saltwater hook.
Thread: Clear, fine monofilament.
Eyes: Tie-in small dumbbell eyes behind the eye of the hook.
Tail: Tie-in flash (copper, gold, pearl or silver).
Claws: Tie-in three stiff grizzly hackles.
Body/Legs: Tie-in a small amount of deer hair on point side of hook. Spin the deer hair and tie in rubber legs so they hang off either side of hook shank. Tie on and spin an additional clump of deer hair and stack it snug against the first bunch. Clip deer hair flat on top and bottom and close to the hook shank.
Wing: Tie-in a sparse clump of squirrel tail as a wing.
Overwing: Tie-in hackle feather over the primary wing.

Wiggle Fly

Tom Herrington | Historic Ocean Springs Saltwater Fly Fishing Club

This swimming fly was designed for gamefish that forage on crabs. Especially effective for redfish and bonefish, its design creates a built-in wiggle action upon fluttering down or when retrieved.

Hook: Jig hook; either 90-degree or 60-degree turn will work.
Thread: Monofilament.
Body 1: Make a mold by cutting a glue pad to the desired configuration. Cut three sections that will be sandwiched together. The bottom section functions to receive the epoxy; the middle and top sections are cut to shape and notched to receive the tail and upward bend of the jig hook. Wrap hook with non-toxic heavy wire or barbell eyes.
Tail: Tie-in Polar Flash tail or any other suitable material.
Body 2: Place hook inside the mold with the tail positioned between the bottom and middle layers of the glue pad. Use small plastic clamps to hold the layers together. Mix epoxy and add glitter. Pour mixture into mold. Allow to set and dry.
Eyes: Eyes may be added at any point after the epoxy has been poured.
Finish: Cover the fly with Hard-As-Nails or other similar coating to heighten the sheen.

Wiggly | Captain Dino Torino

This modified Clouser utilizes a plastic wiggle tail for added motion and appeal. The pattern is ideal for any situation where the additional weight of a jigging-type fly offers an advantage. It is an effective fly for most gamefish.

Hook: Size 2/0.
Thread: White 3/0 monofilament.
Eyes: Tie in a set of barbell eyes.
Tail: Tie in a short length of 30-pound stiff monofilament and then tie the white Fly Tail directly on the extension.
Underwing: Tie in a clump of white bucktail on the underside of the hook shank.
Body: Tie-in a length of pearl Bill's Body Braid and wind it forward to a point immediately behind the eyes.
Top Wing: Tie-in several strands of pearl Krystal Flash, and then tie in a clump of olive bucktail equal in length to the underwing.
Head: Build a head with thread, tie off and apply head cement.

Wiggy Hi Tie Baitfish | Valerio A. Grendanin

This baitfish pattern is effective at imitating larger baits like blue runners or big-eye scad. The design takes advantage of the non-water-absorbent characteristics of Kanekalon Wig Hair. It generates enticing action while maintaining its shape. It can be fished with either a dead drift as an injured baitfish or stripped at varying speeds.

Hook: Owner Gorilla Light, 5107-141, 4/0 or 5/0.
Thread: Fine clear monofilament.
Body: Cut 6- to 8-inch lengths of Kanekalon Wig Hair (white, light blue and dark blue) and blend with fine pearl shredded Mylar. Wrap a layer of thread around hook shank from eye to 1/8 inch of bend. Add a small amount of blended white wig hair at the bend and on top of the hook; tie down in the middle of the bunch. Fold forward-facing end of bunch back and wrap thread in front of bunch, forcing hair back. Pulling both ends of the hair up, wrap about five turns of thread around the bunch over the hook shank. This is done only for the first bunch to help keep hair sticking straight up and not fouling. Continue adding small bunches of hair, tying in the middle and folding back. Change and intermix different colors until you reach the eye.
Gills: At a point about 1/8 inch from the eye, add a small bunch of red wig hair to each side as gills.

Winter Flats Fly | Angelo Tirico

This fly was designed for crystal-clear flats where fish are exceptionally spooky. The fly should be fished on a ten-foot leader with an eight-pound tippet. The extra-long leader gives you the ability to cast the fly close to fish without spooking them. The fly has a slow, falling motion with undulating fibers that motivate lethargic fish to eat. This go-to flats pattern has accounted for many five-pound-plus trout and redfish on clear winter flats.

Hook: Eagle Claw 254 SS, size 4.
Thread: Danville flat waxed nylon.
Wing: Using extra-select Craft Fur in olive and white tie in the top and bottom wing so it extends two times the hook length past the bend. When tying in wings, make certain the wing material extends past the hook eye approximately 3/8 of an inch.
Head: To form the head base fold back the top and bottom wing extensions toward the hook bend and secure in place with three or four wraps. Whip finish but do not cut thread.
Weed Guard: Form the weed guard with a three-inch piece of 30-pound fluorocarbon folded in half. Tie in place by wrapping thread around tag ends just behind eye, forming a V. Trim to extend past the hook point 1/16 of an inch.
Eyes: To finish the head place 4.5 mm medium decal eyes on each side of the head. Epoxy in place and form head.

Woven Body Shrimp | Lawrence Clemens

This simple yet effective generic shrimp pattern is used for any number of gamefish species feeding on small crustaceans.

Hook: Trey Combs Big Game or Gamakatsu, sizes 6 through 1/0.
Thread: Monofilament, fine.
Tail: Tie-in a sparse clump of olive marabou.
Antennae: Tie-in strands of clear Krystal Flash on either side of the marabou.
Eye: Tie-in a set of small or mini-sized dumbbell eyes on the topside of the hook shank, at a point near the hook shank.
Body: Tie-in woven micro chenille in brown/orange tones. Other effective shrimp-type colors can be substituted.
Beard: Tie-in soft gray/white hackle at the head region and on the underside of the hook shank.
Head: Build a small head with the thread, whip finish and apply head cement.

Index of Fly Patterns

Index of Fly Tiers

Art and Photo Index

Art

Gyotaku Art images are the work of artist, Charlie Brown, of Shell Creek Ink, Fort Myers, Florida. www.shellcreekink.com

Photographs

All digital fly images and still life images are the work of Angelo Peluso. www.angelopeluso.com

Recommended Reading

—Adams, Aaron, *Fly Fisherman's Guide to Saltwater Prey: How to Match Coastal Prey Fish and Invertebrates With the Fly Patterns That Imitate Them*, 2008, Stackpole Books

—Bates, Joseph D, Jr., *Streamers and Bucktails*, 1950, Knopf

—Brooks, Joe. *Complete Book of Fly Fishing*, 1958, Outdoor Life Books

—Caolo, Alan, *A Guide to Atlantic Baitfish & Other Food Sources*, 1995, Frank Amato Publications

—Cooper, Peter, *Fly Fishing the Louisiana Coast*, 2004 Countryman Press

—Curcione, Nick, *Tug-O-War: A Fly-Fisher's Game - Successful Techniques For Saltwater Fly-Fishing*, 2001, Frank Amato Publications

—Jacobs, Jimmy, *Fly-Fishing the South Atlantic Coast*, 2000, Backcountry Guides

—Kells, Val – Carpenter, Kent, *A Field Guide to Coastal Fishes: From Maine to Texas*, 2011, The Johns Hopkins University Press

—Kreh, Bernard Lefty, *Fly Fishing in Salt Waters*, 1974, Crown

—Kreh, Bernard Lefty, *Fly Casting*, 1974, Lippincott

—Kreh, Bernard Lefty, *Fly Fishing for Bonefish, Permit and Tarpon*, 2002, The Lyons Press

—Leiser, Eric, *The Complete Book of Fly Tying*, 1977, Knopf

—Maizler, Jan, *Fishing Florida's Flats: A Guide to Bonefish*, Tarpon, Permit, 2007, University Press of Florida

—McClane, A.J., *Practical Fly Fisherman*, 1953, Prentice-Hall

—Peluso, Angelo, *Saltwater Flies of the Northeast*, 2006, Frank Amato Publications

—Peluso, Angelo, *Fly Fishing Long Island*, 2007, WW Norton and Co./Countryman Press

—Samson, Jack, *Fly Fishing for Permit* , 2003, Countryman Press

—Sand, George X, *Saltwater Fly Fishing*, 1970, Knopf

—Shook, Phil H., Scates, Chuck, *Fly Fishing the Texas Coast: Backcountry Flats to Bluewater*, Pruett Publishing Company

—Sorrells, Colby, *Flyfisher's Guide to the Texas Coast*, 2009, Wilderness Adventures Press

—Swisher, Doug – Richards, Carl, *Backcountry Fly Fishing in Salt Water*, 2000, The Lyons Press

—Tabory, Lou, *Guide to Saltwater Baits & Their Imitations*, 1995, Lyons and Burford